BLACK PANTHER
AVENGERS OF THE NEW WORLD
BOOK ONE

writer TA-NEHISI COATES
artists WILFREDO TORRES #13-15 & 18
with JACEN BURROWS #14 & ADAM GORHAM #15
& CHRIS SPROUSE #16-18
inkers JACEN BURROWS, TERRY PALLOT, ADAM GORHAM,
KARL STORY, DEXTER VINES & WALDEN WONG
colour artists LAURA MARTIN & ANDREW CROSSLEY
letterer VC's JOE SABINO
design MANNY MEDEROS
logo by RIAN HUGHES
cover by BRIAN STELFREEZE & LAURA MARTIN

assistant editors CHRIS ROBINSON & CHARLES BEACHAM
associate editor SARAH BRUNSTAD
editor WIL MOSS

executive editor TOM BREVOORT
editor in chief AXEL ALONSO chief creative officer JOE QUESADA
publisher DAN BUCKLEY executive producer ALAN FINE

BLACK PANTHER created by STAN LEE & JACK KIRBY

Do you have any comments or queries about Black Panther Vol. 4: Avengers of the New World Book One?
Email us at graphicnovels@panini.co.uk Join us on Facebook at Panini/Marvel Graphic Novels

 First impression 2017. Published by Panini Publishing, a division of Panini UK Limited. Mike Riddell, Managing Director. Alan O'Keefe, Managing Editor. Mark Irvine, Production Manager. Marco M. Lupoi, Publishing Director Europe. Brady Webb, Reprint Editor. Charlotte Harvey, Designer. Office of publication: Brockbourne House, 77 Mount Ephraim, Tunbridge Wells, Kent TN4 8BS. This publication may not be sold, except by authorised dealers, and is sold subject to the condition that it shall not be sold or distributed with any part of its cover or markings removed, nor in a mutilated condition. Printed in Italy by Lito Terrazzi. ISBN: 978-1-84653-833-9.

BLACK PANTHER

In the aftermath of a rebellion that set change against tradition, the nation against their king, and even the living against the dead... Wakanda must now rebuild.

The forces of rebellion have quieted with the arrest of Tetu, one of the rebel leaders, while the other, Zenzi, remains at large. The royal family and the people of Wakanda are attempting to move forward together. T'Challa began this process by calling together a council of representatives from each region to write a new constitution and enact a new government. In discussions with his mother Ramonda and sister Shuri, T'Challa has expressed both trepidation and hope for this new era in Wakandan history.

But just as T'Challa moves forward, he keeps one eye on his past...

MARVEL GRAPHIC NOVEL

BLACK PANTHER #13

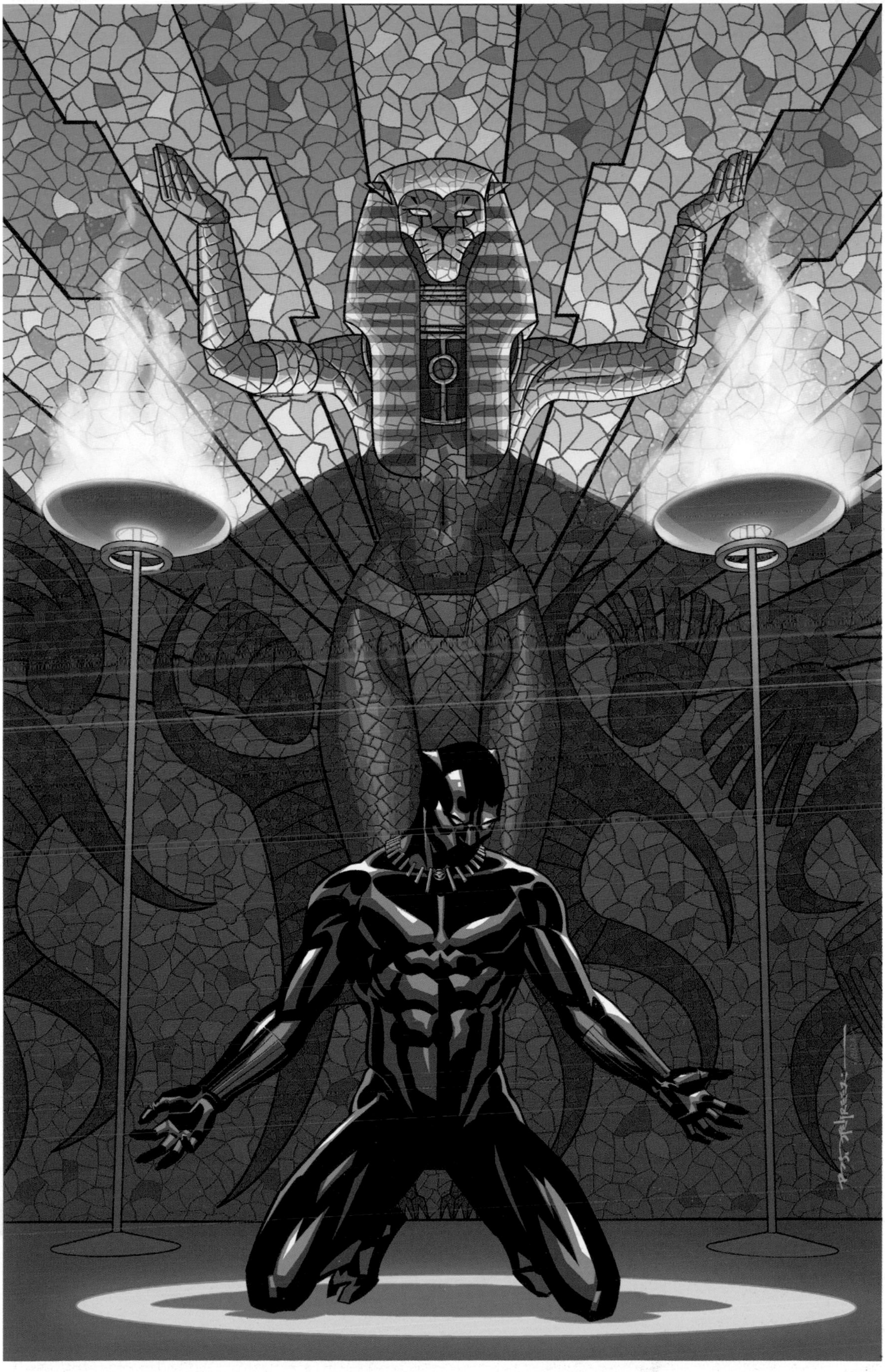

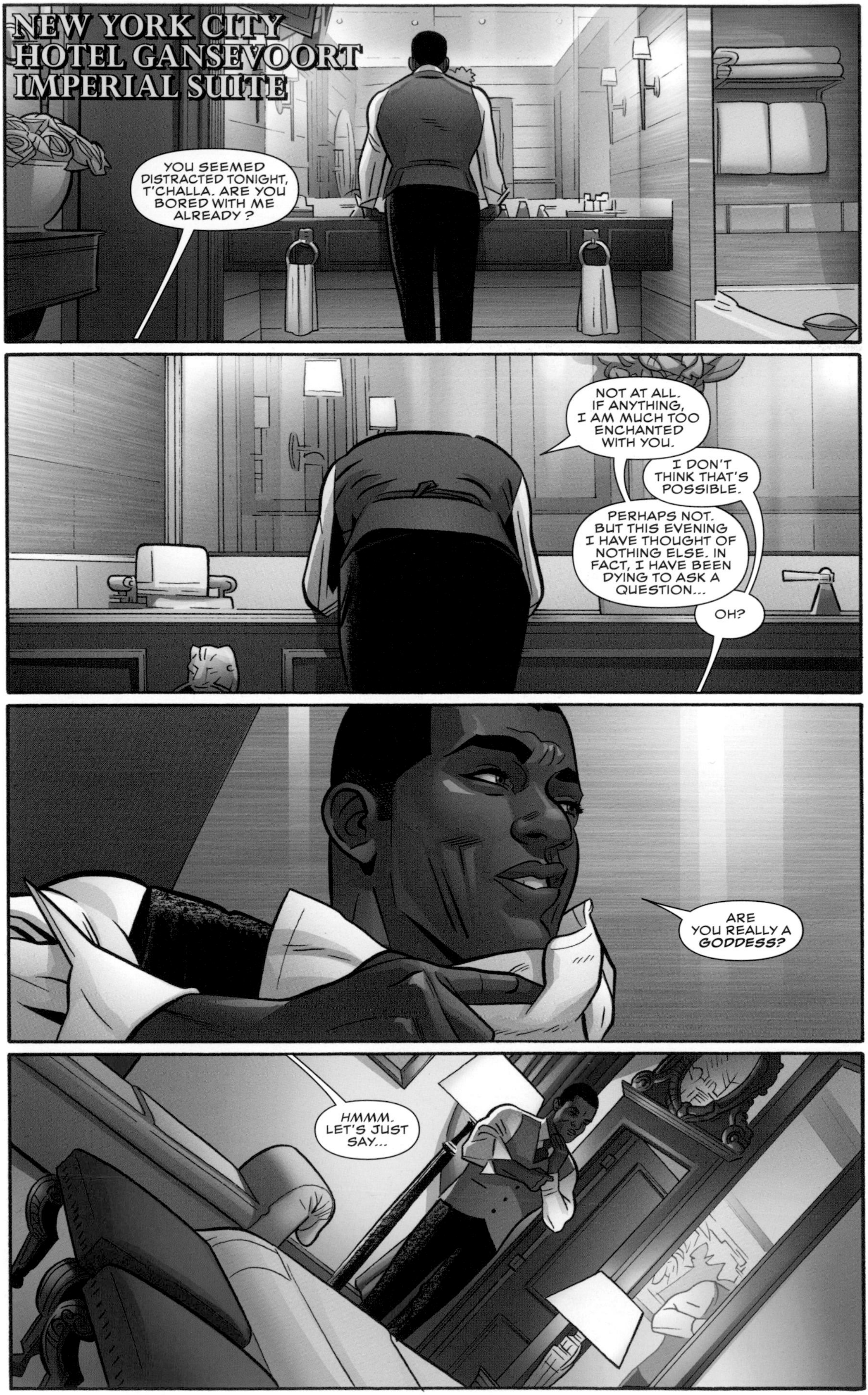
NEW YORK CITY
HOTEL GANSEVOORT
IMPERIAL SUITE
YOU SEEMED DISTRACTED TONIGHT, T'CHALLA. ARE YOU BORED WITH ME ALREADY?
NOT AT ALL. IF ANYTHING, I AM MUCH TOO ENCHANTED WITH YOU.
I DON'T THINK THAT'S POSSIBLE.
PERHAPS NOT. BUT THIS EVENING I HAVE THOUGHT OF NOTHING ELSE. IN FACT, I HAVE BEEN DYING TO ASK A QUESTION...
OH?
ARE YOU REALLY A GODDESS?
HMMM. LET'S JUST SAY...

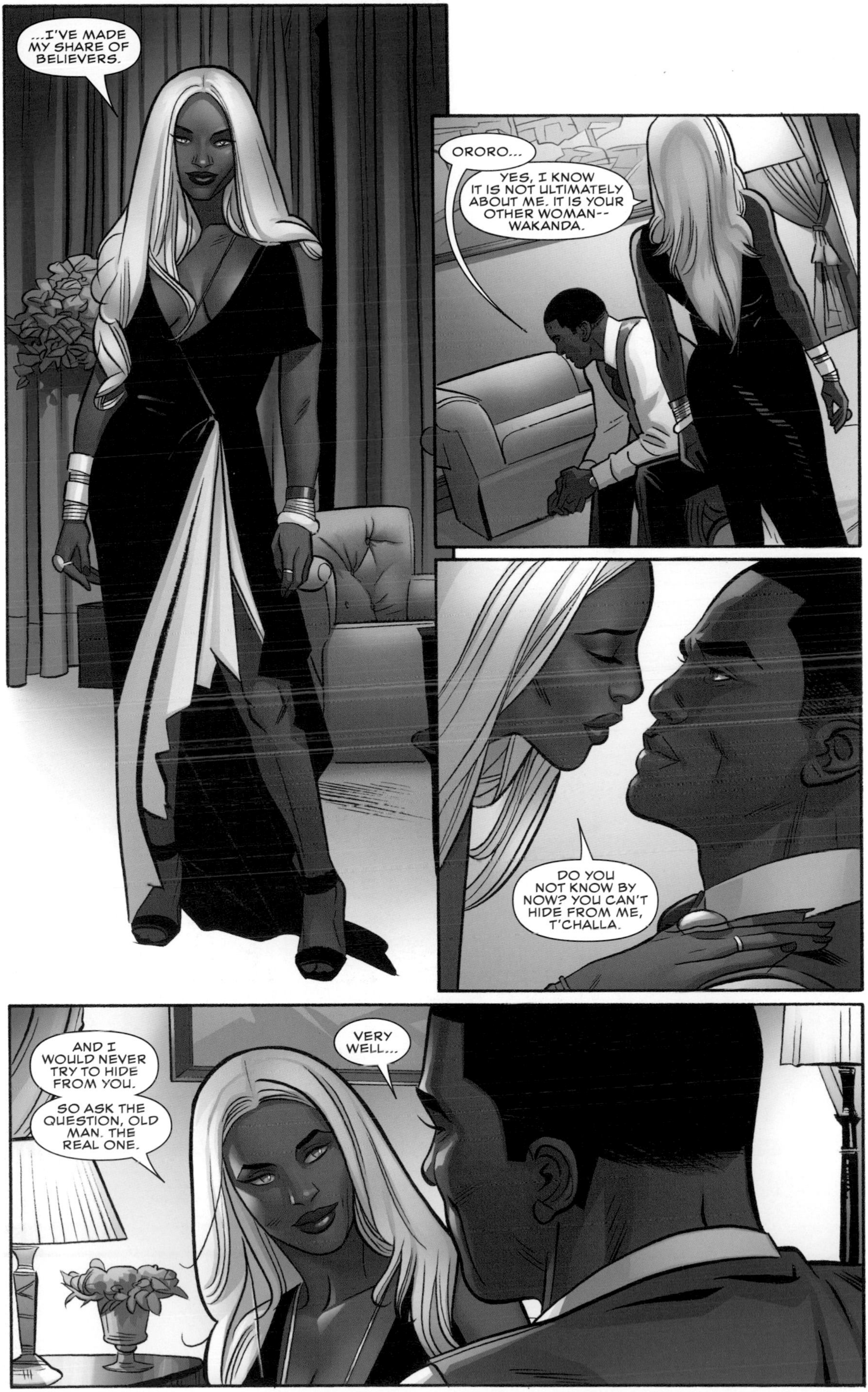
...I'VE MADE MY SHARE OF BELIEVERS.
ORORO...
YES, I KNOW IT IS NOT ULTIMATELY ABOUT ME. IT IS YOUR OTHER WOMAN-- WAKANDA.
DO YOU NOT KNOW BY NOW? YOU CAN'T HIDE FROM ME, T'CHALLA.
AND I WOULD NEVER TRY TO HIDE FROM YOU.
SO ASK THE QUESTION, OLD MAN. THE REAL ONE.
VERY WELL...

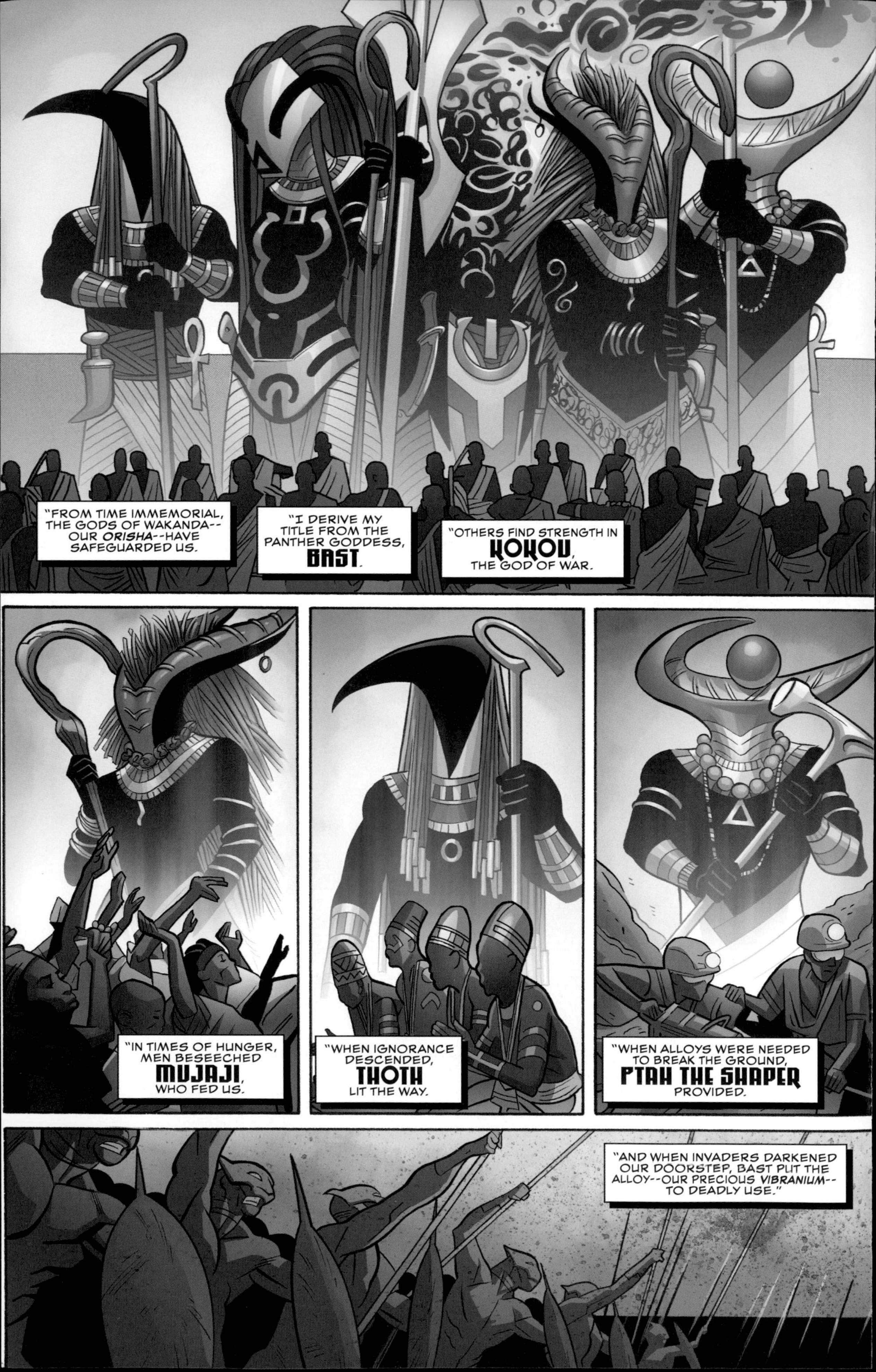
"FROM TIME IMMEMORIAL, THE GODS OF WAKANDA--OUR ORISHA--HAVE SAFEGUARDED US.
"I DERIVE MY TITLE FROM THE PANTHER GODDESS, BAST.
"OTHERS FIND STRENGTH IN KOKOU, THE GOD OF WAR.
"IN TIMES OF HUNGER, MEN BESEECHED MUJAJI, WHO FED US.
"WHEN IGNORANCE DESCENDED, THOTH LIT THE WAY.
"WHEN ALLOYS WERE NEEDED TO BREAK THE GROUND, PTAH THE SHAPER PROVIDED.
"AND WHEN INVADERS DARKENED OUR DOORSTEP, BAST PUT THE ALLOY--OUR PRECIOUS VIBRANIUM--TO DEADLY USE."

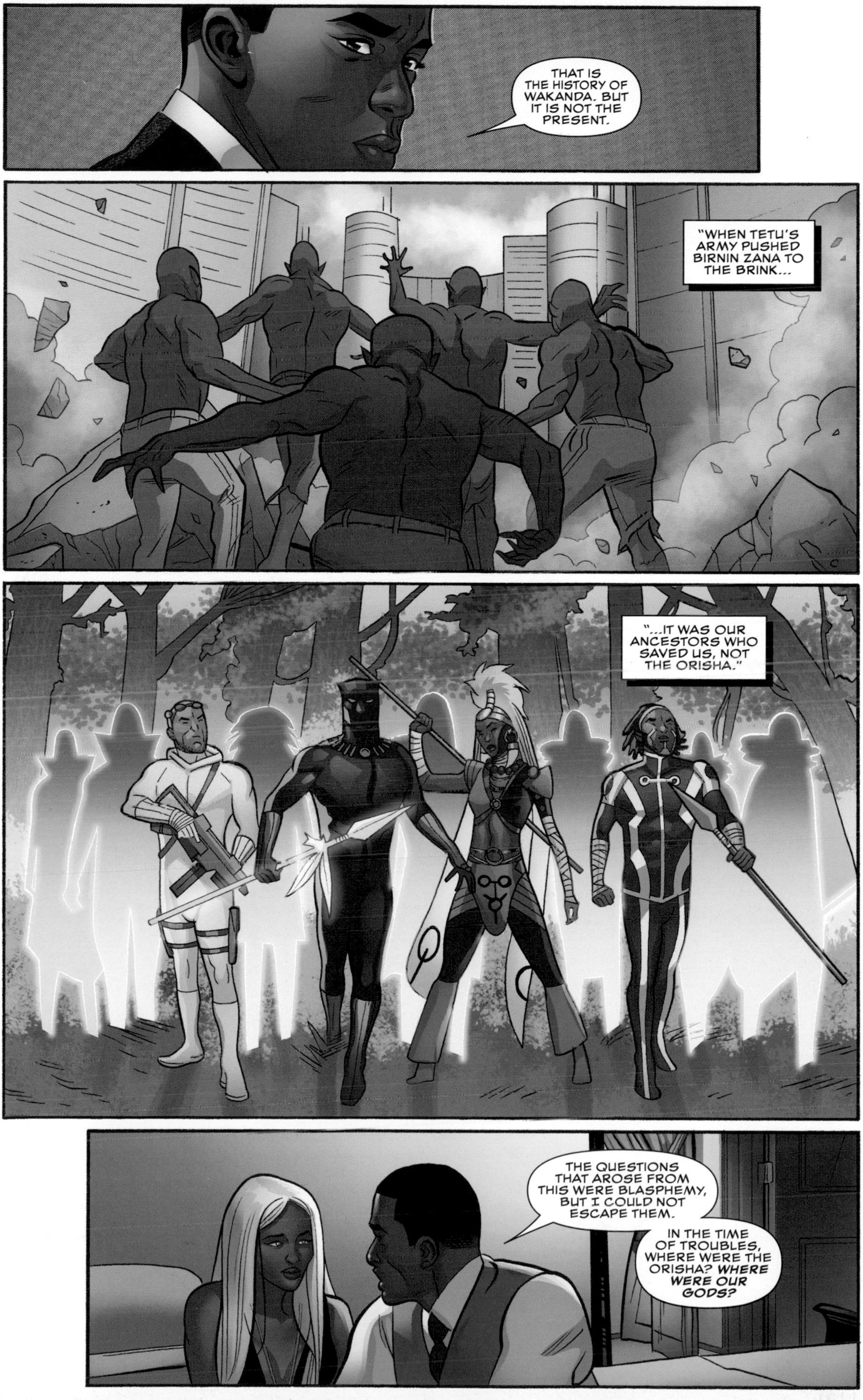
THAT IS THE HISTORY OF WAKANDA. BUT IT IS NOT THE PRESENT.
"WHEN TETU'S ARMY PUSHED BIRNIN ZANA TO THE BRINK...
"...IT WAS OUR ANCESTORS WHO SAVED US, NOT THE ORISHA."
THE QUESTIONS THAT AROSE FROM THIS WERE BLASPHEMY, BUT I COULD NOT ESCAPE THEM.
IN THE TIME OF TROUBLES, WHERE WERE THE ORISHA? ***WHERE WERE OUR GODS?***

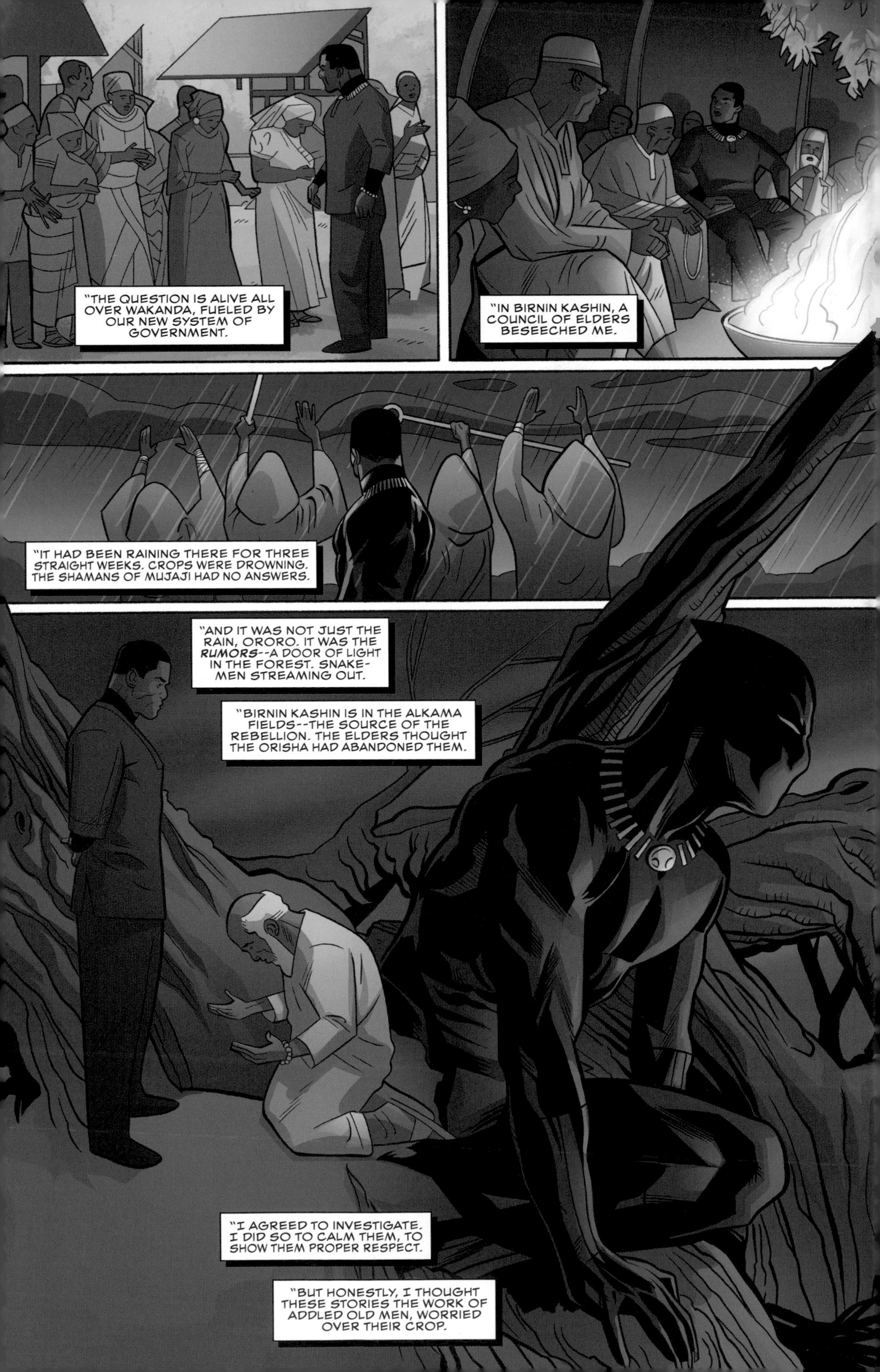
"THE QUESTION IS ALIVE ALL OVER WAKANDA, FUELED BY OUR NEW SYSTEM OF GOVERNMENT.
"IN BIRNIN KASHIN, A COUNCIL OF ELDERS BESEECHED ME.
"IT HAD BEEN RAINING THERE FOR THREE STRAIGHT WEEKS. CROPS WERE DROWNING. THE SHAMANS OF MUJAJI HAD NO ANSWERS.
"AND IT WAS NOT JUST THE RAIN, ORORO. IT WAS THE RUMORS--A DOOR OF LIGHT IN THE FOREST. SNAKE-MEN STREAMING OUT.
"BIRNIN KASHIN IS IN THE ALKAMA FIELDS--THE SOURCE OF THE REBELLION. THE ELDERS THOUGHT THE ORISHA HAD ABANDONED THEM.
"I AGREED TO INVESTIGATE. I DID SO TO CALM THEM, TO SHOW THEM PROPER RESPECT.
"BUT HONESTLY, I THOUGHT THESE STORIES THE WORK OF ADDLED OLD MEN, WORRIED OVER THEIR CROP.

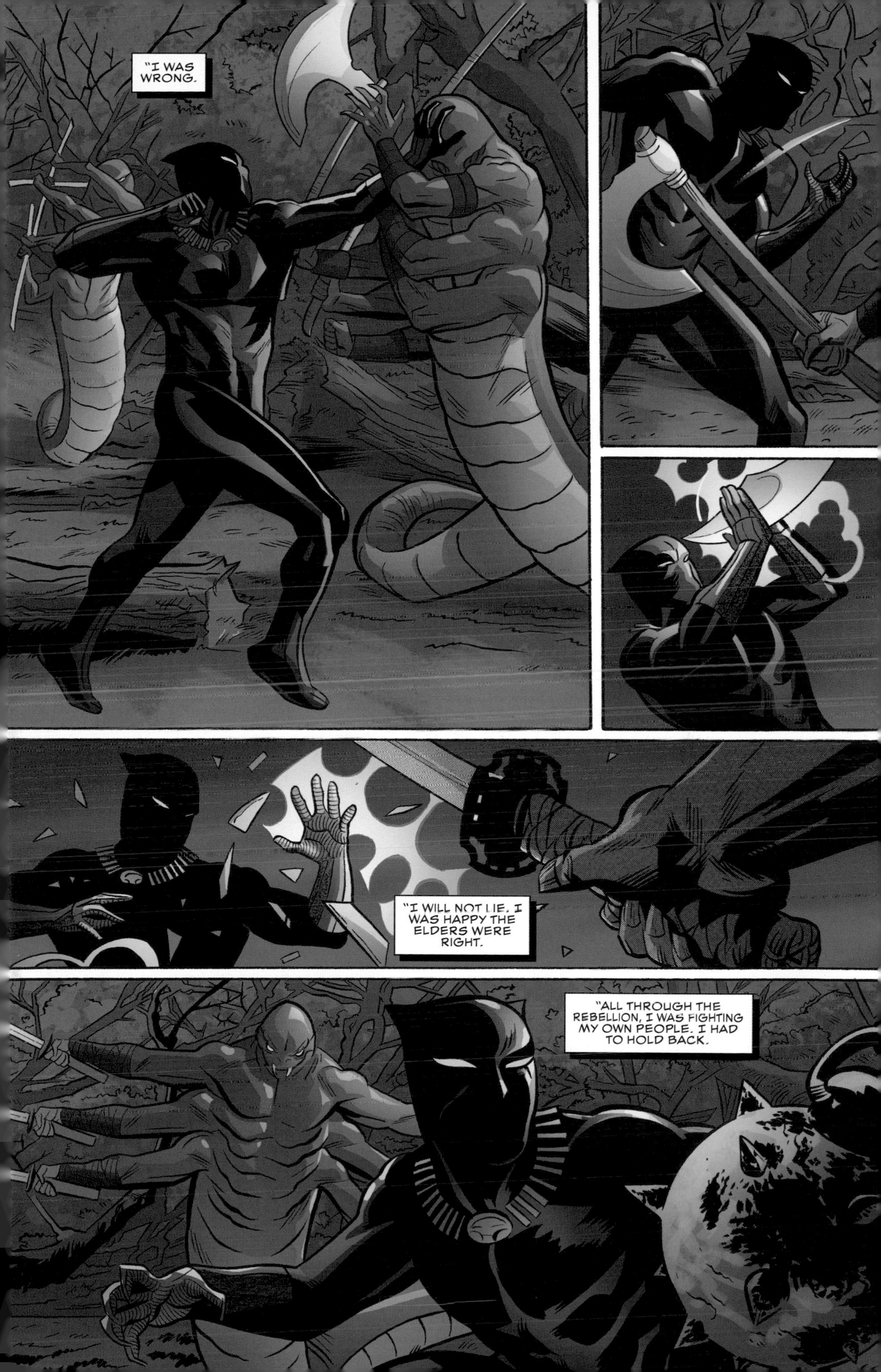
"I WAS WRONG.
"I WILL NOT LIE. I WAS HAPPY THE ELDERS WERE RIGHT.
"ALL THROUGH THE REBELLION, I WAS FIGHTING MY OWN PEOPLE. I HAD TO HOLD BACK.

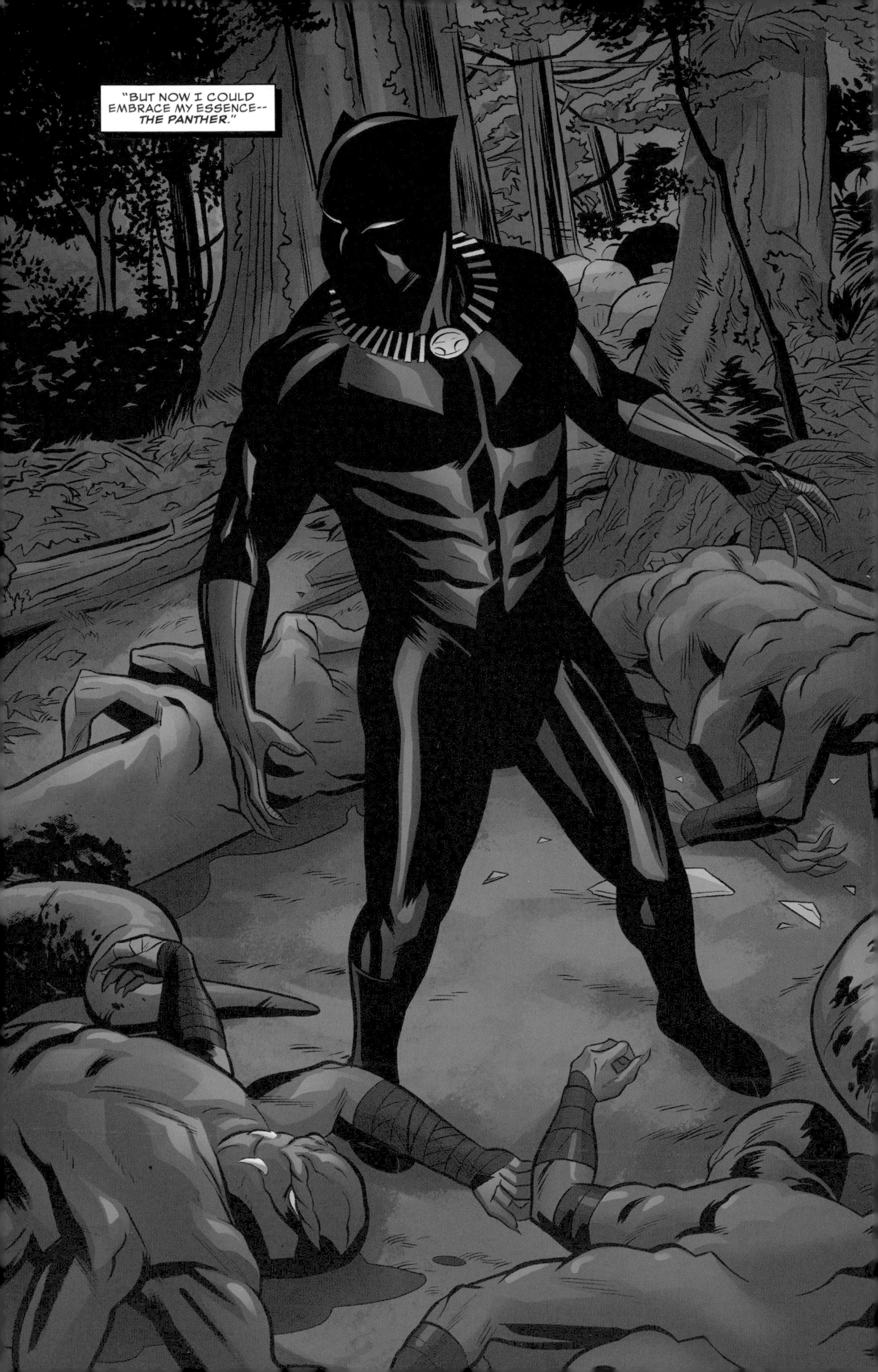
"BUT NOW I COULD EMBRACE MY ESSENCE-- THE PANTHER."

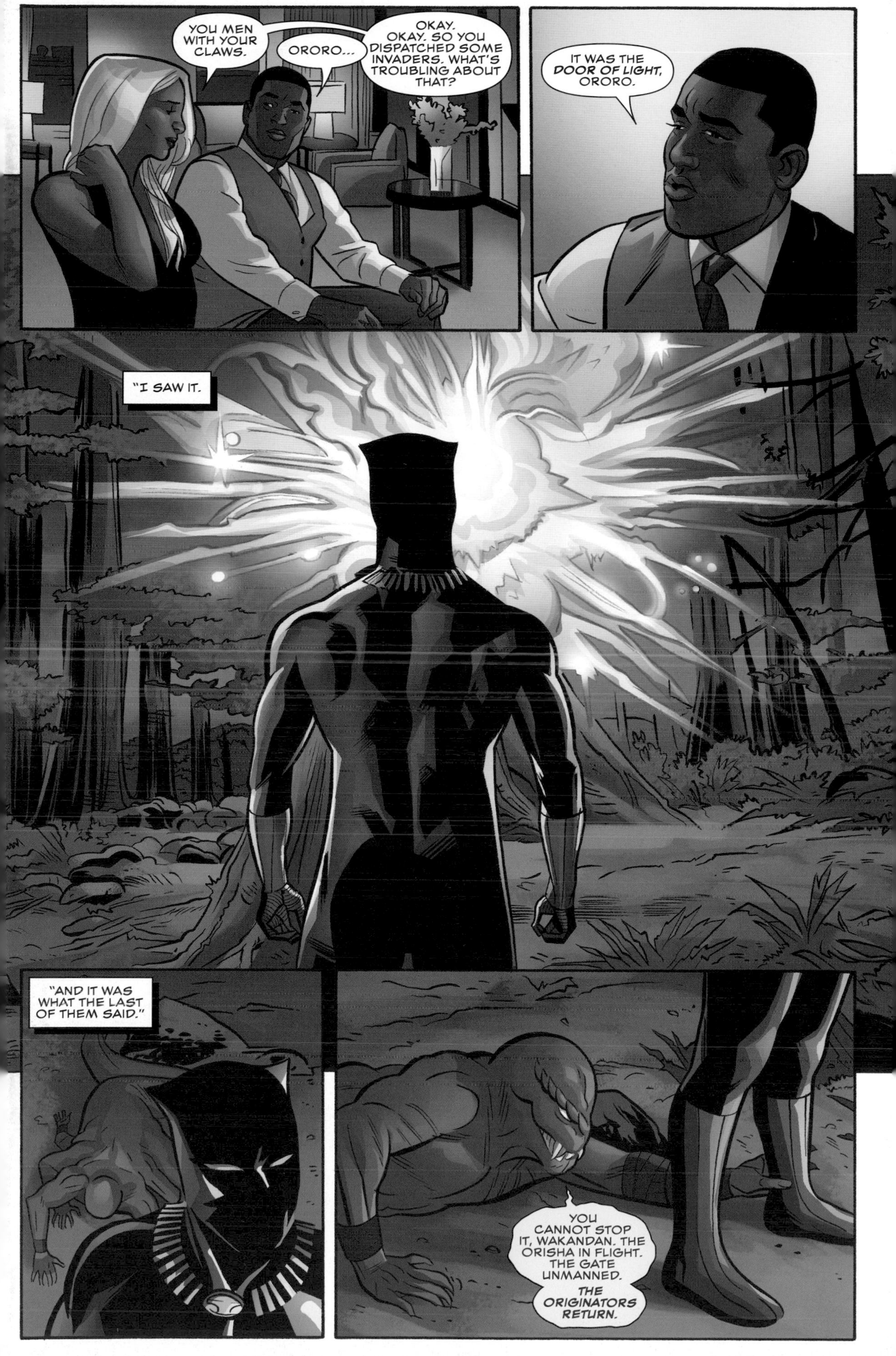
YOU MEN WITH YOUR CLAWS.
ORORO...
OKAY. OKAY. SO YOU DISPATCHED SOME INVADERS. WHAT'S TROUBLING ABOUT THAT?
IT WAS THE *DOOR OF LIGHT*, ORORO.
"I SAW IT.
"AND IT WAS WHAT THE LAST OF THEM SAID."
YOU CANNOT STOP IT, WAKANDAN. THE ORISHA IN FLIGHT. THE GATE UNMANNED.
THE ORIGINATORS RETURN.

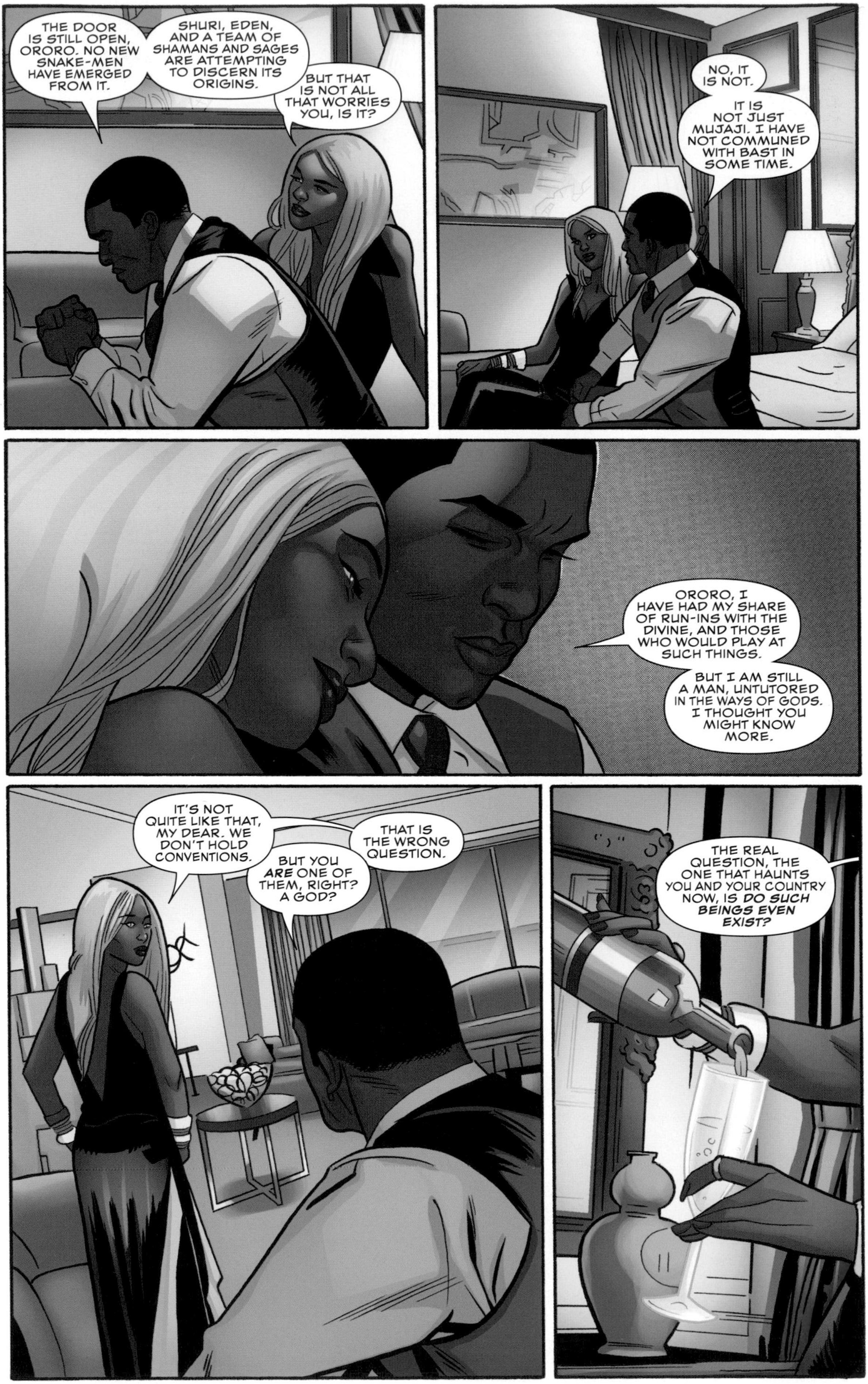
THE DOOR IS STILL OPEN, ORORO. NO NEW SNAKE-MEN HAVE EMERGED FROM IT.
SHURI, EDEN, AND A TEAM OF SHAMANS AND SAGES ARE ATTEMPTING TO DISCERN ITS ORIGINS.
BUT THAT IS NOT ALL THAT WORRIES YOU, IS IT?
NO, IT IS NOT.
IT IS NOT JUST MUJAJI. I HAVE NOT COMMUNED WITH BAST IN SOME TIME.
ORORO, I HAVE HAD MY SHARE OF RUN-INS WITH THE DIVINE, AND THOSE WHO WOULD PLAY AT SUCH THINGS.
BUT I AM STILL A MAN, UNTUTORED IN THE WAYS OF GODS. I THOUGHT YOU MIGHT KNOW MORE.
IT'S NOT QUITE LIKE THAT, MY DEAR. WE DON'T HOLD CONVENTIONS.
BUT YOU ***ARE*** ONE OF THEM, RIGHT? A GOD?
THAT IS THE WRONG QUESTION.
THE REAL QUESTION, THE ONE THAT HAUNTS YOU AND YOUR COUNTRY NOW, IS ***DO SUCH BEINGS EVEN EXIST?***

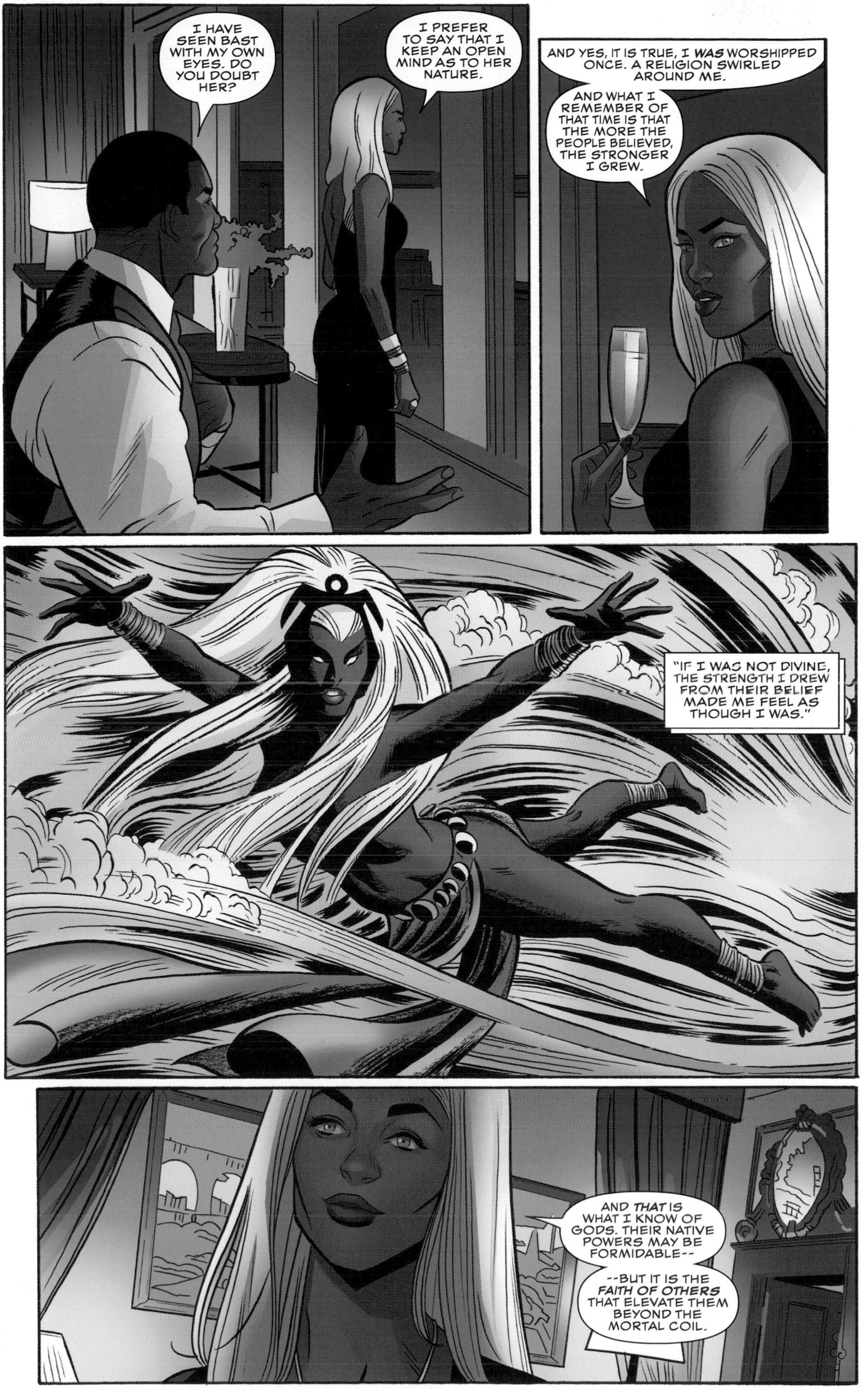
I HAVE SEEN BAST WITH MY OWN EYES. DO YOU DOUBT HER?
I PREFER TO SAY THAT I KEEP AN OPEN MIND AS TO HER NATURE.
AND YES, IT IS TRUE, I WAS WORSHIPPED ONCE. A RELIGION SWIRLED AROUND ME.
AND WHAT I REMEMBER OF THAT TIME IS THAT THE MORE THE PEOPLE BELIEVED, THE STRONGER I GREW.
"IF I WAS NOT DIVINE, THE STRENGTH I DREW FROM THEIR BELIEF MADE ME FEEL AS THOUGH I WAS."
AND THAT IS WHAT I KNOW OF GODS. THEIR NATIVE POWERS MAY BE FORMIDABLE--
--BUT IT IS THE FAITH OF OTHERS THAT ELEVATE THEM BEYOND THE MORTAL COIL.

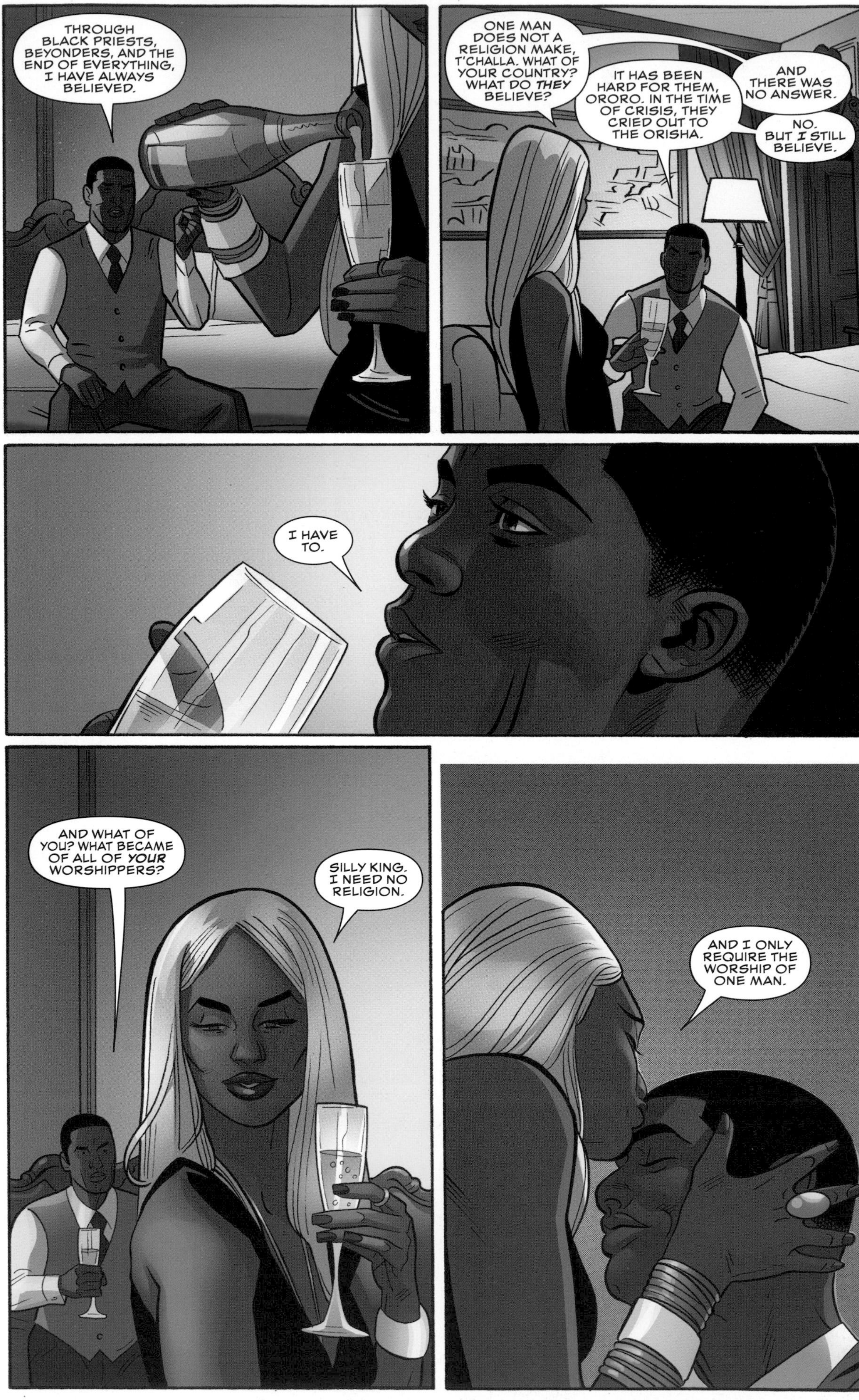
THROUGH BLACK PRIESTS, BEYONDERS, AND THE END OF EVERYTHING, I HAVE ALWAYS BELIEVED.
ONE MAN DOES NOT A RELIGION MAKE, T'CHALLA. WHAT OF YOUR COUNTRY? WHAT DO *THEY* BELIEVE?
IT HAS BEEN HARD FOR THEM, ORORO. IN THE TIME OF CRISIS, THEY CRIED OUT TO THE ORISHA.
AND THERE WAS NO ANSWER.
NO. BUT *I* STILL BELIEVE.
I HAVE TO.
AND WHAT OF YOU? WHAT BECAME OF ALL OF *YOUR* WORSHIPPERS?
SILLY KING. I NEED NO RELIGION.
AND I ONLY REQUIRE THE WORSHIP OF ONE MAN.

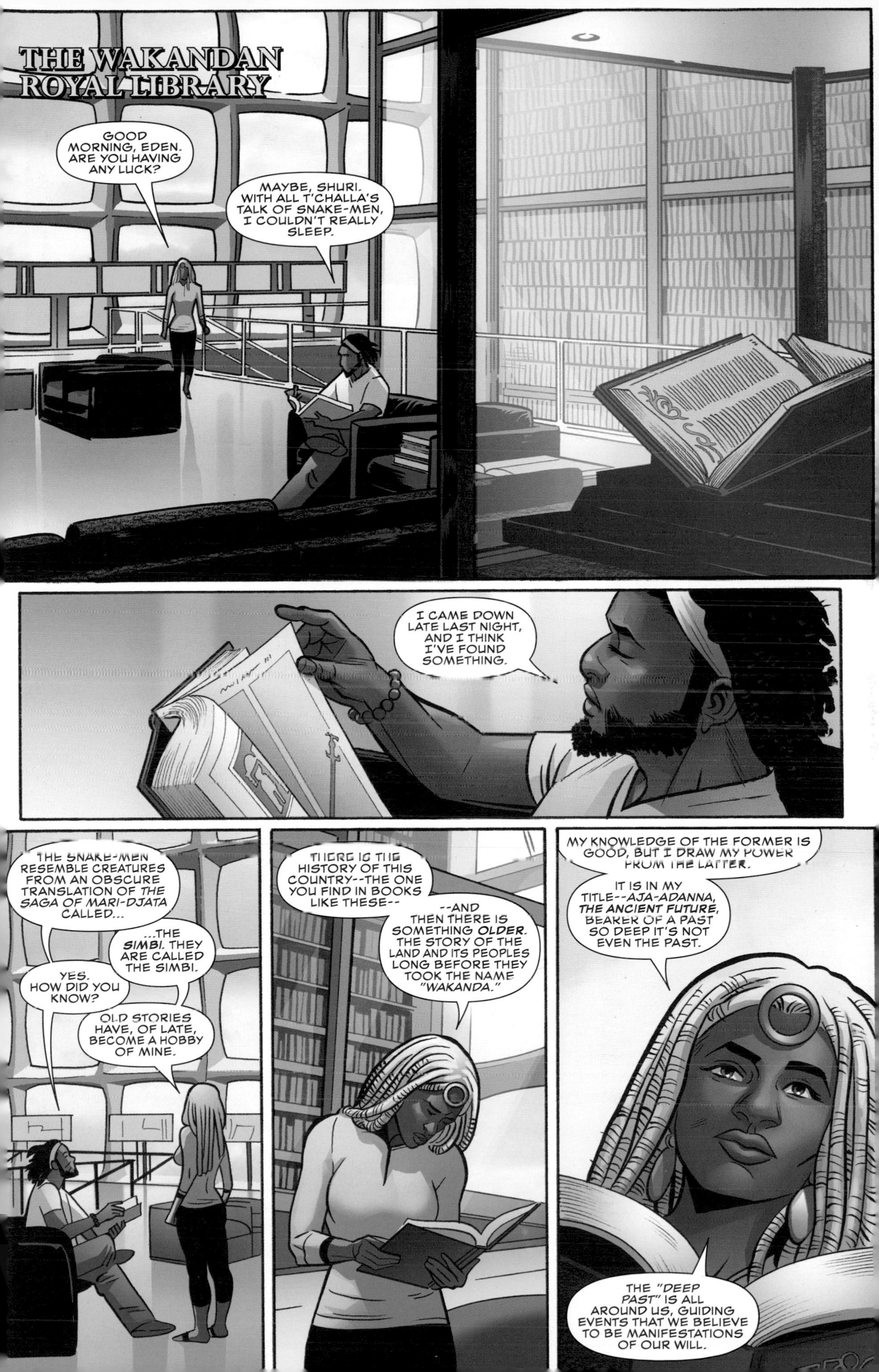
THE WAKANDAN ROYAL LIBRARY
GOOD MORNING, EDEN. ARE YOU HAVING ANY LUCK?
MAYBE, SHURI. WITH ALL T'CHALLA'S TALK OF SNAKE-MEN, I COULDN'T REALLY SLEEP.
I CAME DOWN LATE LAST NIGHT, AND I THINK I'VE FOUND SOMETHING.
THE SNAKE-MEN RESEMBLE CREATURES FROM AN OBSCURE TRANSLATION OF THE SAGA OF MARI-DJATA CALLED...
...THE SIMBI. THEY ARE CALLED THE SIMBI.
YES. HOW DID YOU KNOW?
OLD STORIES HAVE, OF LATE, BECOME A HOBBY OF MINE.
THERE IS THE HISTORY OF THIS COUNTRY--THE ONE YOU FIND IN BOOKS LIKE THESE--
--AND THEN THERE IS SOMETHING OLDER. THE STORY OF THE LAND AND ITS PEOPLES LONG BEFORE THEY TOOK THE NAME "WAKANDA."
MY KNOWLEDGE OF THE FORMER IS GOOD, BUT I DRAW MY POWER FROM THE LATTER.
IT IS IN MY TITLE--AJA-ADANNA, THE ANCIENT FUTURE, BEARER OF A PAST SO DEEP IT'S NOT EVEN THE PAST.
THE "DEEP PAST" IS ALL AROUND US, GUIDING EVENTS THAT WE BELIEVE TO BE MANIFESTATIONS OF OUR WILL.

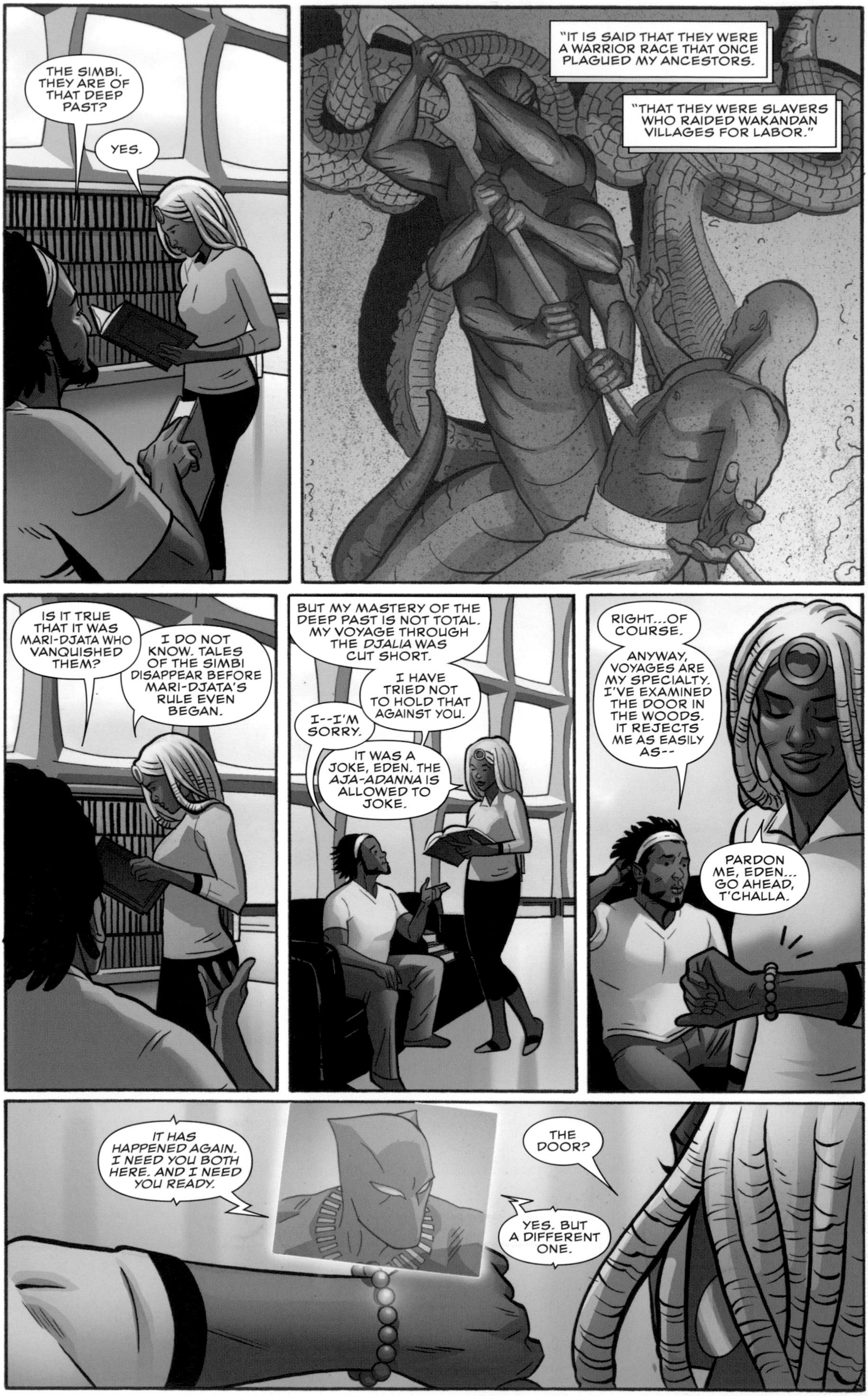
THE SIMBI. THEY ARE OF THAT DEEP PAST?
YES.
"IT IS SAID THAT THEY WERE A WARRIOR RACE THAT ONCE PLAGUED MY ANCESTORS.
"THAT THEY WERE SLAVERS WHO RAIDED WAKANDAN VILLAGES FOR LABOR."
IS IT TRUE THAT IT WAS MARI-DJATA WHO VANQUISHED THEM?
I DO NOT KNOW. TALES OF THE SIMBI DISAPPEAR BEFORE MARI-DJATA'S RULE EVEN BEGAN.
BUT MY MASTERY OF THE DEEP PAST IS NOT TOTAL. MY VOYAGE THROUGH THE *DJALIA* WAS CUT SHORT.
I HAVE TRIED NOT TO HOLD THAT AGAINST YOU.
I--I'M SORRY.
IT WAS A JOKE, EDEN. THE *AJA-ADANNA* IS ALLOWED TO JOKE.
RIGHT...OF COURSE.
ANYWAY, VOYAGES ARE MY SPECIALTY. I'VE EXAMINED THE DOOR IN THE WOODS. IT REJECTS ME AS EASILY AS--
PARDON ME, EDEN... GO AHEAD, T'CHALLA.
IT HAS HAPPENED AGAIN. I NEED YOU BOTH HERE. AND I NEED YOU READY.
THE DOOR?
YES. BUT A DIFFERENT ONE.

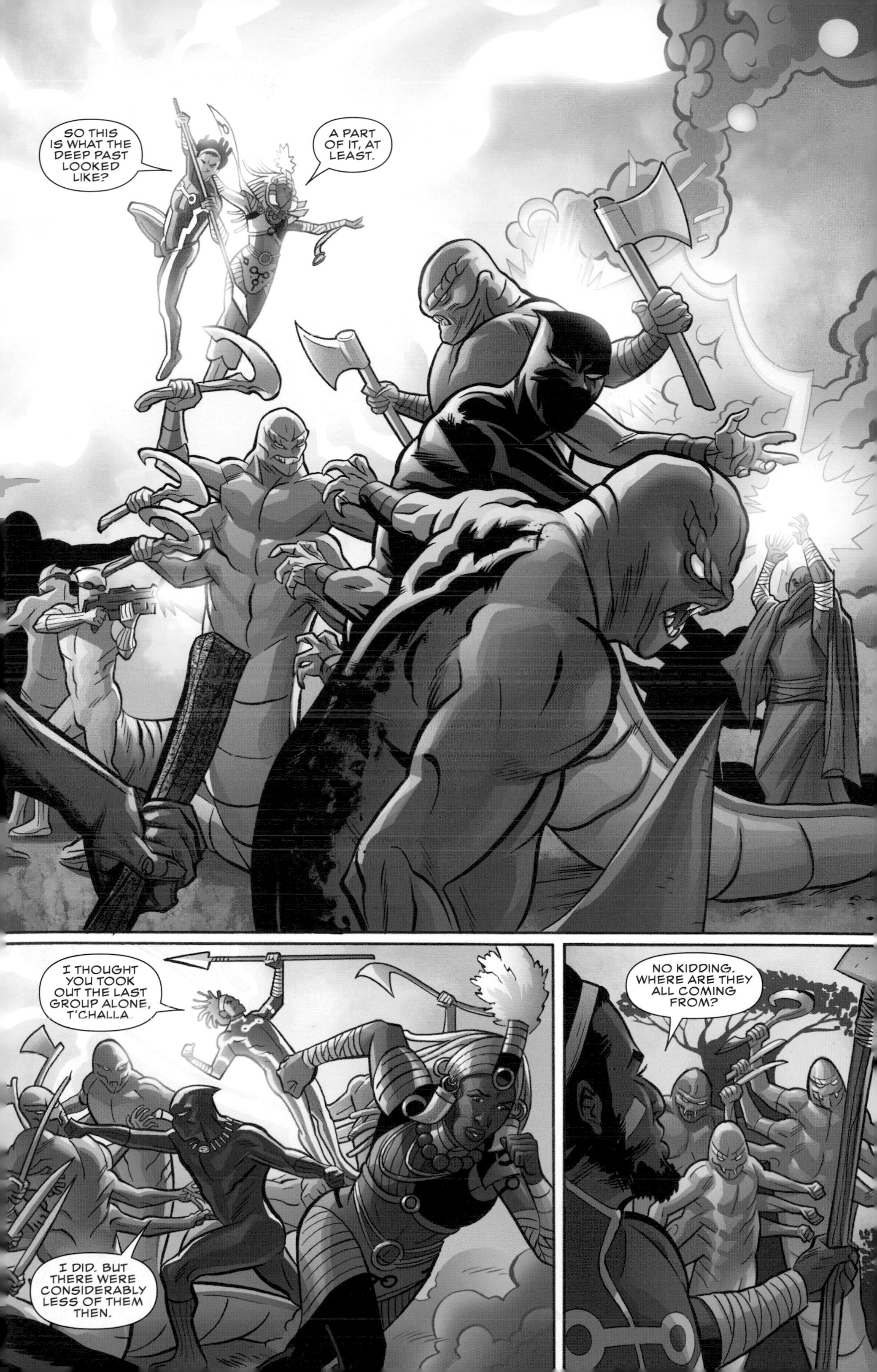
SO THIS IS WHAT THE DEEP PAST LOOKED LIKE?
A PART OF IT, AT LEAST.
I THOUGHT YOU TOOK OUT THE LAST GROUP ALONE, T'CHALLA.
I DID. BUT THERE WERE CONSIDERABLY LESS OF THEM THEN.
NO KIDDING. WHERE ARE THEY ALL COMING FROM?

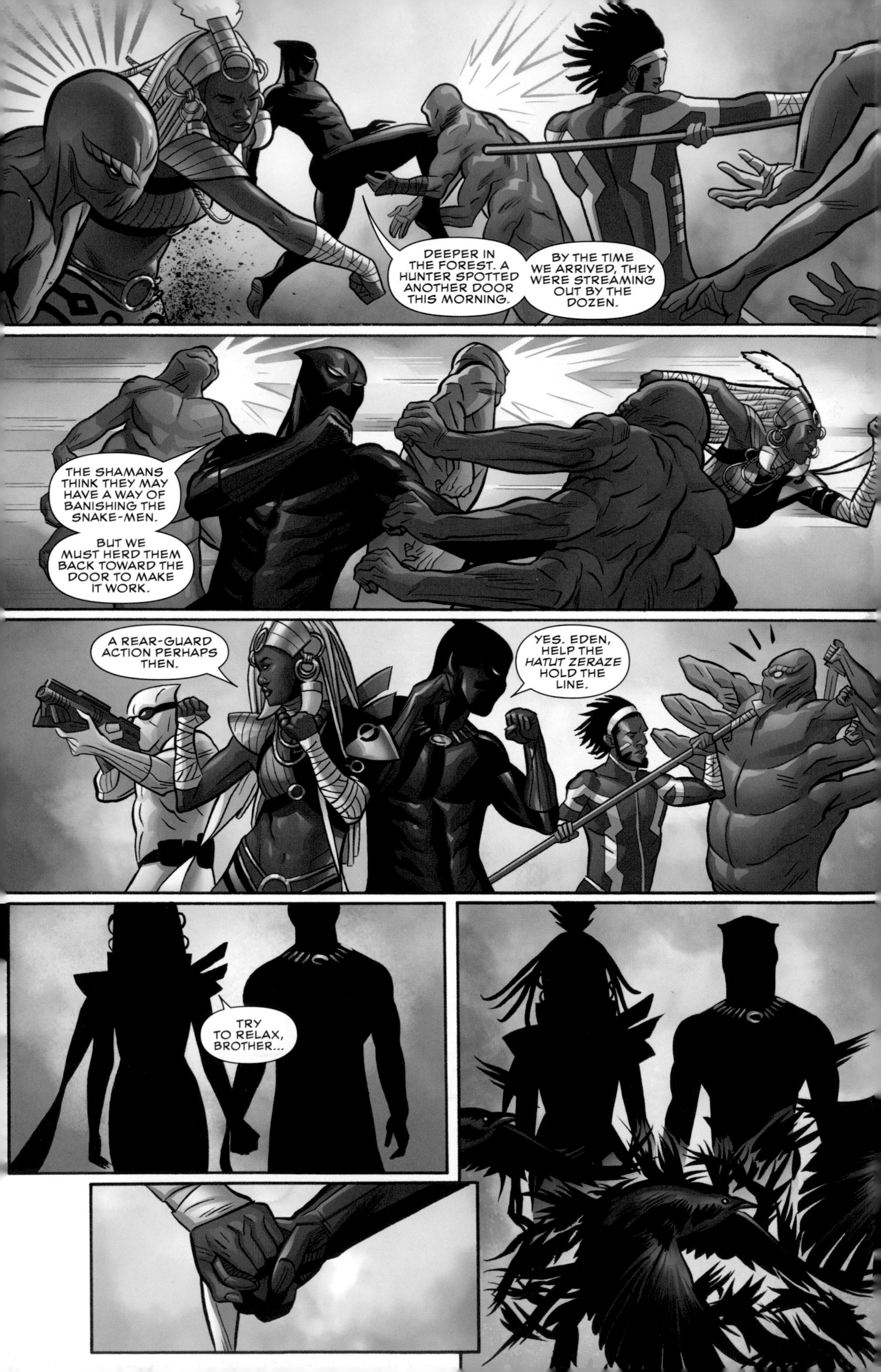
DEEPER IN THE FOREST. A HUNTER SPOTTED ANOTHER DOOR THIS MORNING.
BY THE TIME WE ARRIVED, THEY WERE STREAMING OUT BY THE DOZEN.
THE SHAMANS THINK THEY MAY HAVE A WAY OF BANISHING THE SNAKE-MEN.
BUT WE MUST HERD THEM BACK TOWARD THE DOOR TO MAKE IT WORK.
A REAR-GUARD ACTION PERHAPS THEN.
YES. EDEN, HELP THE *HATUT ZERAZE* HOLD THE LINE.
TRY TO RELAX, BROTHER...

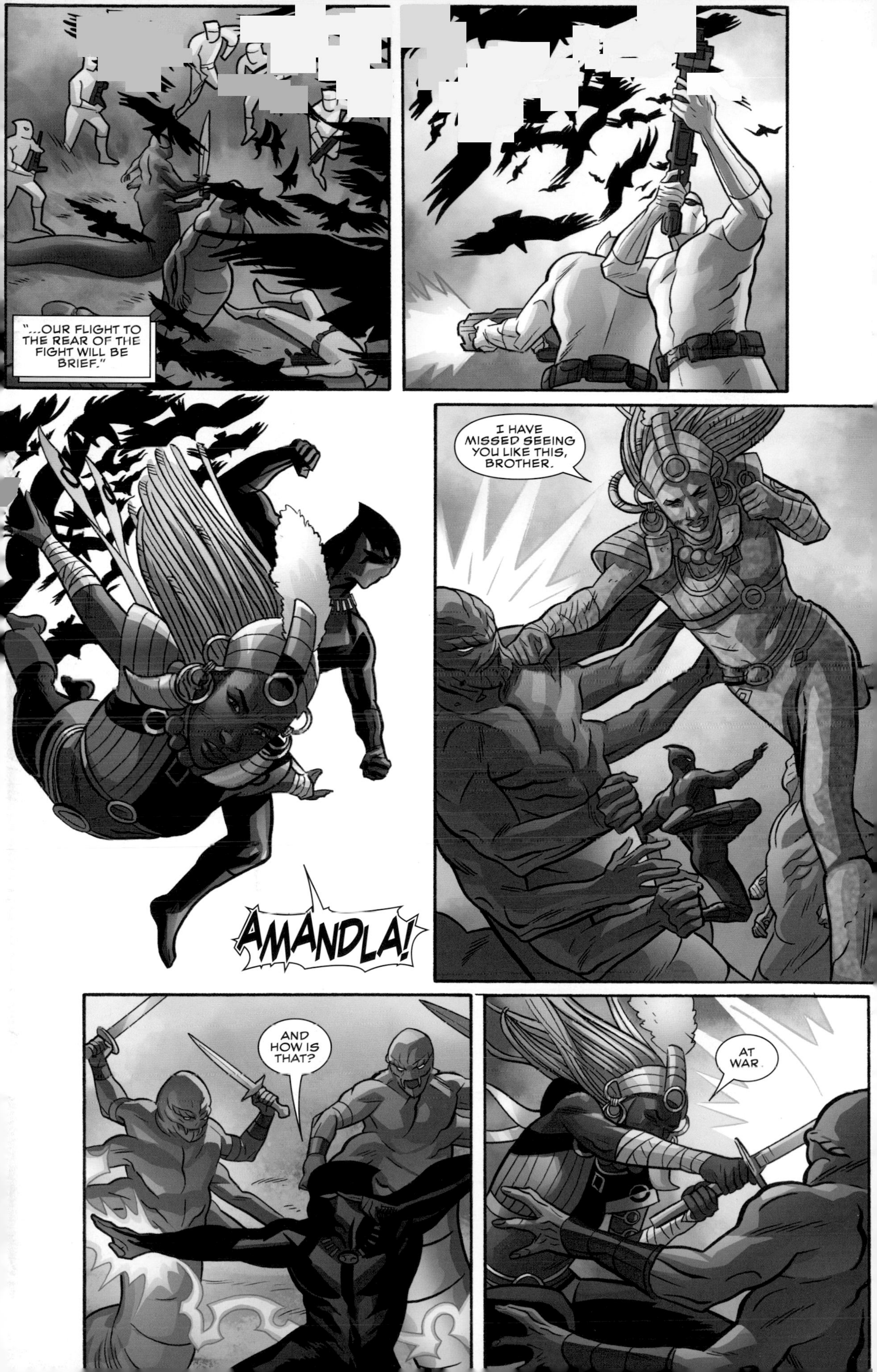
"...OUR FLIGHT TO THE REAR OF THE FIGHT WILL BE BRIEF."
AMANDLA!
I HAVE MISSED SEEING YOU LIKE THIS, BROTHER.
AND HOW IS THAT?
AT WAR.

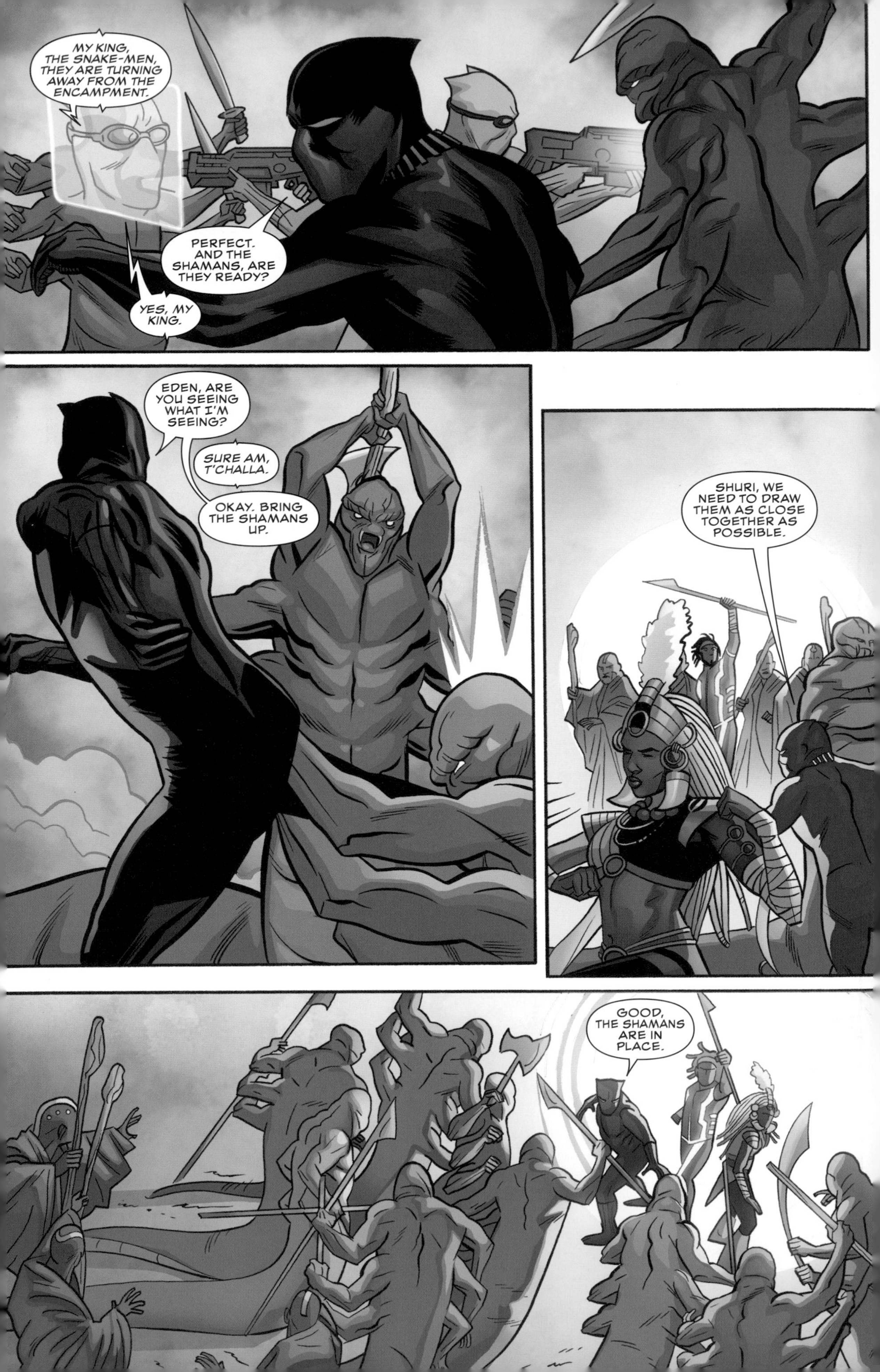
MY KING, THE SNAKE-MEN, THEY ARE TURNING AWAY FROM THE ENCAMPMENT.
PERFECT. AND THE SHAMANS, ARE THEY READY?
YES, MY KING.
EDEN, ARE YOU SEEING WHAT I'M SEEING?
SURE AM, T'CHALLA.
OKAY. BRING THE SHAMANS UP.
SHURI, WE NEED TO DRAW THEM AS CLOSE TOGETHER AS POSSIBLE.
GOOD, THE SHAMANS ARE IN PLACE.

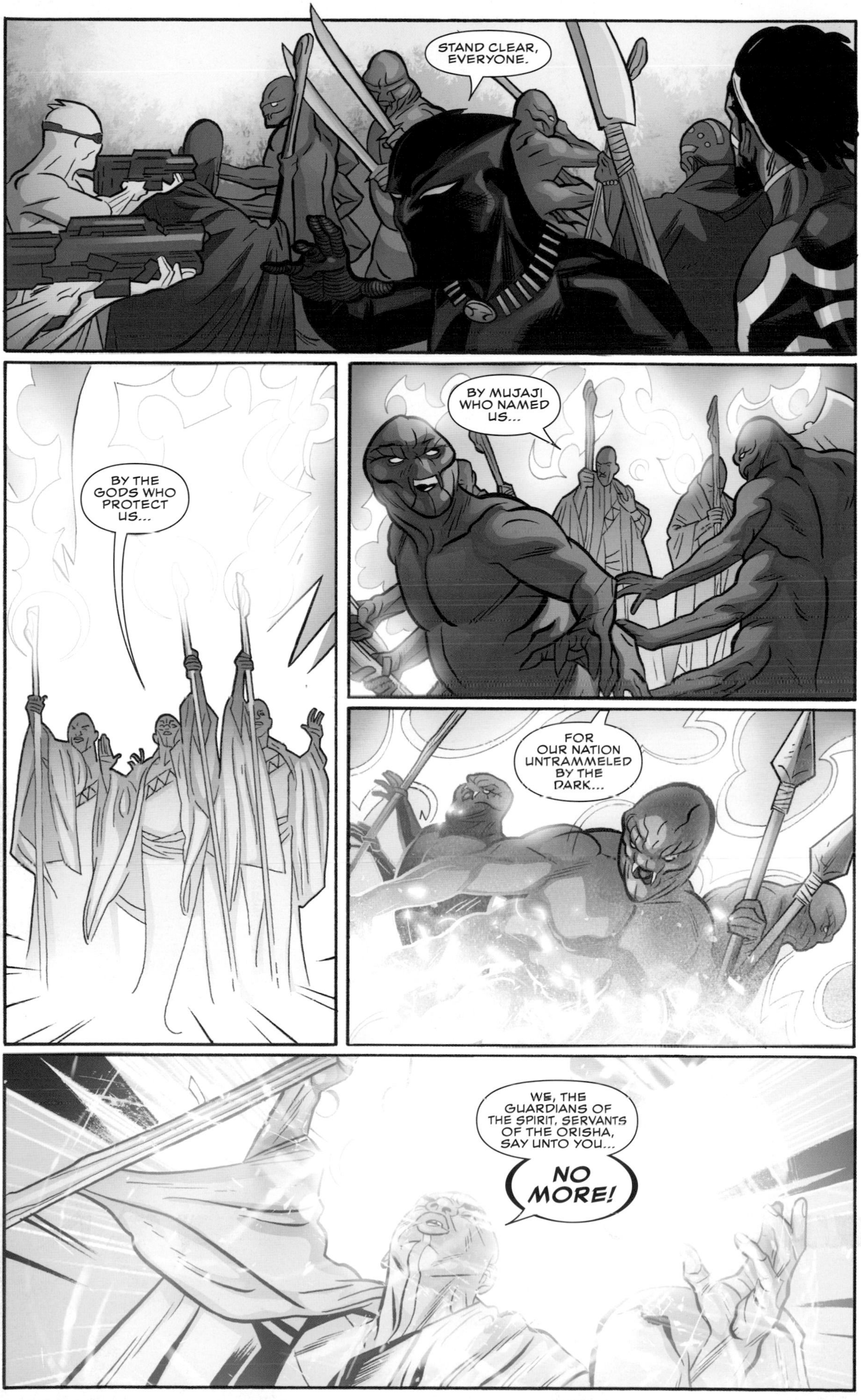
STAND CLEAR, EVERYONE.
BY THE GODS WHO PROTECT US...
BY MUJAJI WHO NAMED US...
FOR OUR NATION UNTRAMMELED BY THE DARK...
WE, THE GUARDIANS OF THE SPIRIT, SERVANTS OF THE ORISHA, SAY UNTO YOU...
NO MORE!

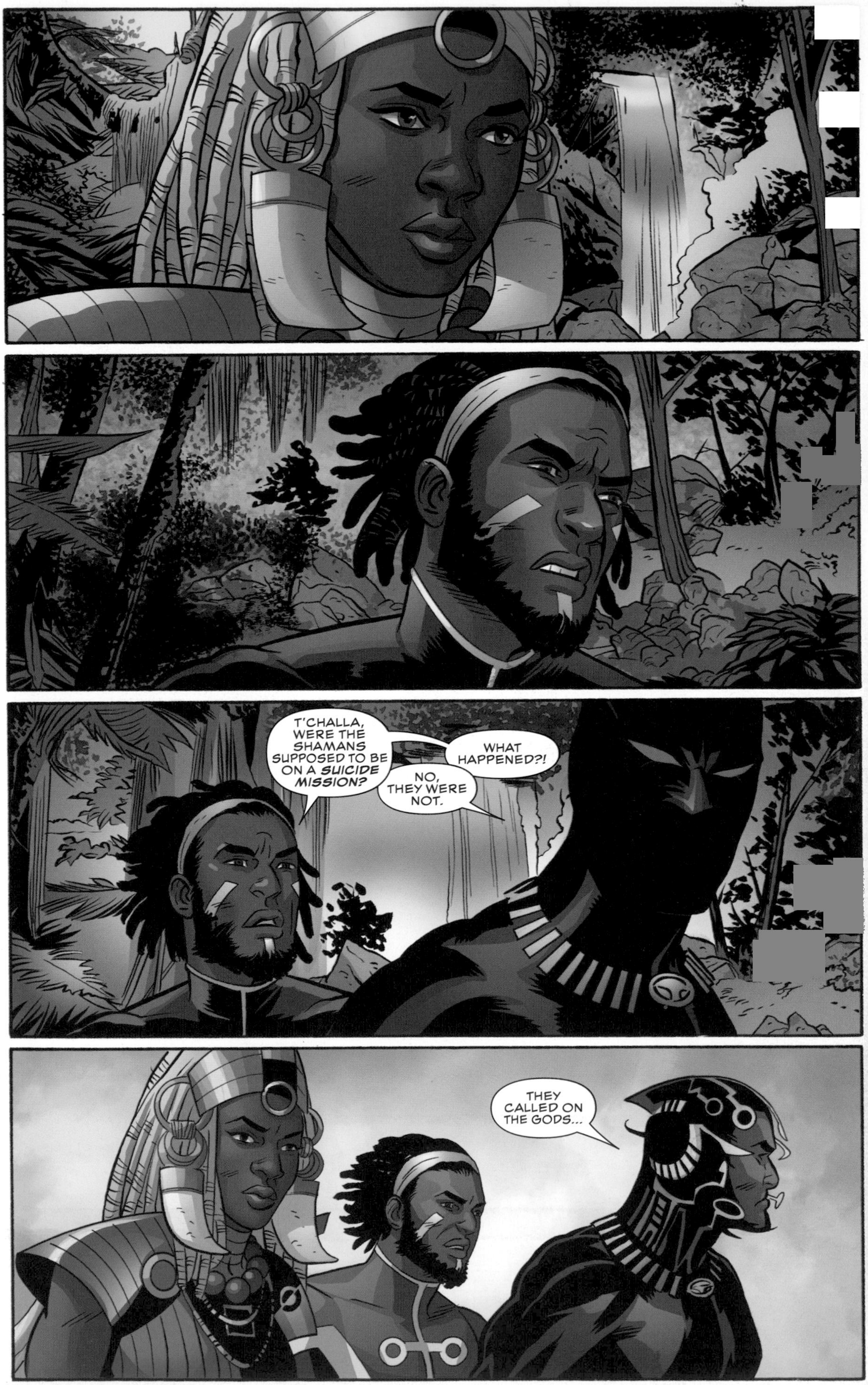
T'CHALLA, WERE THE SHAMANS SUPPOSED TO BE ON A SUICIDE MISSION?
WHAT HAPPENED?!
NO, THEY WERE NOT.
THEY CALLED ON THE GODS...

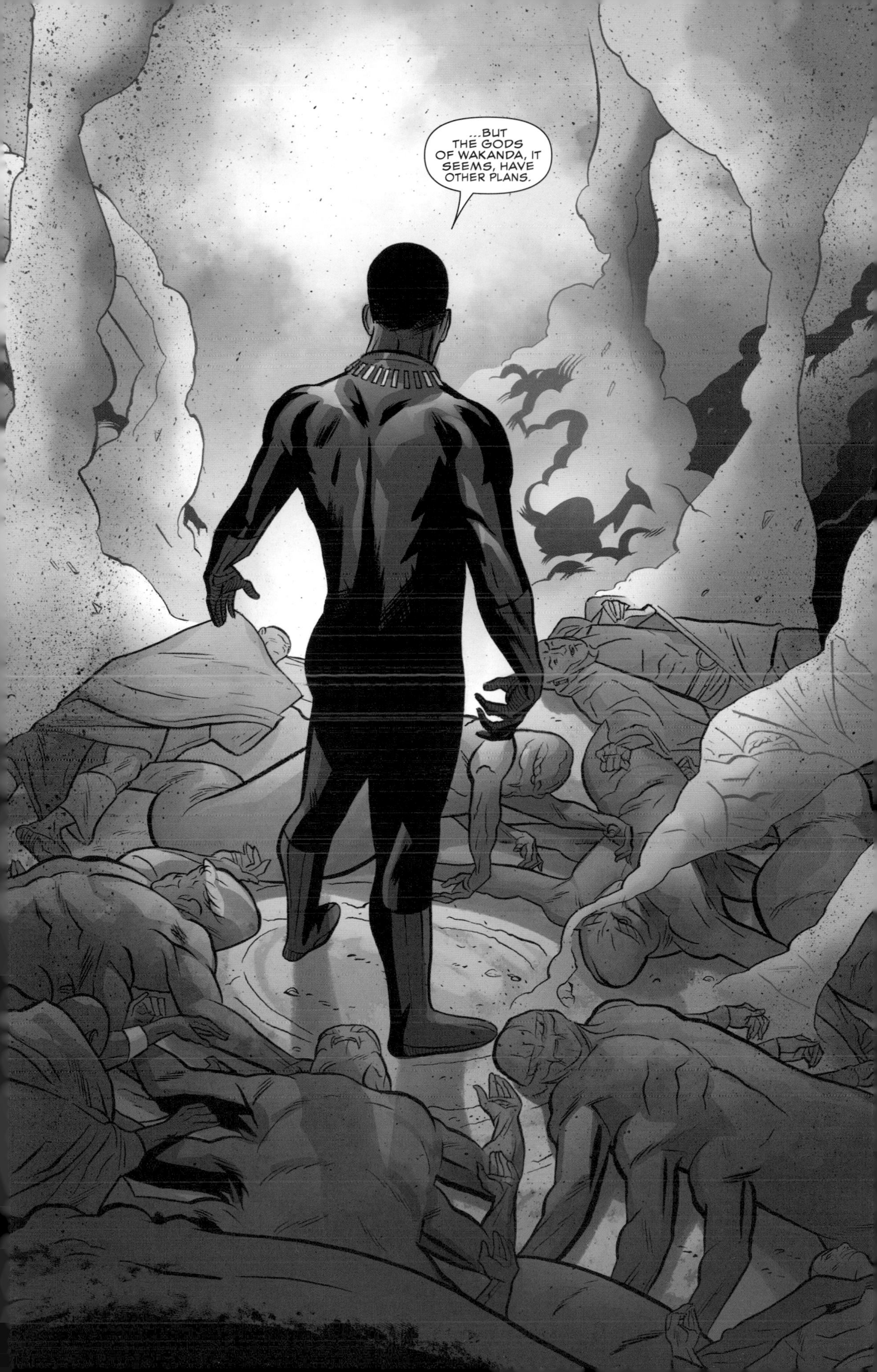
...BUT THE GODS OF WAKANDA, IT SEEMS, HAVE OTHER PLANS.

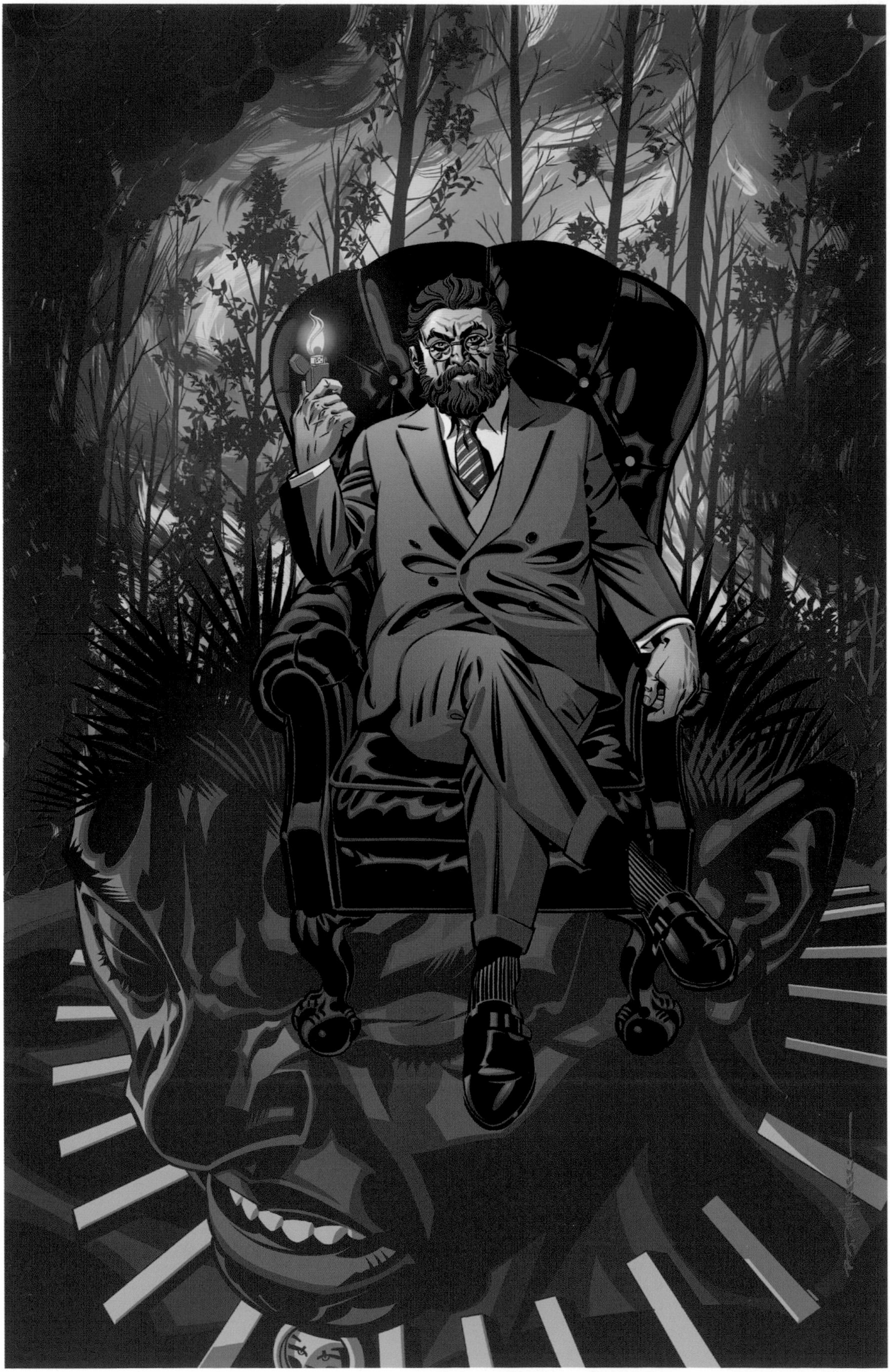

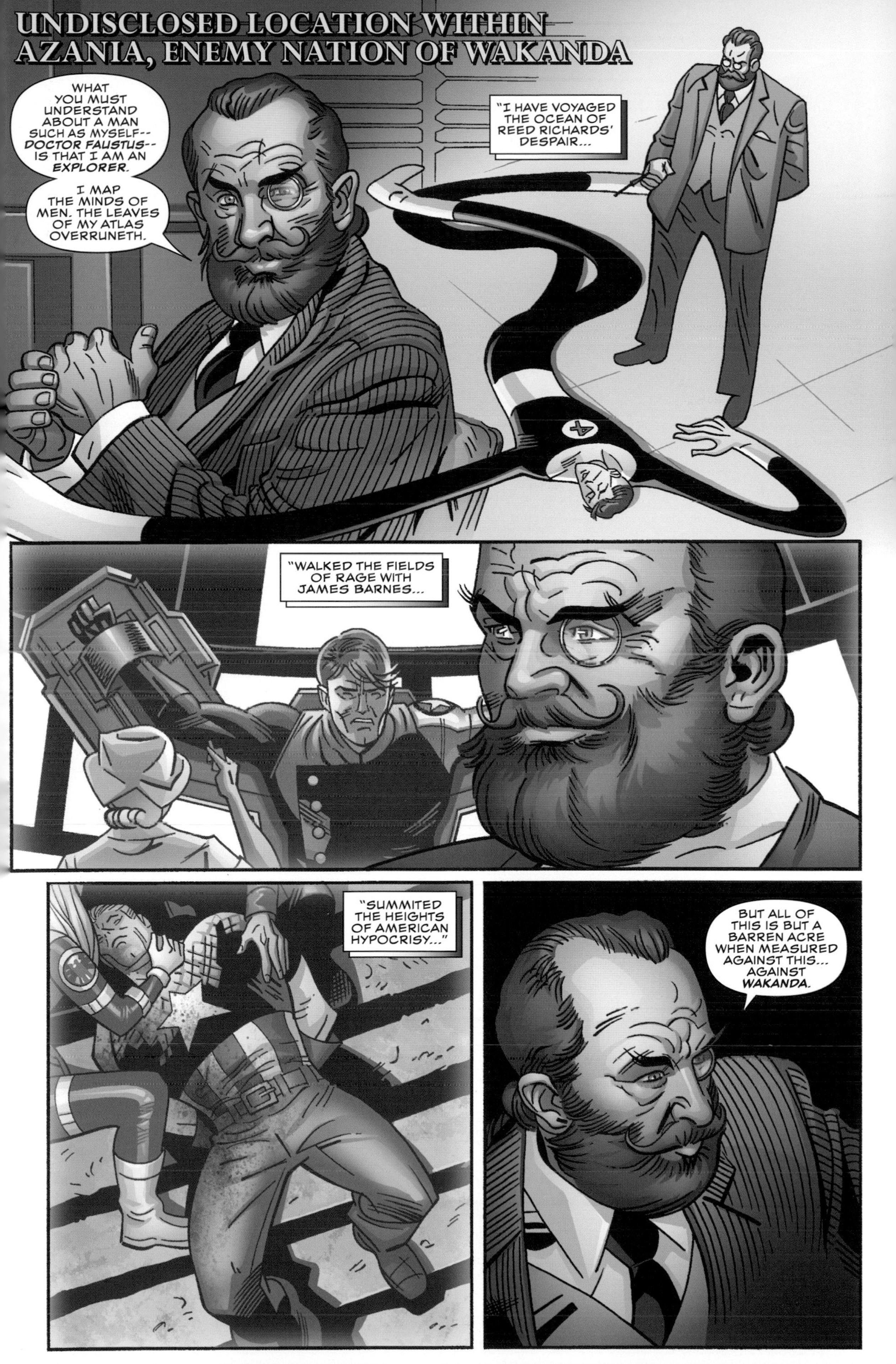
UNDISCLOSED LOCATION WITHIN AZANIA, ENEMY NATION OF WAKANDA
WHAT YOU MUST UNDERSTAND ABOUT A MAN SUCH AS MYSELF-- DOCTOR FAUSTUS-- IS THAT I AM AN EXPLORER.
I MAP THE MINDS OF MEN. THE LEAVES OF MY ATLAS OVERRUNETH.
"I HAVE VOYAGED THE OCEAN OF REED RICHARDS' DESPAIR...
"WALKED THE FIELDS OF RAGE WITH JAMES BARNES...
"SUMMITED THE HEIGHTS OF AMERICAN HYPOCRISY..."
BUT ALL OF THIS IS BUT A BARREN ACRE WHEN MEASURED AGAINST THIS... AGAINST WAKANDA.

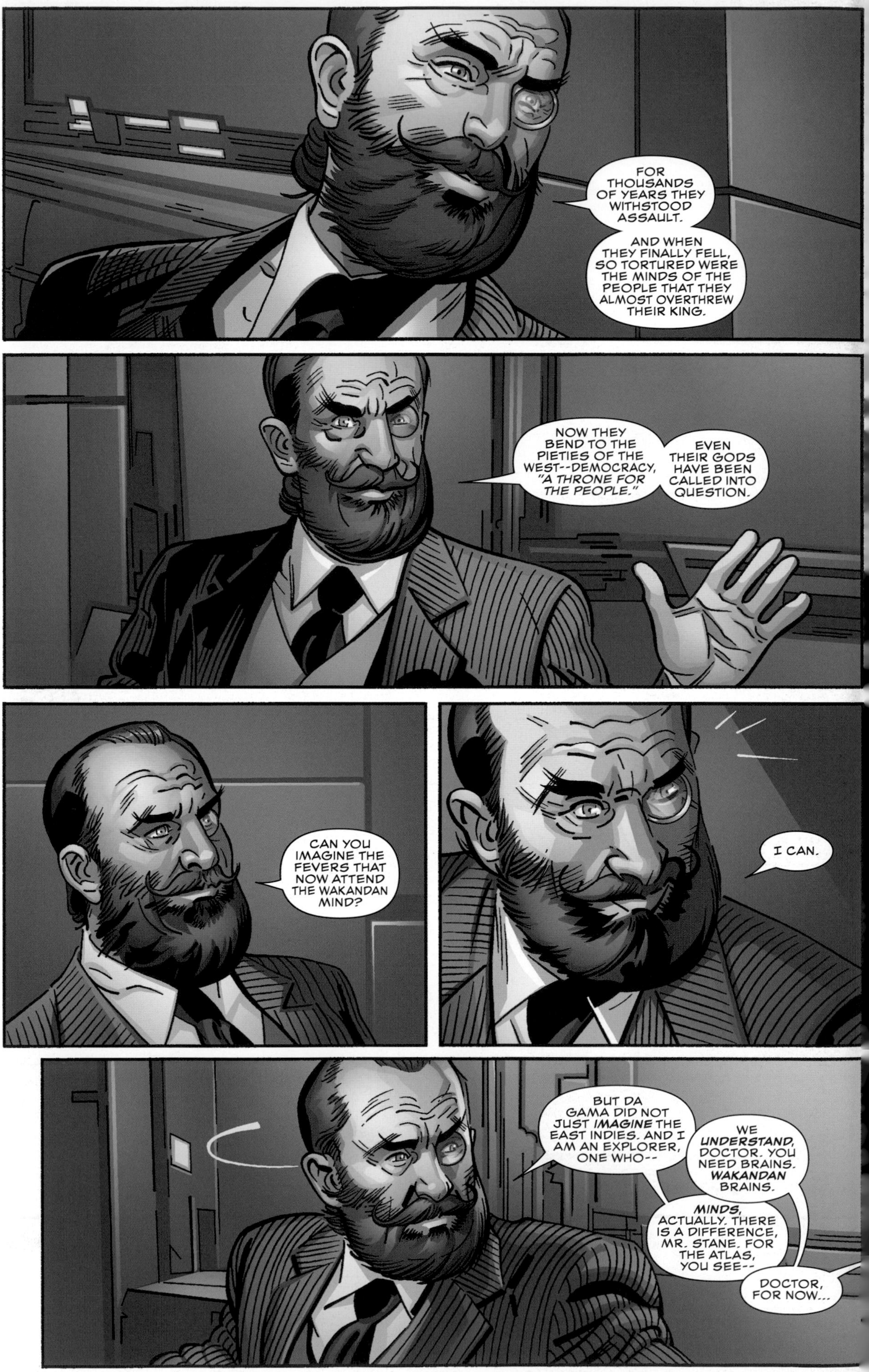
FOR THOUSANDS OF YEARS THEY WITHSTOOD ASSAULT.
AND WHEN THEY FINALLY FELL, SO TORTURED WERE THE MINDS OF THE PEOPLE THAT THEY ALMOST OVERTHREW THEIR KING.
NOW THEY BEND TO THE PIETIES OF THE WEST--DEMOCRACY, "A THRONE FOR THE PEOPLE."
EVEN THEIR GODS HAVE BEEN CALLED INTO QUESTION.
CAN YOU IMAGINE THE FEVERS THAT NOW ATTEND THE WAKANDAN MIND?
I CAN.
BUT DA GAMA DID NOT JUST IMAGINE THE EAST INDIES. AND I AM AN EXPLORER, ONE WHO--
WE UNDERSTAND, DOCTOR. YOU NEED BRAINS. WAKANDAN BRAINS.
MINDS, ACTUALLY. THERE IS A DIFFERENCE, MR. STANE. FOR THE ATLAS, YOU SEE--
DOCTOR, FOR NOW...

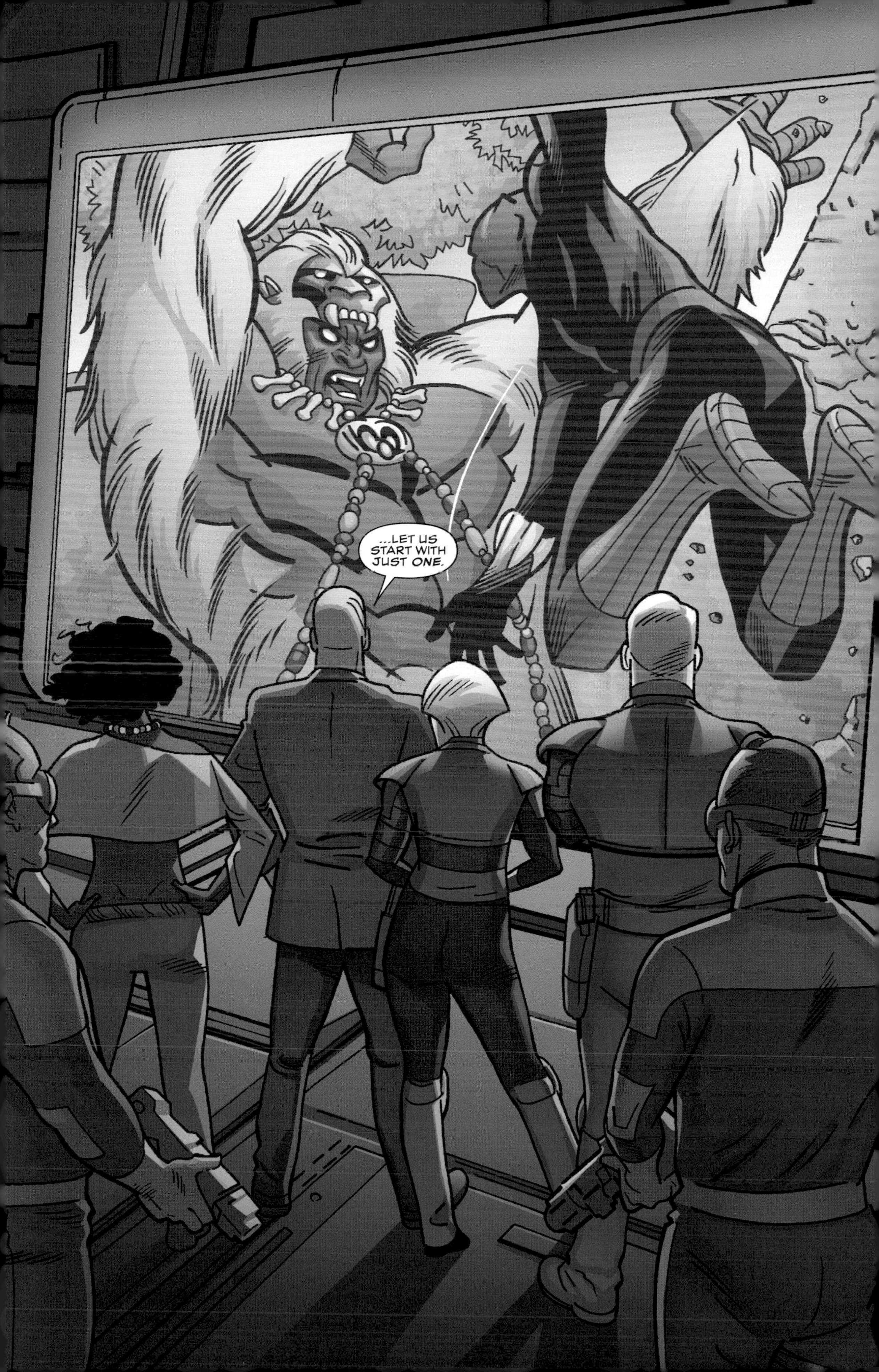
...LET US START WITH JUST ONE.

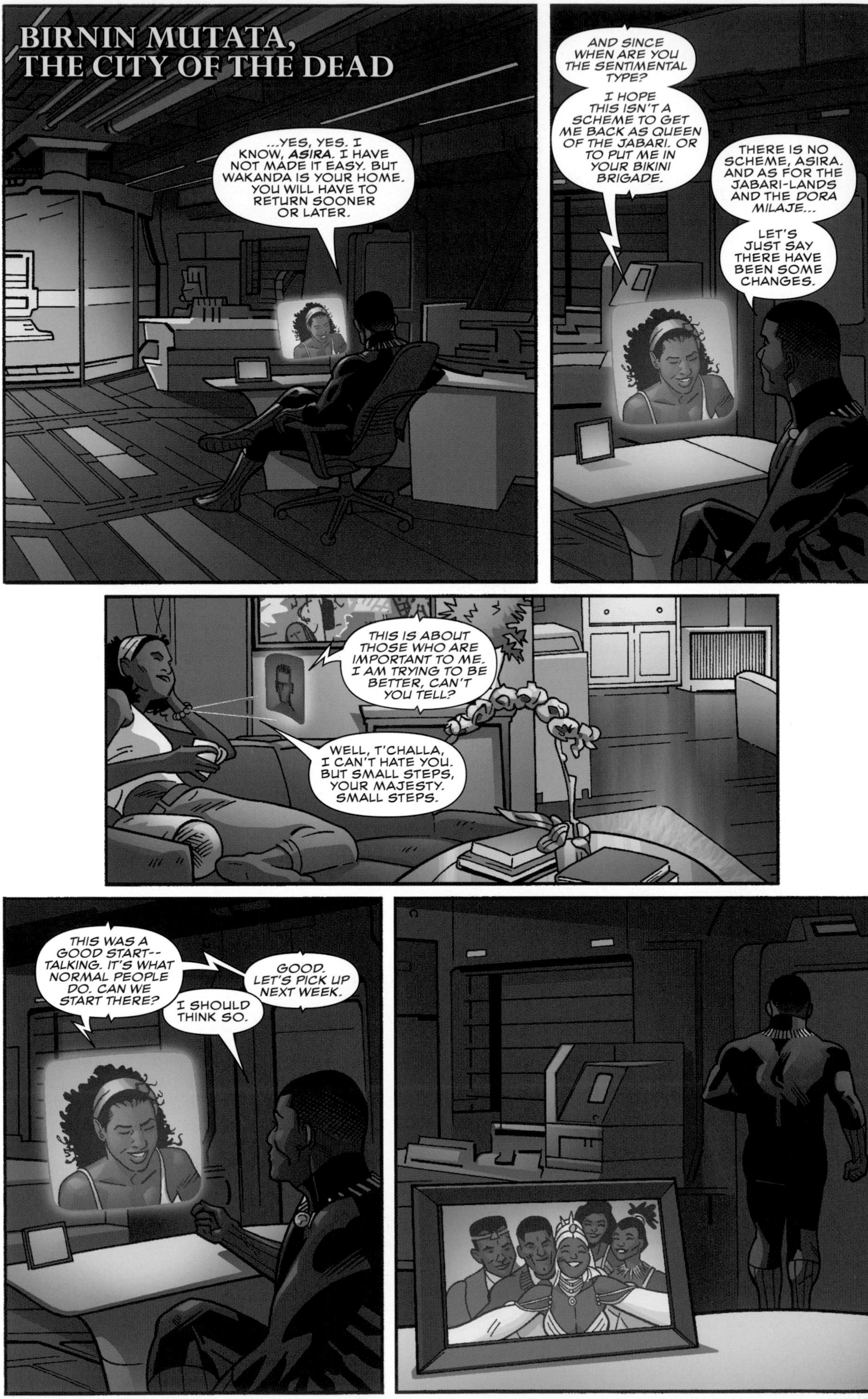
BIRNIN MUTATA, THE CITY OF THE DEAD
...YES, YES. I KNOW, ASIRA. I HAVE NOT MADE IT EASY. BUT WAKANDA IS YOUR HOME. YOU WILL HAVE TO RETURN SOONER OR LATER.
AND SINCE WHEN ARE YOU THE SENTIMENTAL TYPE?
I HOPE THIS ISN'T A SCHEME TO GET ME BACK AS QUEEN OF THE JABARI. OR TO PUT ME IN YOUR BIKINI BRIGADE.
THERE IS NO SCHEME, ASIRA. AND AS FOR THE JABARI-LANDS AND THE DORA MILAJE...
LET'S JUST SAY THERE HAVE BEEN SOME CHANGES.
THIS IS ABOUT THOSE WHO ARE IMPORTANT TO ME. I AM TRYING TO BE BETTER, CAN'T YOU TELL?
WELL, T'CHALLA, I CAN'T HATE YOU. BUT SMALL STEPS, YOUR MAJESTY. SMALL STEPS.
THIS WAS A GOOD START-- TALKING. IT'S WHAT NORMAL PEOPLE DO. CAN WE START THERE?
I SHOULD THINK SO.
GOOD. LET'S PICK UP NEXT WEEK.

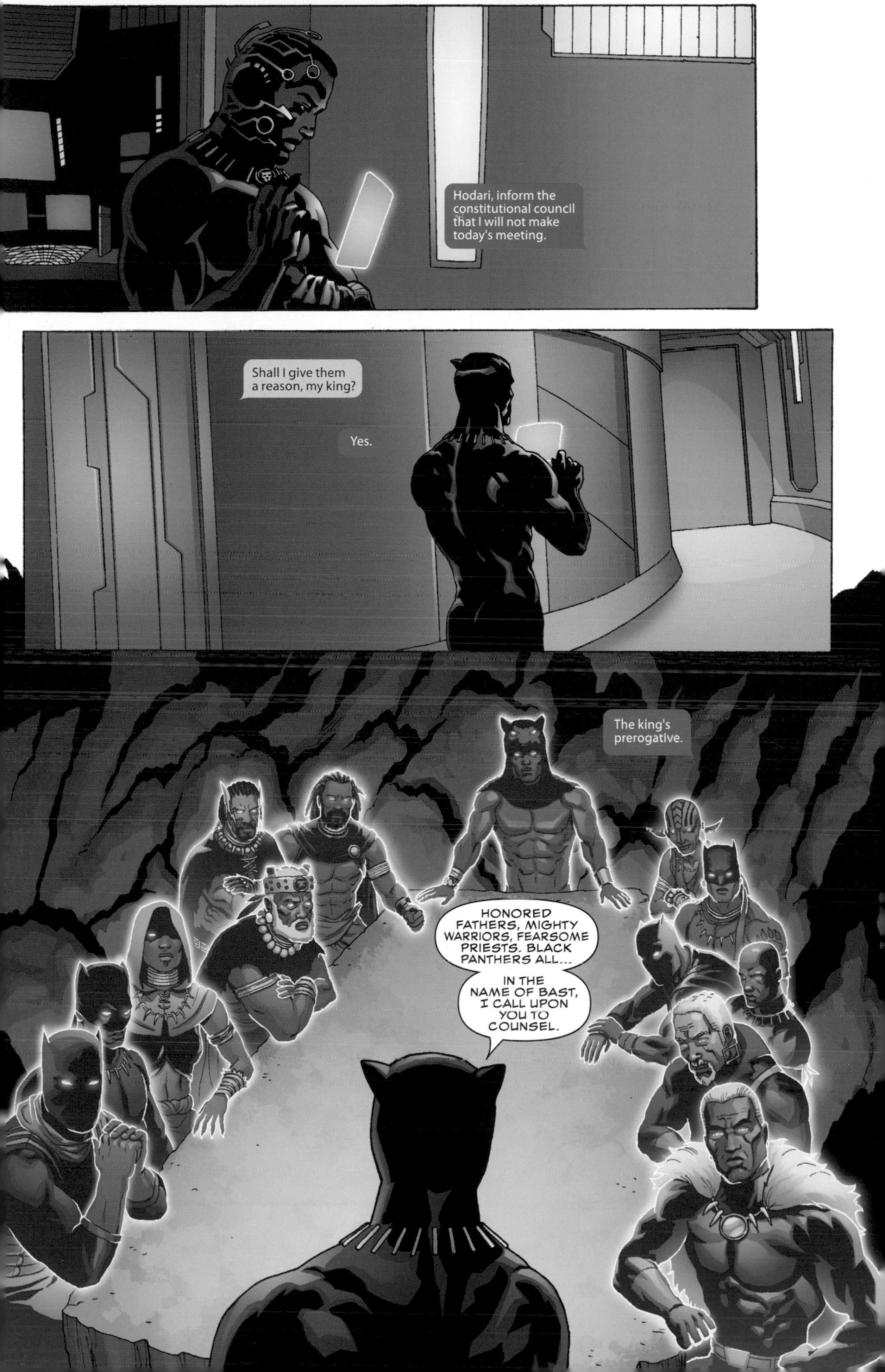
Hodari, inform the constitutional council that I will not make today's meeting.
Shall I give them a reason, my king?
Yes.
The king's prerogative.
HONORED FATHERS, MIGHTY WARRIORS, FEARSOME PRIESTS. BLACK PANTHERS ALL...
IN THE NAME OF BAST, I CALL UPON YOU TO COUNSEL.

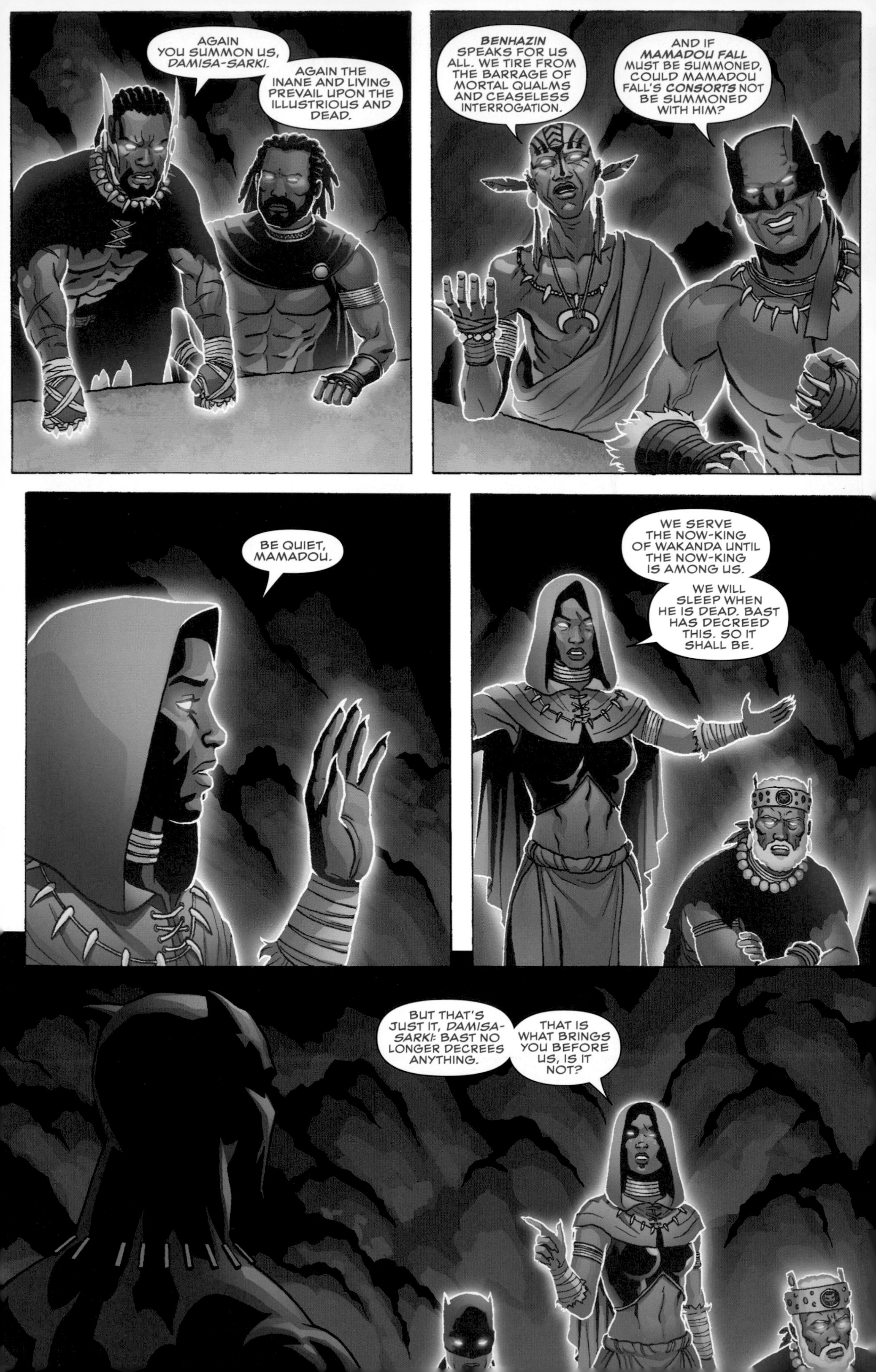
AGAIN YOU SUMMON US, DAMISA-SARKI.
AGAIN THE INANE AND LIVING PREVAIL UPON THE ILLUSTRIOUS AND DEAD.
BENHAZIN SPEAKS FOR US ALL. WE TIRE FROM THE BARRAGE OF MORTAL QUALMS AND CEASELESS INTERROGATION.
AND IF MAMADOU FALL MUST BE SUMMONED, COULD MAMADOU FALL'S CONSORTS NOT BE SUMMONED WITH HIM?
BE QUIET, MAMADOU.
WE SERVE THE NOW-KING OF WAKANDA UNTIL THE NOW-KING IS AMONG US.
WE WILL SLEEP WHEN HE IS DEAD. BAST HAS DECREED THIS. SO IT SHALL BE.
BUT THAT'S JUST IT, DAMISA-SARKI: BAST NO LONGER DECREES ANYTHING.
THAT IS WHAT BRINGS YOU BEFORE US, IS IT NOT?

IT IS.

YES, YES. I SEE IT NOW. LOOK HERE, BROTHERS. MY SIGHT IS YOUR SIGHT.

NEHANDA IS RIGHT. THE RAIN CLOUDS HOLD OVER WAKANDA LIKE A VENUE OF BUZZARDS OVER A DYING HERD.

WHOSE SORCERY IS THIS? NAMOR, WHOM THE NOW-KING DID NOT SLAY?

NO. SOMETHING ELSE. THE WOODLANDS CRY OUT. WHERE IS MUJAJI? WHERE IS THOTH WHO CIVILIZED MEN? WHERE IS THE SHAPER?

QUIET BROTHERS, LET MY NEPHEW SPEAK. EVEN THE EYES OF NEHANDA HAVE LIMITS.

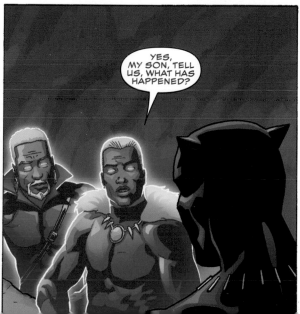

YES, MY SON, TELL US, WHAT HAS HAPPENED?

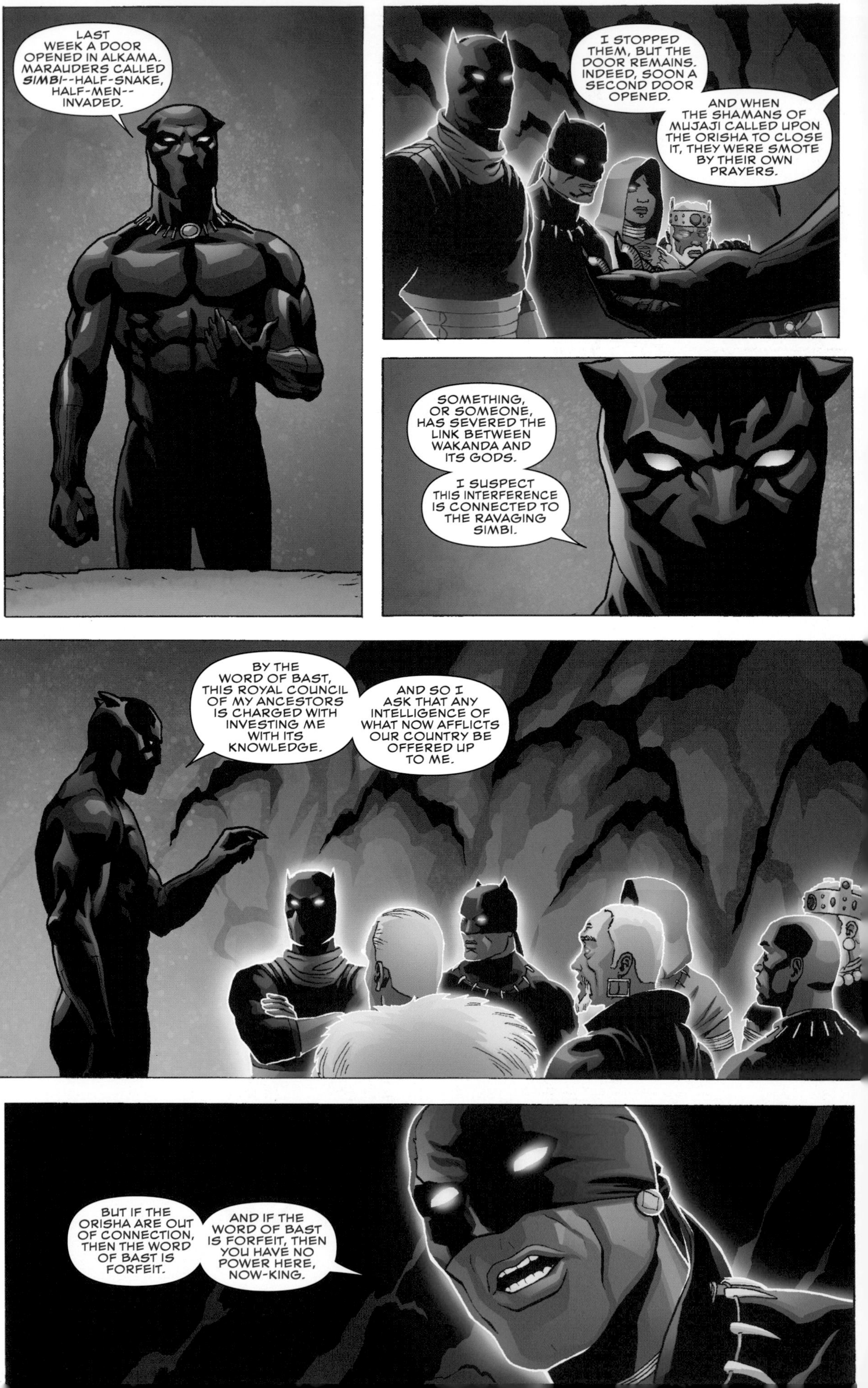
LAST WEEK A DOOR OPENED IN ALKAMA. MARAUDERS CALLED SIMBI--HALF-SNAKE, HALF-MEN--INVADED.
I STOPPED THEM, BUT THE DOOR REMAINS. INDEED, SOON A SECOND DOOR OPENED.
AND WHEN THE SHAMANS OF MUJAJI CALLED UPON THE ORISHA TO CLOSE IT, THEY WERE SMOTE BY THEIR OWN PRAYERS.
SOMETHING, OR SOMEONE, HAS SEVERED THE LINK BETWEEN WAKANDA AND ITS GODS.
I SUSPECT THIS INTERFERENCE IS CONNECTED TO THE RAVAGING SIMBI.
BY THE WORD OF BAST, THIS ROYAL COUNCIL OF MY ANCESTORS IS CHARGED WITH INVESTING ME WITH ITS KNOWLEDGE.
AND SO I ASK THAT ANY INTELLIGENCE OF WHAT NOW AFFLICTS OUR COUNTRY BE OFFERED UP TO ME.
BUT IF THE ORISHA ARE OUT OF CONNECTION, THEN THE WORD OF BAST IS FORFEIT.
AND IF THE WORD OF BAST IS FORFEIT, THEN YOU HAVE NO POWER HERE, NOW-KING.

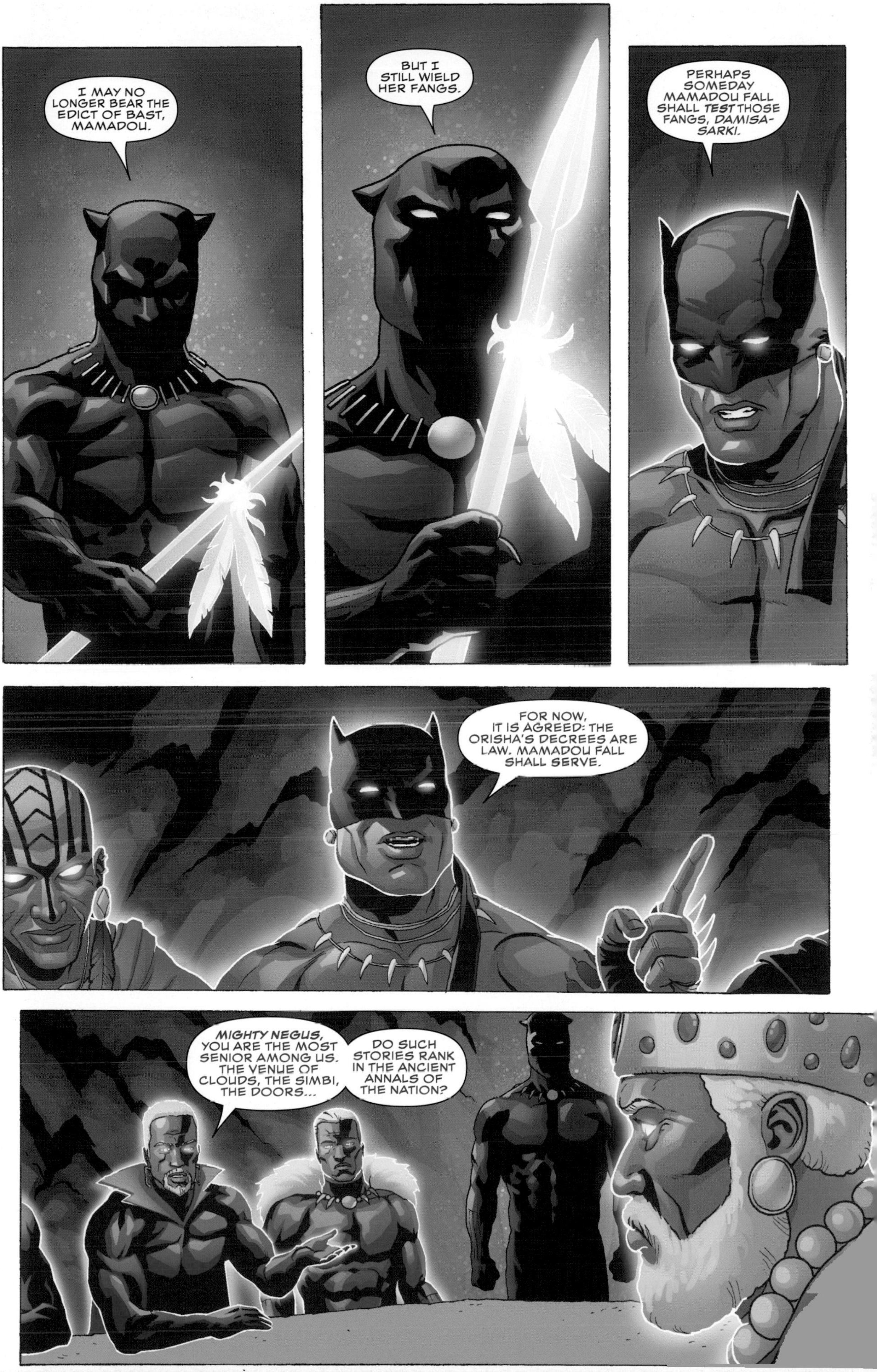
I MAY NO LONGER BEAR THE EDICT OF BAST, MAMADOU.
BUT I STILL WIELD HER FANGS.
PERHAPS SOMEDAY MAMADOU FALL SHALL *TEST* THOSE FANGS, *DAMISA-SARKI.*
FOR NOW, IT IS AGREED: THE ORISHA'S DECREES ARE LAW. MAMADOU FALL SHALL SERVE.
MIGHTY NEGUS, YOU ARE THE MOST SENIOR AMONG US. THE VENUE OF CLOUDS, THE SIMBI, THE DOORS...
DO SUCH STORIES RANK IN THE ANCIENT ANNALS OF THE NATION?

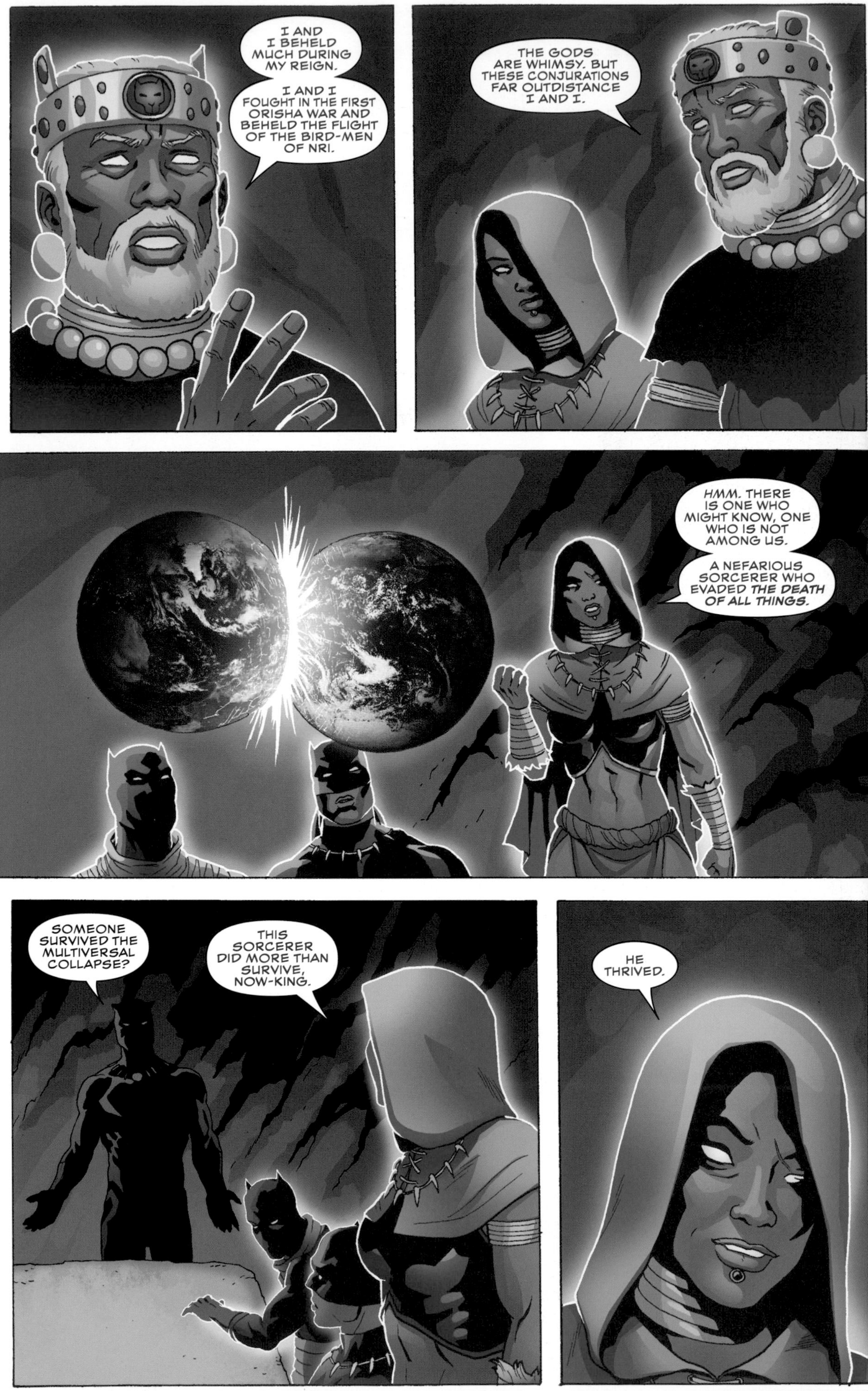
I AND I BEHELD MUCH DURING MY REIGN.
I AND I FOUGHT IN THE FIRST ORISHA WAR AND BEHELD THE FLIGHT OF THE BIRD-MEN OF NRI.
THE GODS ARE WHIMSY. BUT THESE CONJURATIONS FAR OUTDISTANCE I AND I.
HMM. THERE IS ONE WHO MIGHT KNOW, ONE WHO IS NOT AMONG US.
A NEFARIOUS SORCERER WHO EVADED ***THE DEATH OF ALL THINGS.***
SOMEONE SURVIVED THE MULTIVERSAL COLLAPSE?
THIS SORCERER DID MORE THAN SURVIVE, NOW-KING.
HE *THRIVED.*

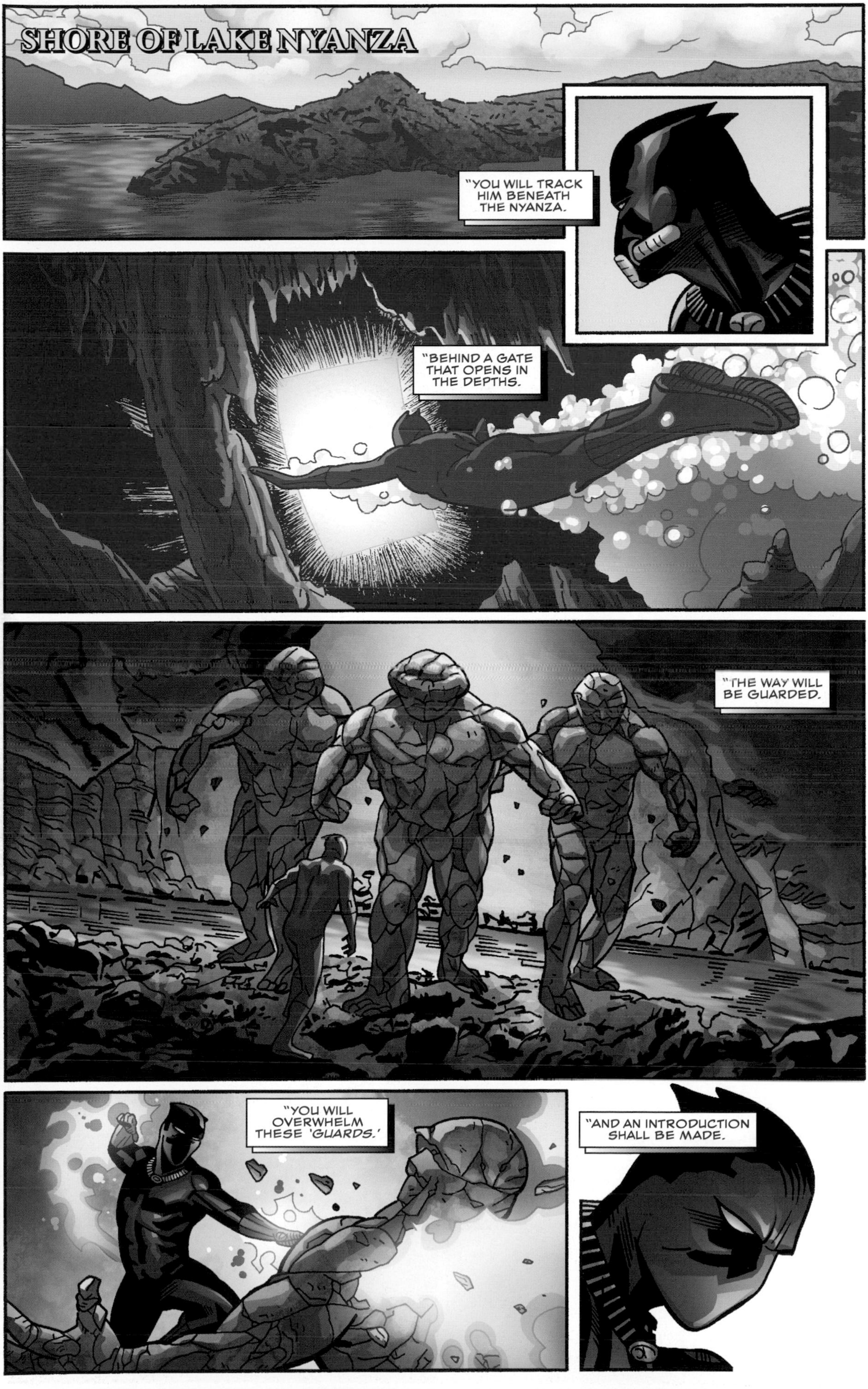
SHORE OF LAKE NYANZA
"YOU WILL TRACK HIM BENEATH THE NYANZA.
"BEHIND A GATE THAT OPENS IN THE DEPTHS.
"THE WAY WILL BE GUARDED.
"YOU WILL OVERWHELM THESE 'GUARDS.'
"AND AN INTRODUCTION SHALL BE MADE.

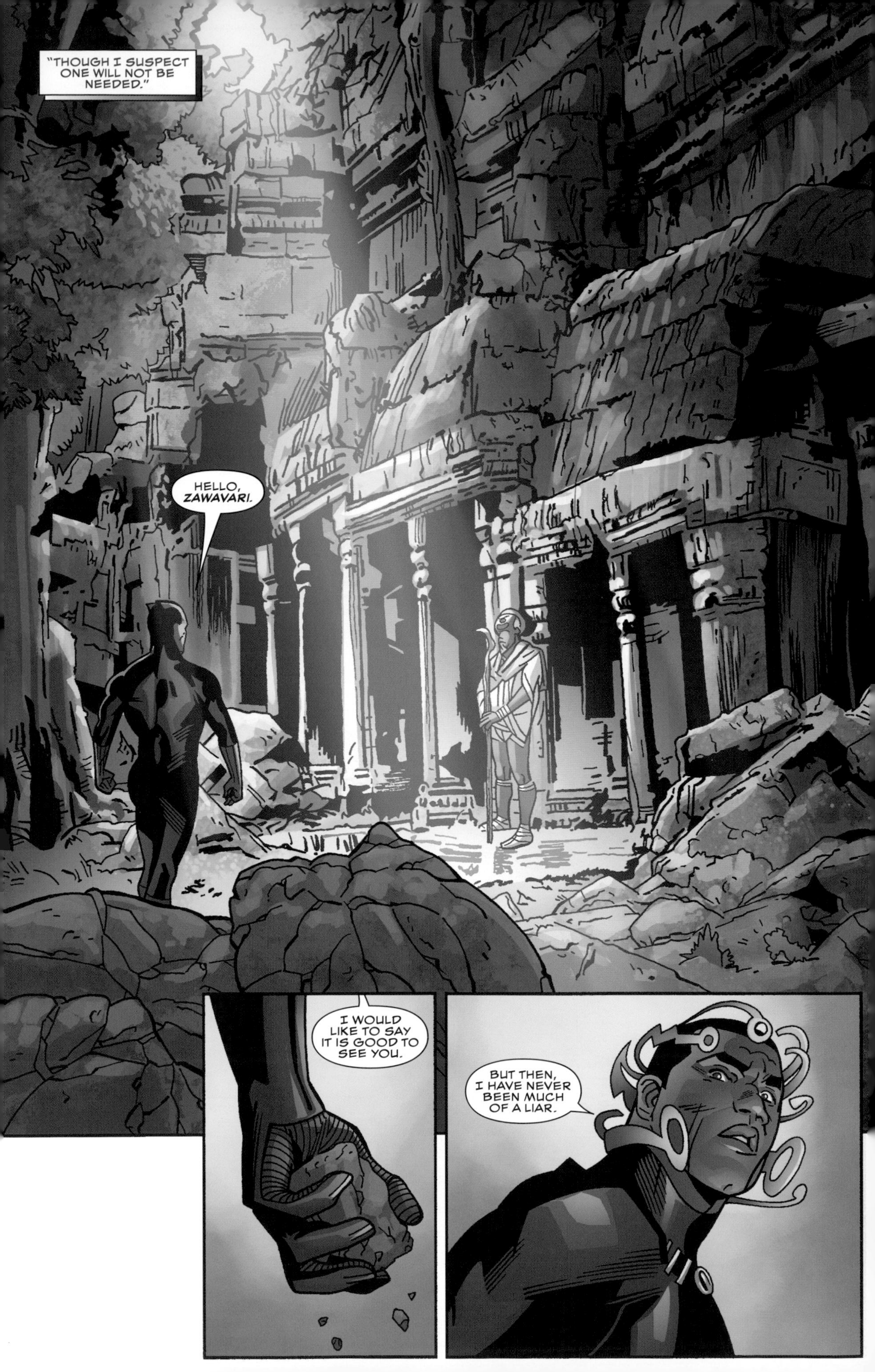
"THOUGH I SUSPECT ONE WILL NOT BE NEEDED."
HELLO, ZAWAVARI.
I WOULD LIKE TO SAY IT IS GOOD TO SEE YOU.
BUT THEN, I HAVE NEVER BEEN MUCH OF A LIAR.

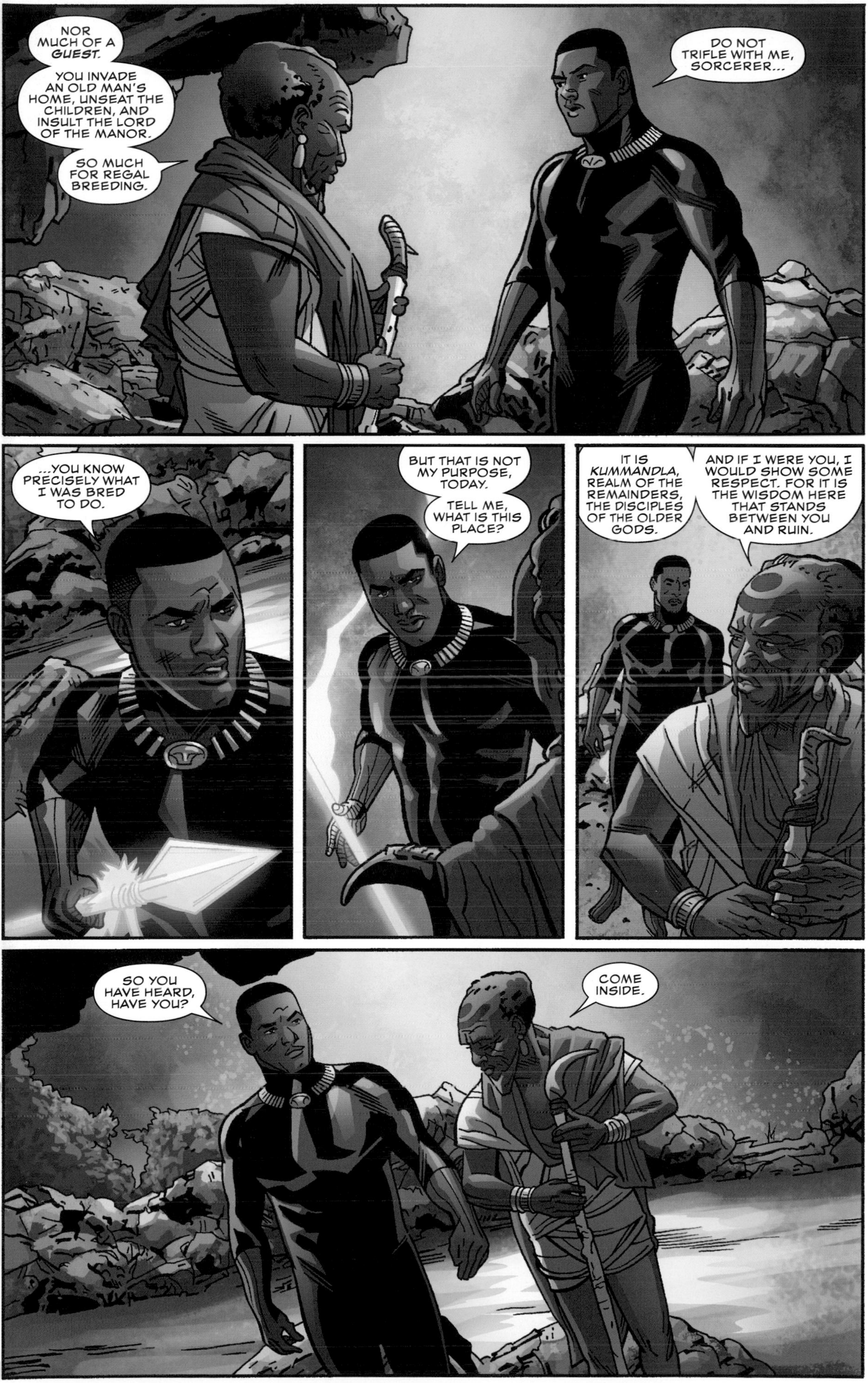
NOR MUCH OF A GUEST.
YOU INVADE AN OLD MAN'S HOME, UNSEAT THE CHILDREN, AND INSULT THE LORD OF THE MANOR.
SO MUCH FOR REGAL BREEDING.
DO NOT TRIFLE WITH ME, SORCERER...
...YOU KNOW PRECISELY WHAT I WAS BRED TO DO.
BUT THAT IS NOT MY PURPOSE, TODAY.
TELL ME, WHAT IS THIS PLACE?
IT IS KUMMANDLA, REALM OF THE REMAINDERS, THE DISCIPLES OF THE OLDER GODS.
AND IF I WERE YOU, I WOULD SHOW SOME RESPECT. FOR IT IS THE WISDOM HERE THAT STANDS BETWEEN YOU AND RUIN.
SO YOU HAVE HEARD, HAVE YOU?
COME INSIDE.

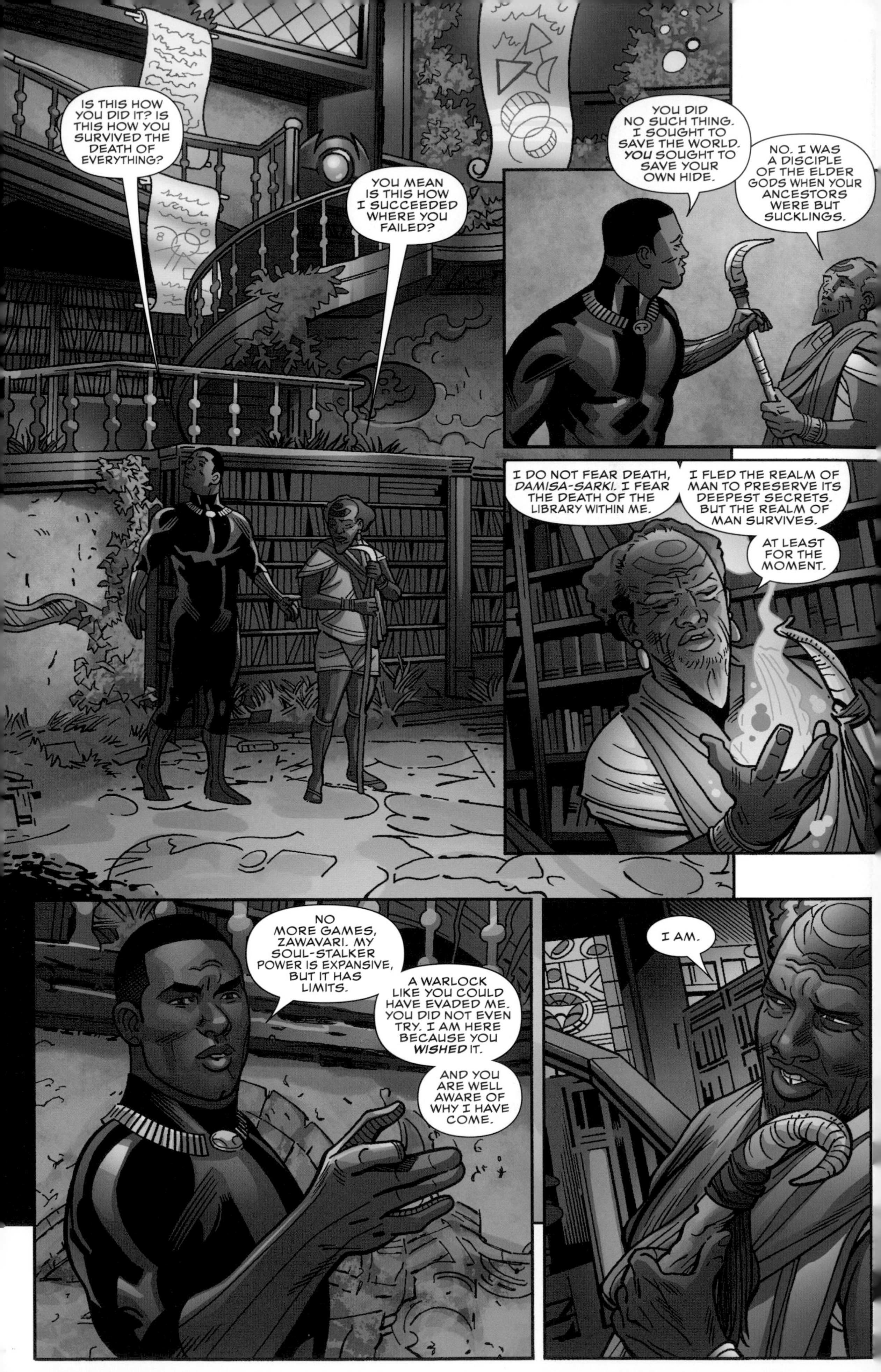
IS THIS HOW YOU DID IT? IS THIS HOW YOU SURVIVED THE DEATH OF EVERYTHING?
YOU MEAN IS THIS HOW I SUCCEEDED WHERE YOU FAILED?
YOU DID NO SUCH THING. I SOUGHT TO SAVE THE WORLD. *YOU* SOUGHT TO SAVE YOUR OWN HIDE.
NO. I WAS A DISCIPLE OF THE ELDER GODS WHEN YOUR ANCESTORS WERE BUT SUCKLINGS.
I DO NOT FEAR DEATH, *DAMISA-SARKI*. I FEAR THE DEATH OF THE LIBRARY WITHIN ME.
I FLED THE REALM OF MAN TO PRESERVE ITS DEEPEST SECRETS. BUT THE REALM OF MAN SURVIVES.
AT LEAST FOR THE MOMENT.
NO MORE GAMES, ZAWAVARI. MY SOUL-STALKER POWER IS EXPANSIVE, BUT IT HAS LIMITS.
A WARLOCK LIKE YOU COULD HAVE EVADED ME. YOU DID NOT EVEN TRY. I AM HERE BECAUSE YOU *WISHED* IT.
AND YOU ARE WELL AWARE OF WHY I HAVE COME.
I AM.

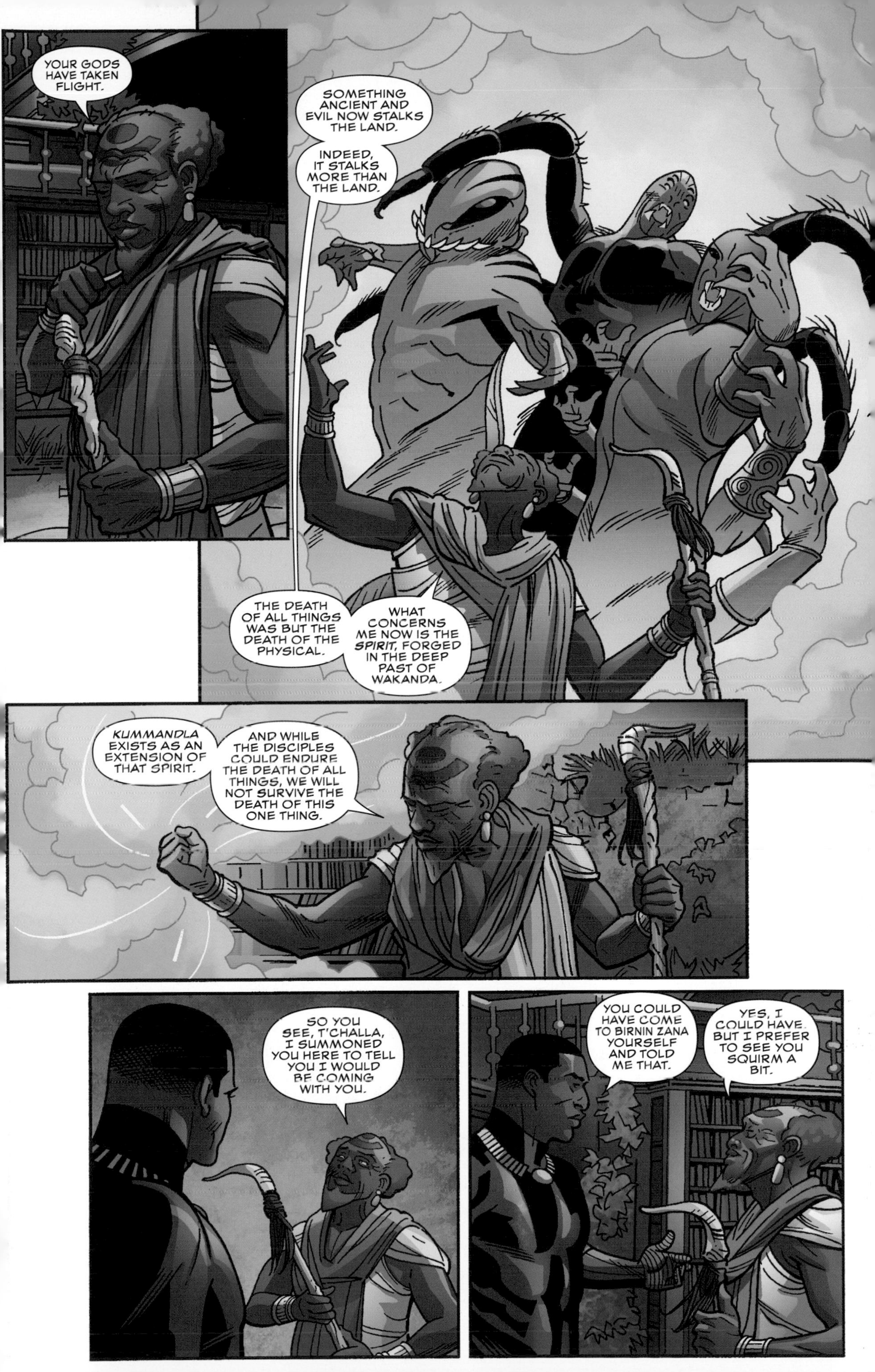

YOUR GODS HAVE TAKEN FLIGHT.
SOMETHING ANCIENT AND EVIL NOW STALKS THE LAND.
INDEED, IT STALKS MORE THAN THE LAND.
THE DEATH OF ALL THINGS WAS BUT THE DEATH OF THE PHYSICAL.
WHAT CONCERNS ME NOW IS THE *SPIRIT*, FORGED IN THE DEEP PAST OF WAKANDA.
KUMMANDLA EXISTS AS AN EXTENSION OF THAT SPIRIT.
AND WHILE THE DISCIPLES COULD ENDURE THE DEATH OF ALL THINGS, WE WILL NOT SURVIVE THE DEATH OF THIS ONE THING.
SO YOU SEE, T'CHALLA, I SUMMONED YOU HERE TO TELL YOU I WOULD BE COMING WITH YOU.
YOU COULD HAVE COME TO BIRNIN ZANA YOURSELF AND TOLD ME THAT.
YES, I COULD HAVE. BUT I PREFER TO SEE YOU SQUIRM A BIT.

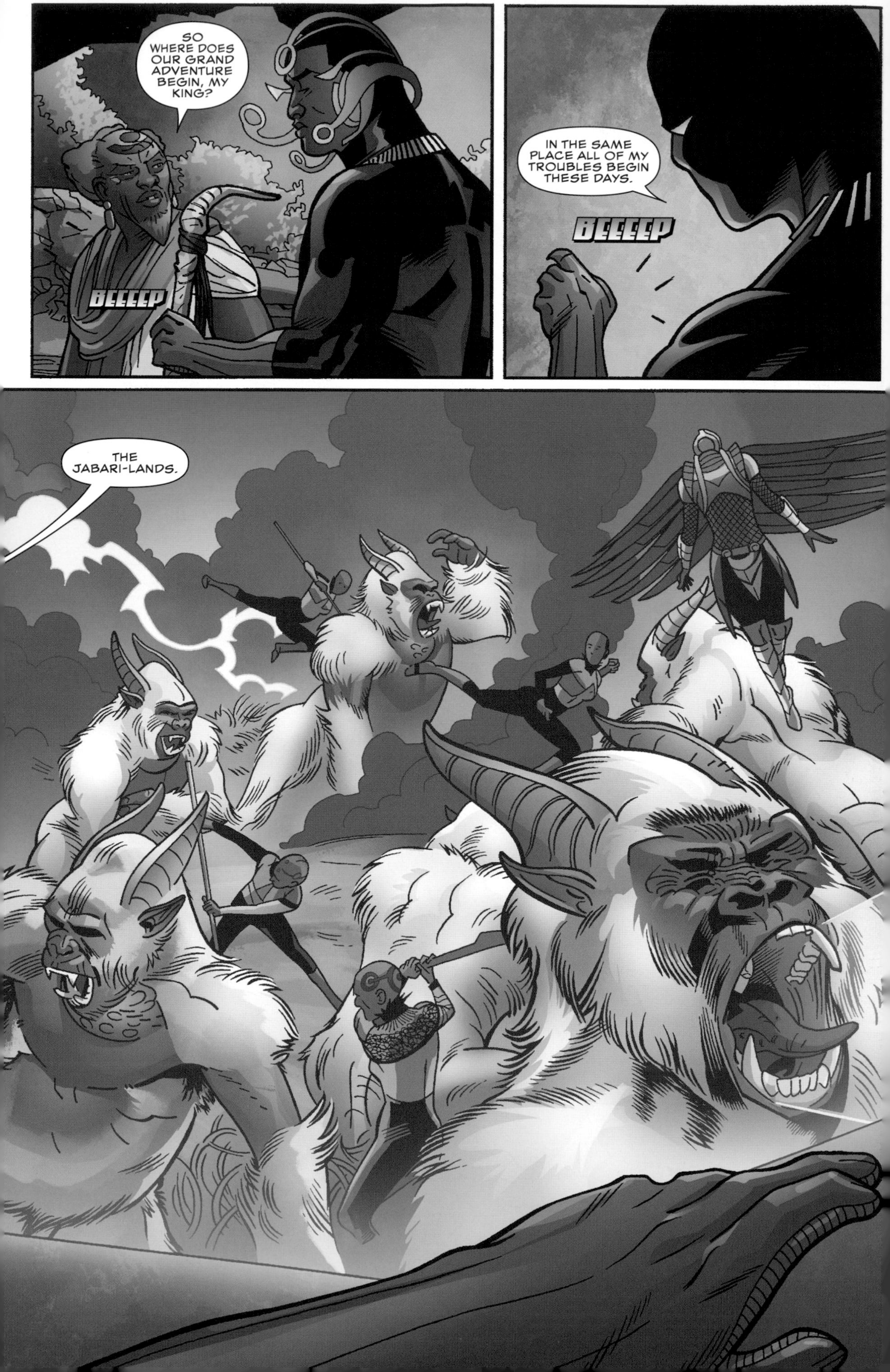
SO WHERE DOES OUR GRAND ADVENTURE BEGIN, MY KING?
BEEEEP
IN THE SAME PLACE ALL OF MY TROUBLES BEGIN THESE DAYS.
BEEEEP
THE JABARI-LANDS.

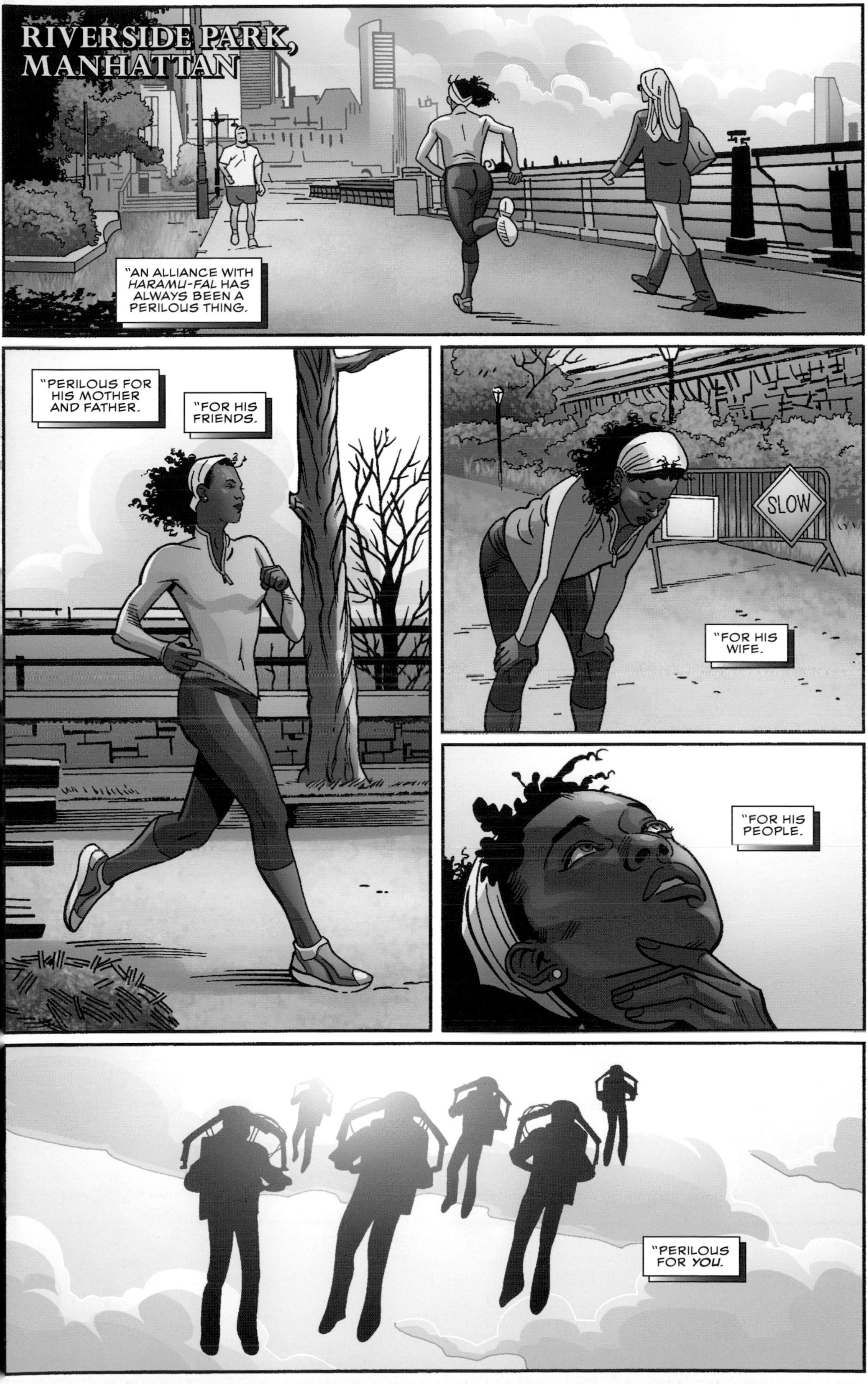
RIVERSIDE PARK, MANHATTAN
"AN ALLIANCE WITH HARAMU-FAL HAS ALWAYS BEEN A PERILOUS THING.
"PERILOUS FOR HIS MOTHER AND FATHER.
"FOR HIS FRIENDS.
"FOR HIS WIFE.
SLOW
"FOR HIS PEOPLE.
"PERILOUS FOR YOU.

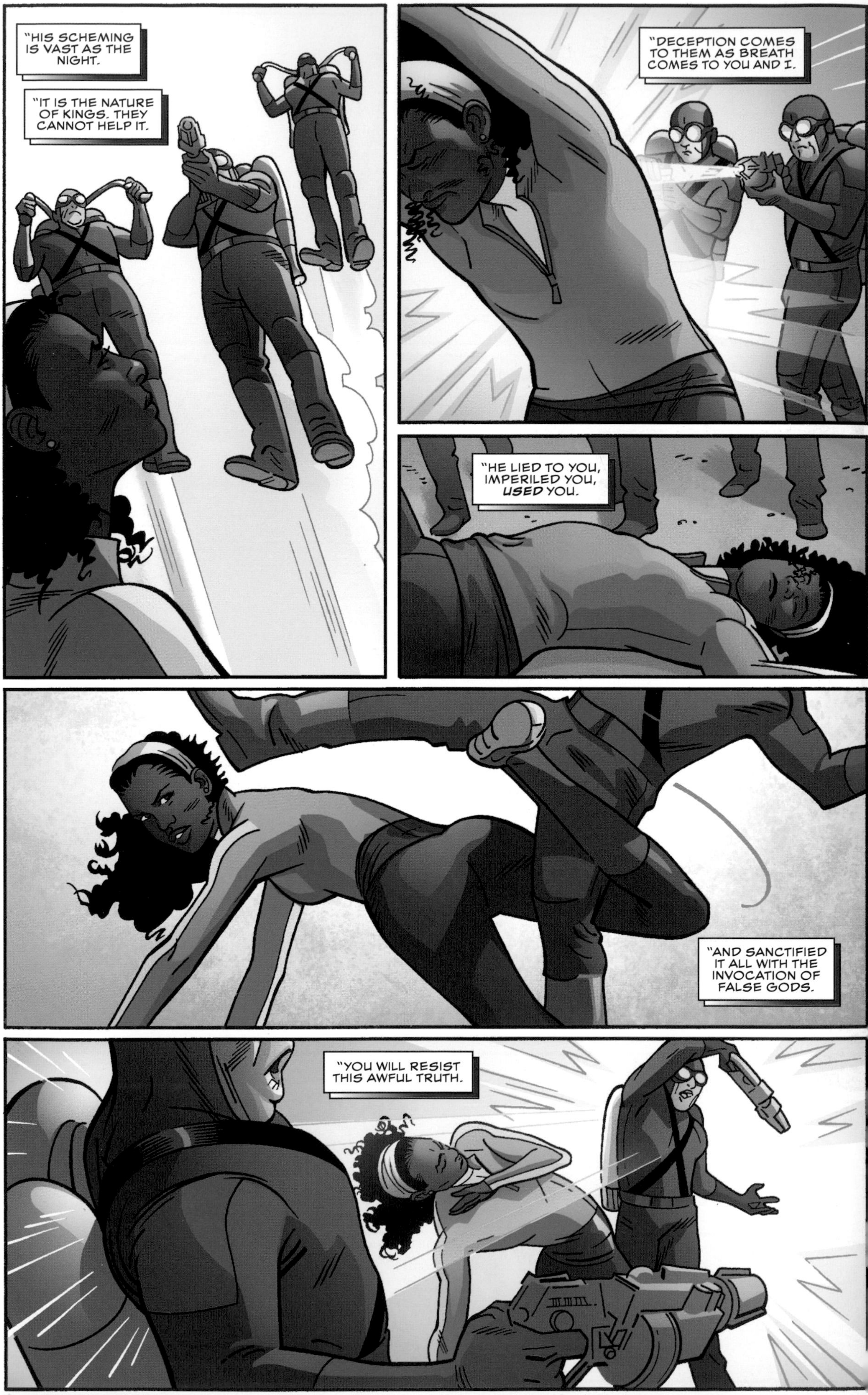
"HIS SCHEMING IS VAST AS THE NIGHT.
"IT IS THE NATURE OF KINGS. THEY CANNOT HELP IT.
"DECEPTION COMES TO THEM AS BREATH COMES TO YOU AND I.
"HE LIED TO YOU, IMPERILED YOU, *USED* YOU.
"AND SANCTIFIED IT ALL WITH THE INVOCATION OF FALSE GODS.
"YOU WILL RESIST THIS AWFUL TRUTH.

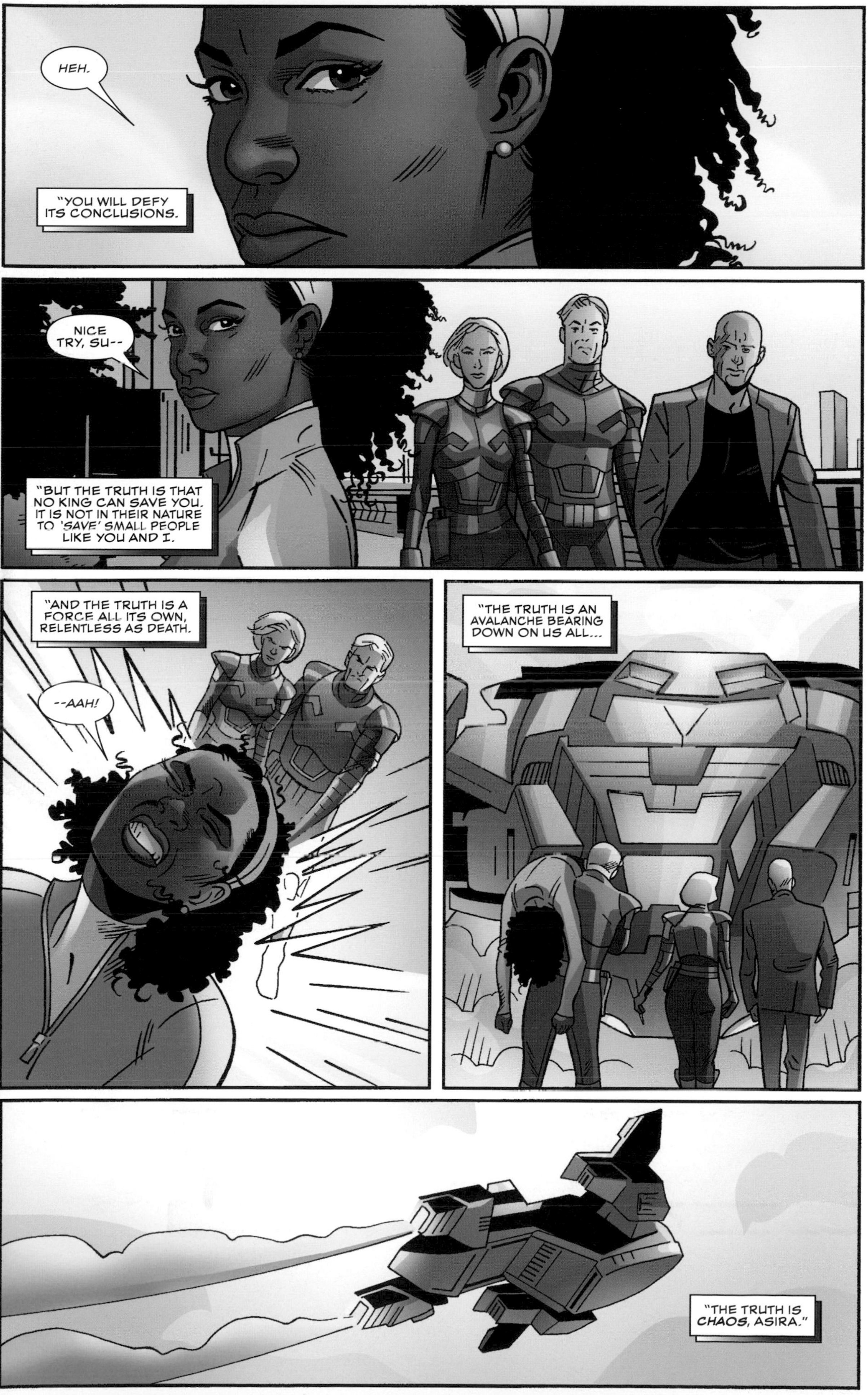
HEH.
"YOU WILL DEFY ITS CONCLUSIONS.
NICE TRY, SU--
"BUT THE TRUTH IS THAT NO KING CAN SAVE YOU. IT IS NOT IN THEIR NATURE TO 'SAVE' SMALL PEOPLE LIKE YOU AND I.
"AND THE TRUTH IS A FORCE ALL ITS OWN, RELENTLESS AS DEATH.
--AAH!
"THE TRUTH IS AN AVALANCHE BEARING DOWN ON US ALL...
"THE TRUTH IS CHAOS, ASIRA."

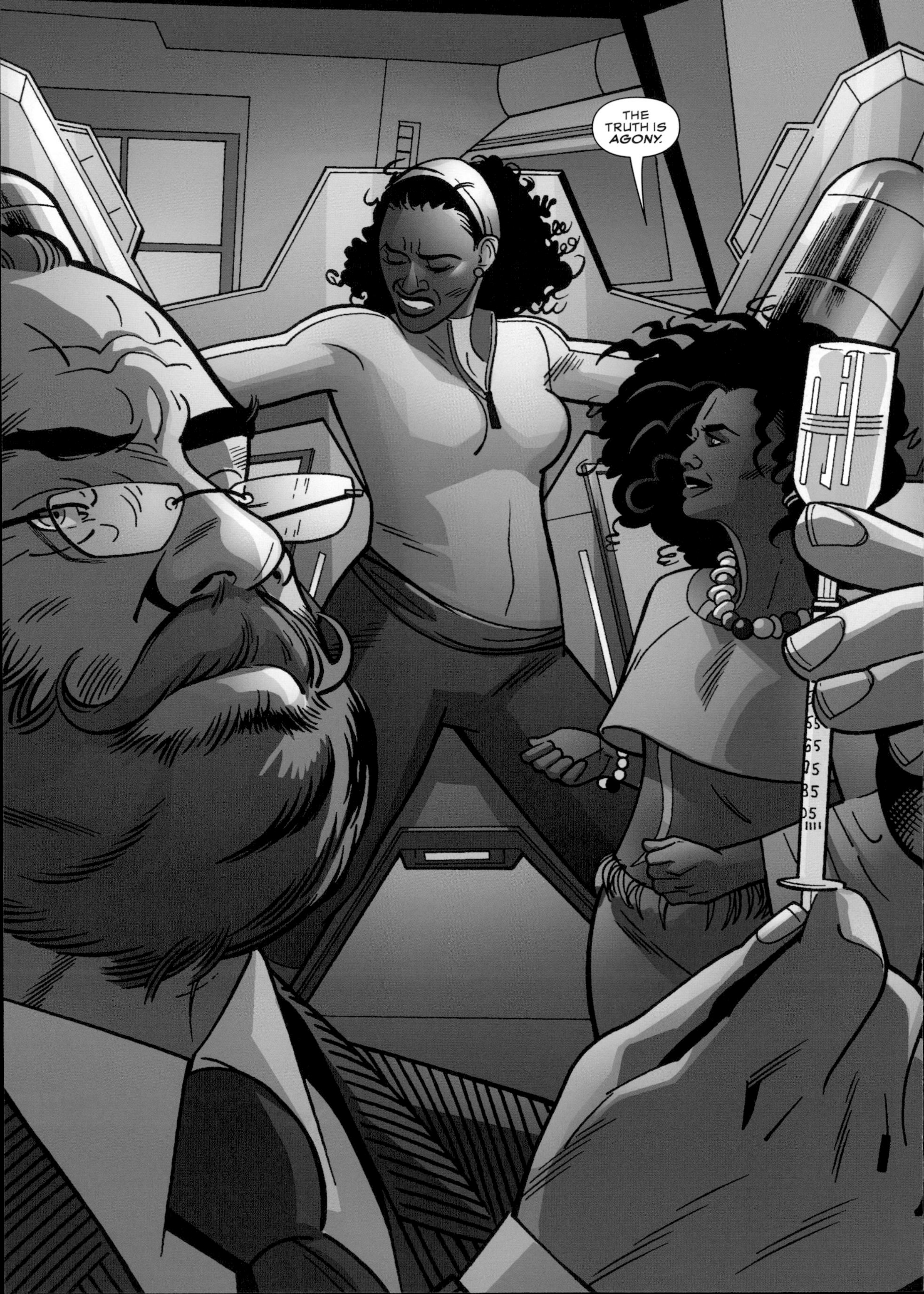
THE TRUTH IS AGONY.

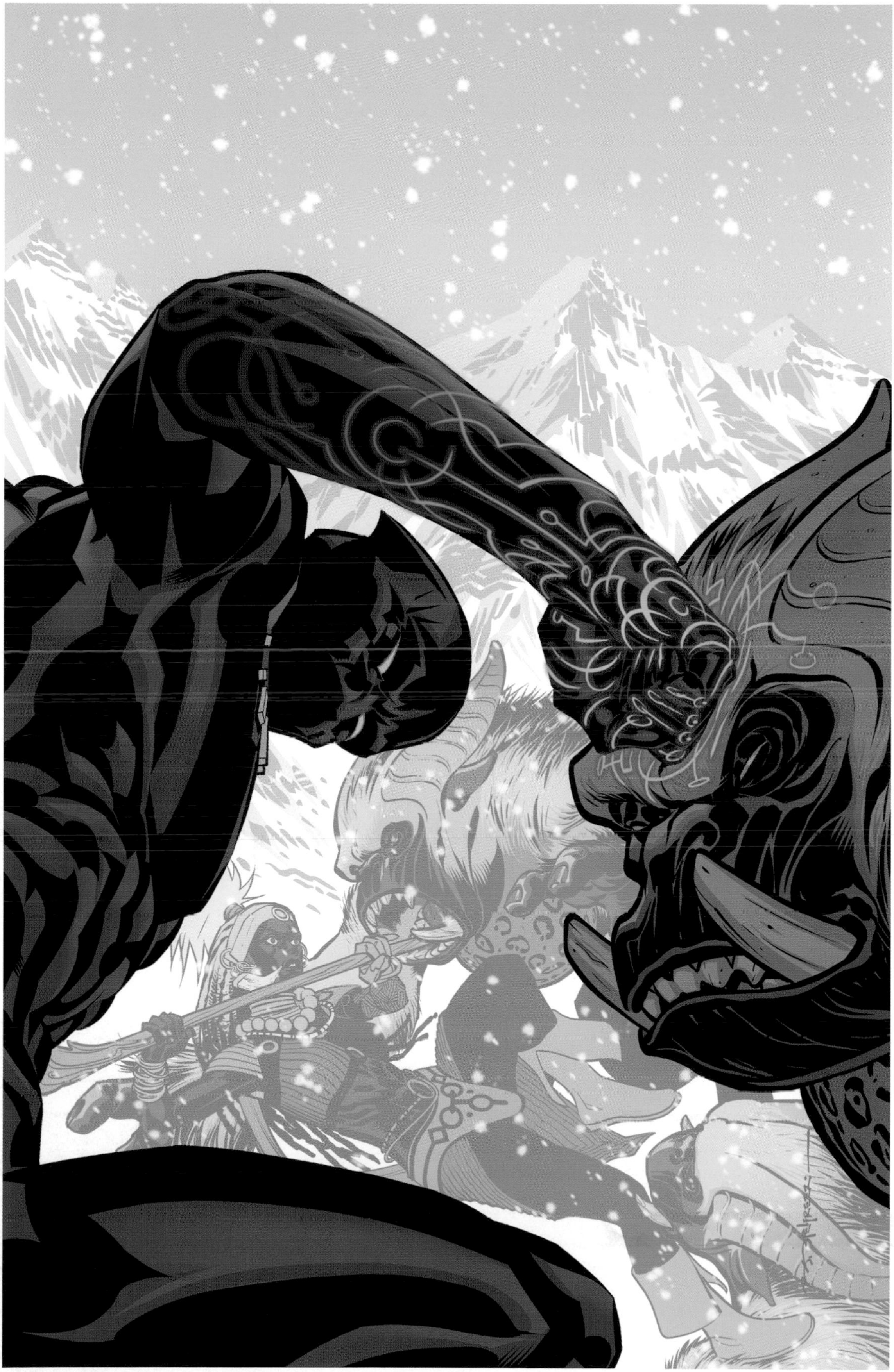

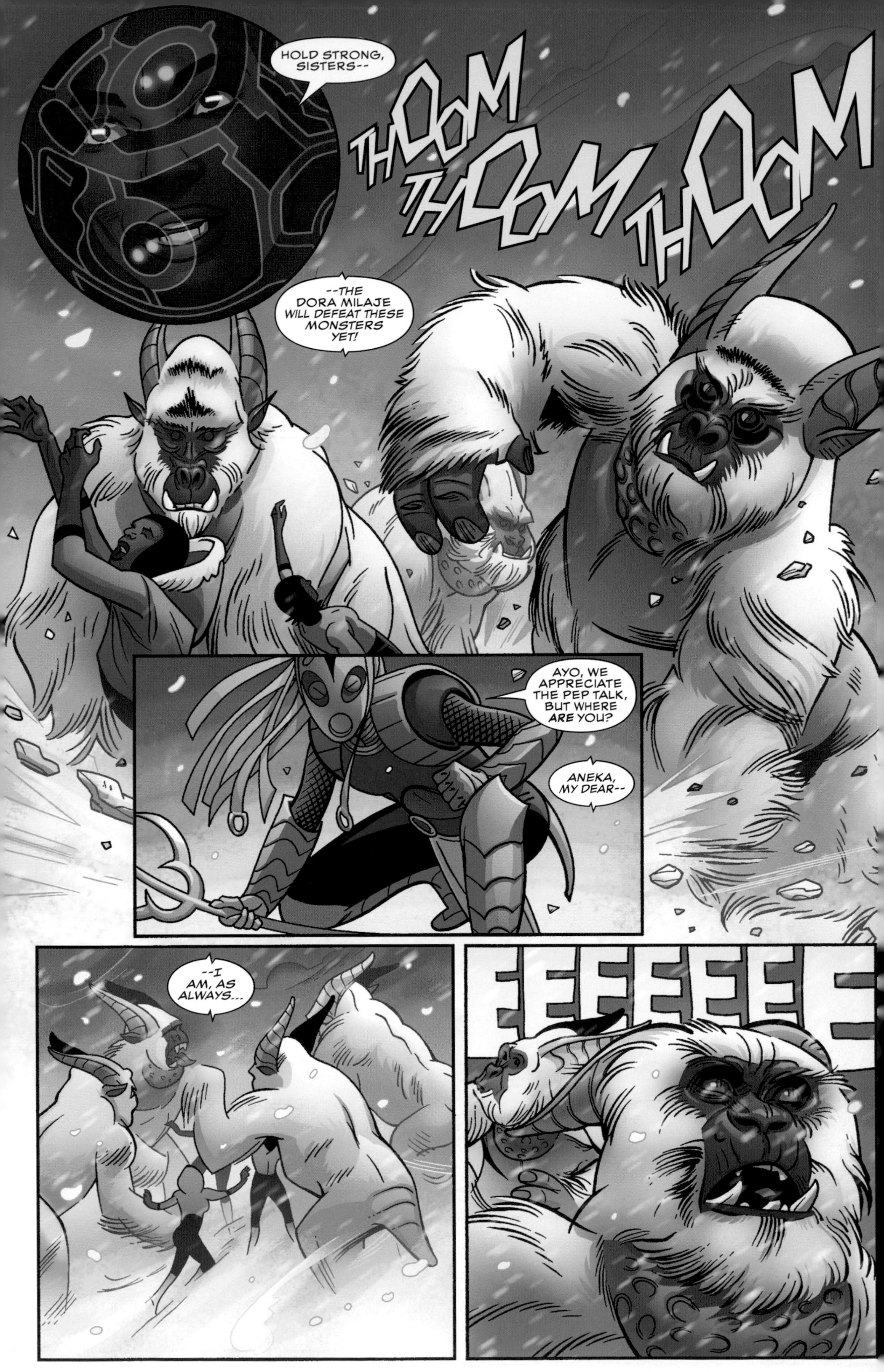
HOLD STRONG, SISTERS--
THOOM THOOM THOOM
--THE DORA MILAJE WILL DEFEAT THESE MONSTERS YET!
AYO, WE APPRECIATE THE PEP TALK, BUT WHERE ARE YOU?
ANEKA, MY DEAR--
--I AM, AS ALWAYS...
EEEEEE

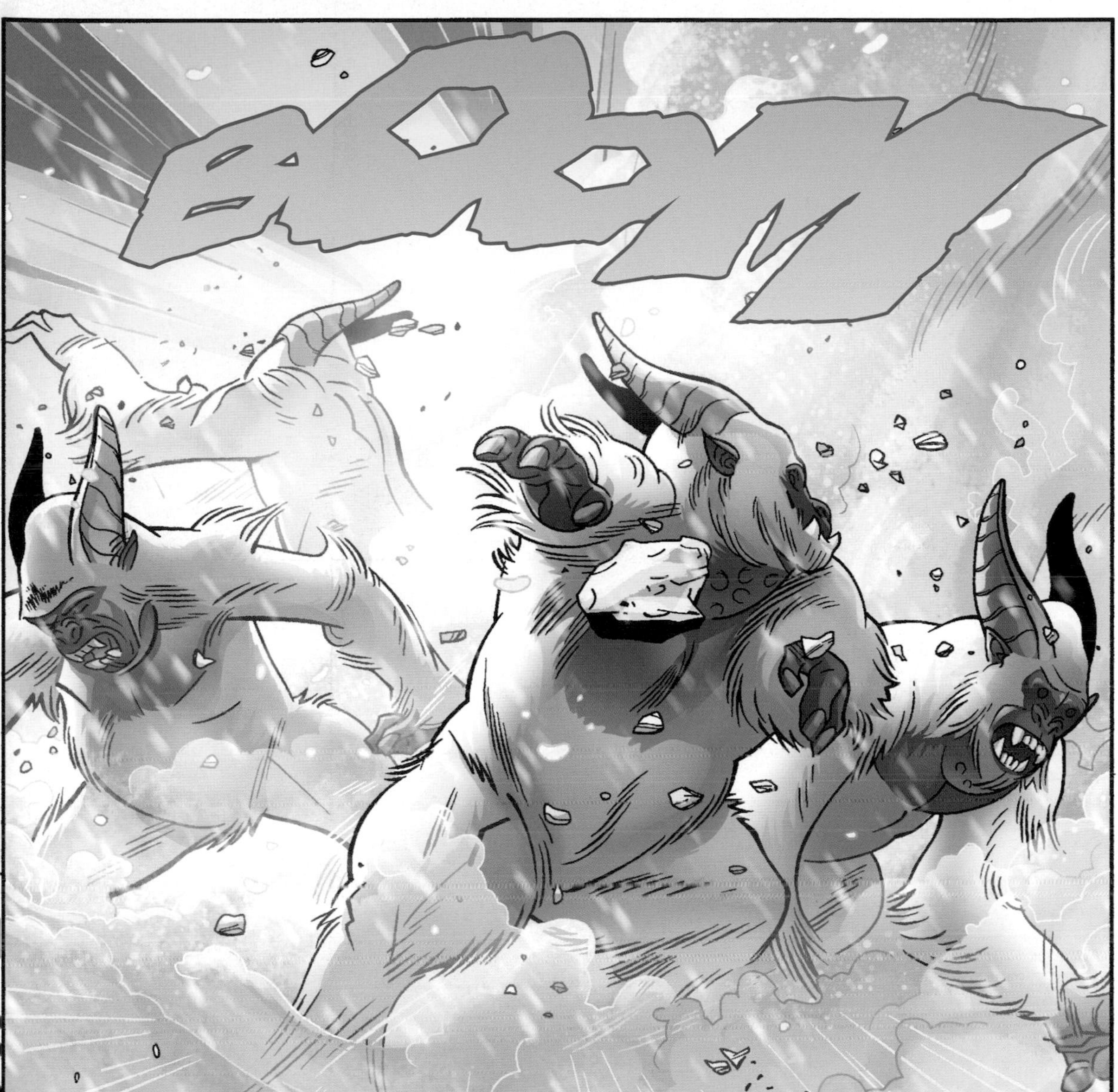
BOOM

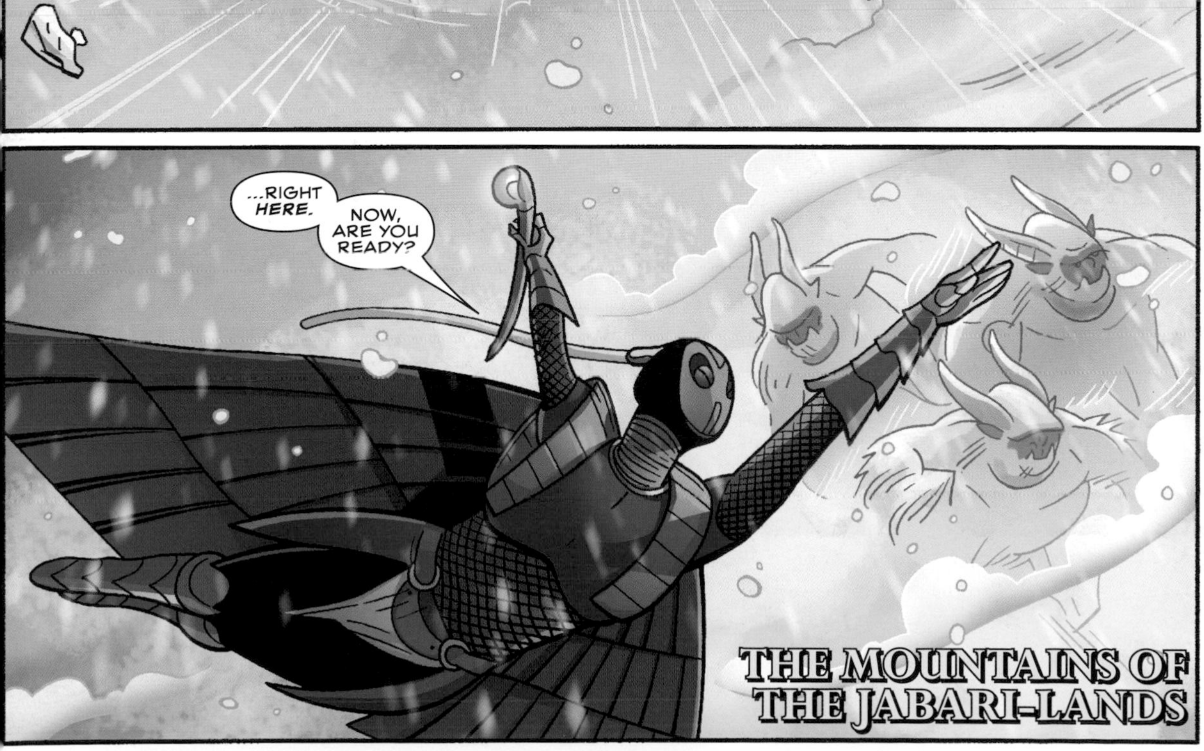
...RIGHT HERE.
NOW, ARE YOU READY?
THE MOUNTAINS OF THE JABARI-LANDS

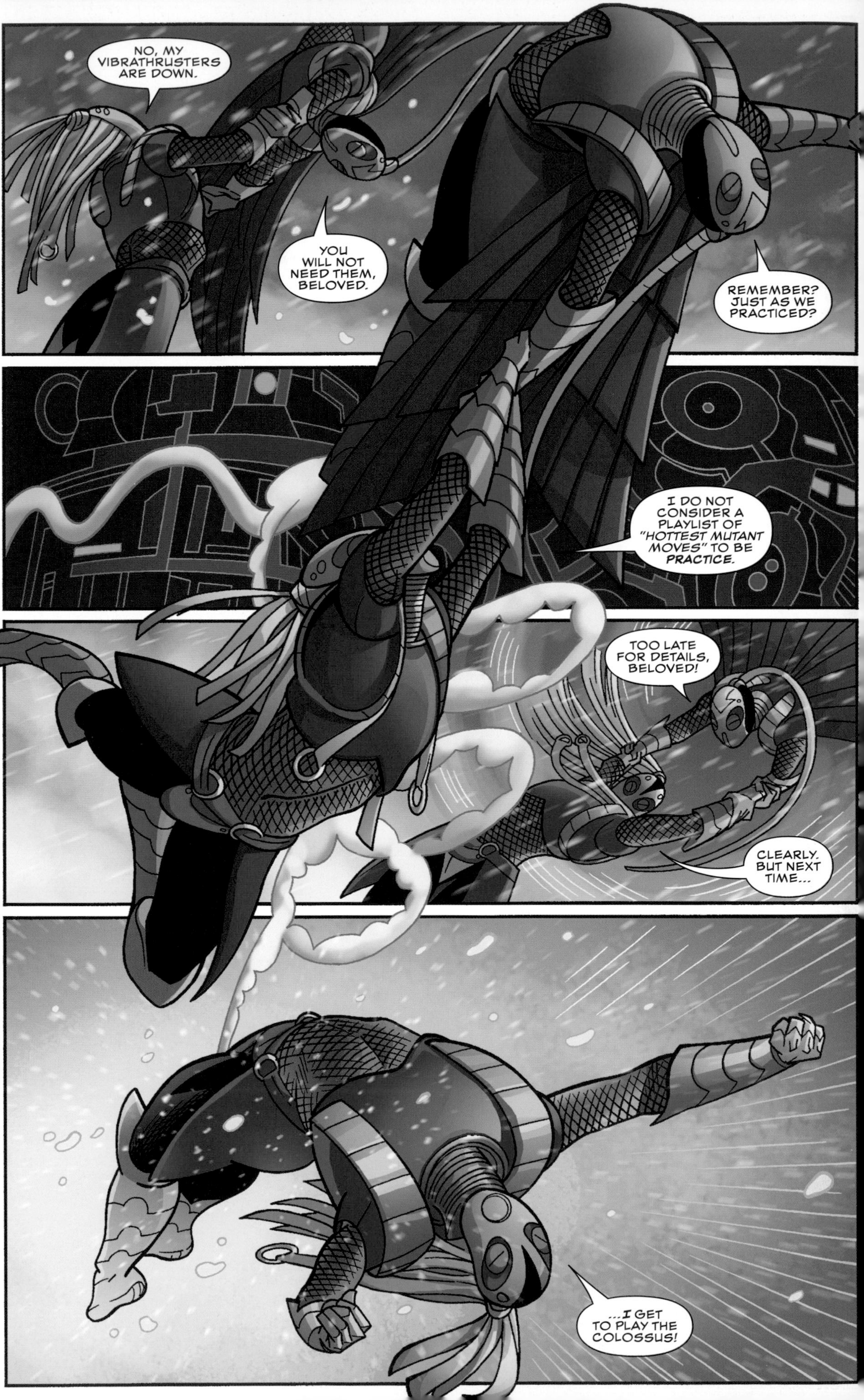
NO, MY VIBRATHRUSTERS ARE DOWN.
YOU WILL NOT NEED THEM, BELOVED.
REMEMBER? JUST AS WE PRACTICED?
I DO NOT CONSIDER A PLAYLIST OF "HOTTEST MUTANT MOVES" TO BE PRACTICE.
TOO LATE FOR DETAILS, BELOVED!
CLEARLY. BUT NEXT TIME...
...I GET TO PLAY THE COLOSSUS!

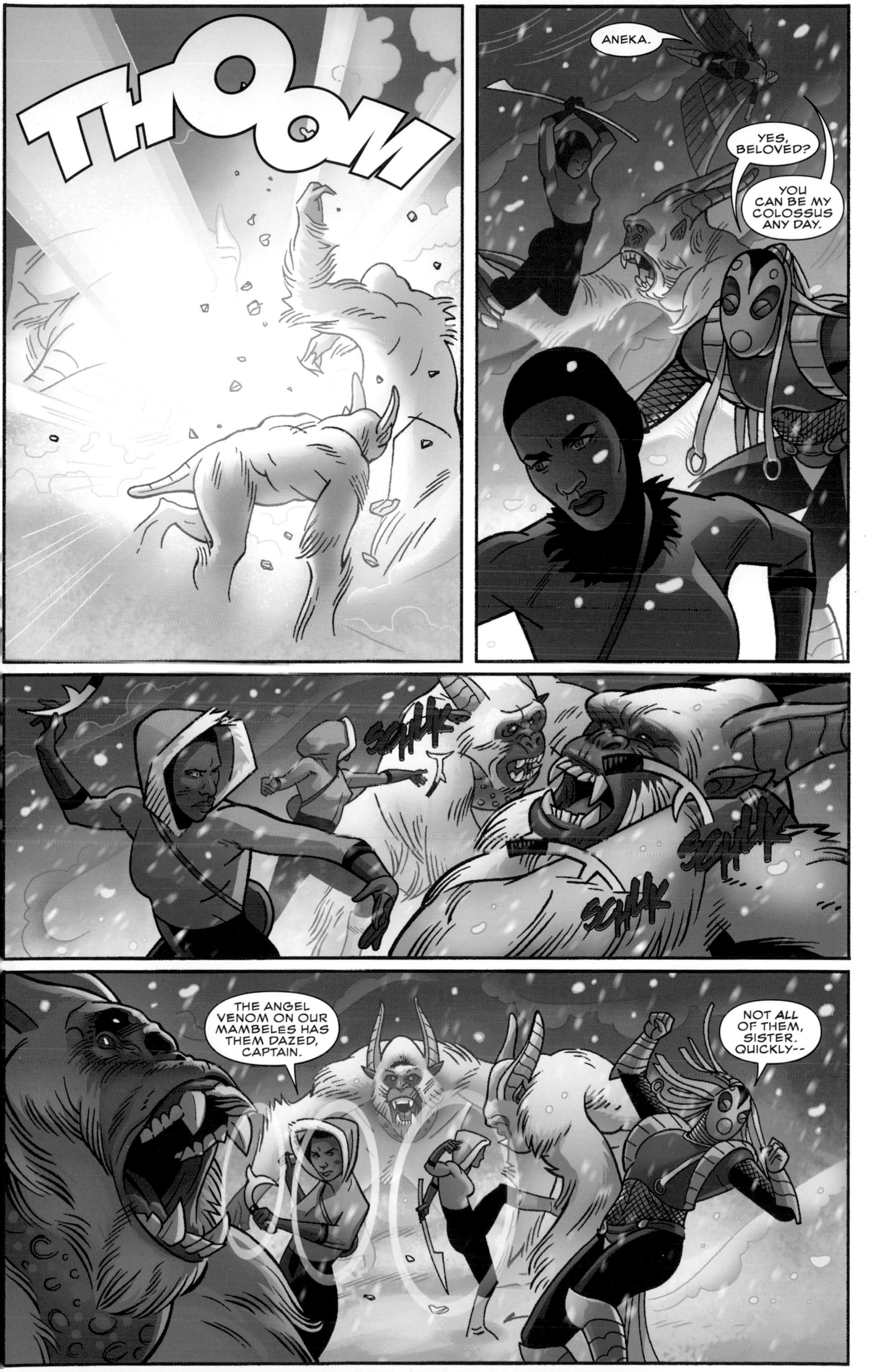
THOOM
ANEKA.
YES, BELOVED?
YOU CAN BE MY COLOSSUS ANY DAY.
SCHLUK
SCHLUK
SCHLUK
THE ANGEL VENOM ON OUR MAMBELES HAS THEM DAZED, CAPTAIN.
NOT ALL OF THEM, SISTER. QUICKLY--

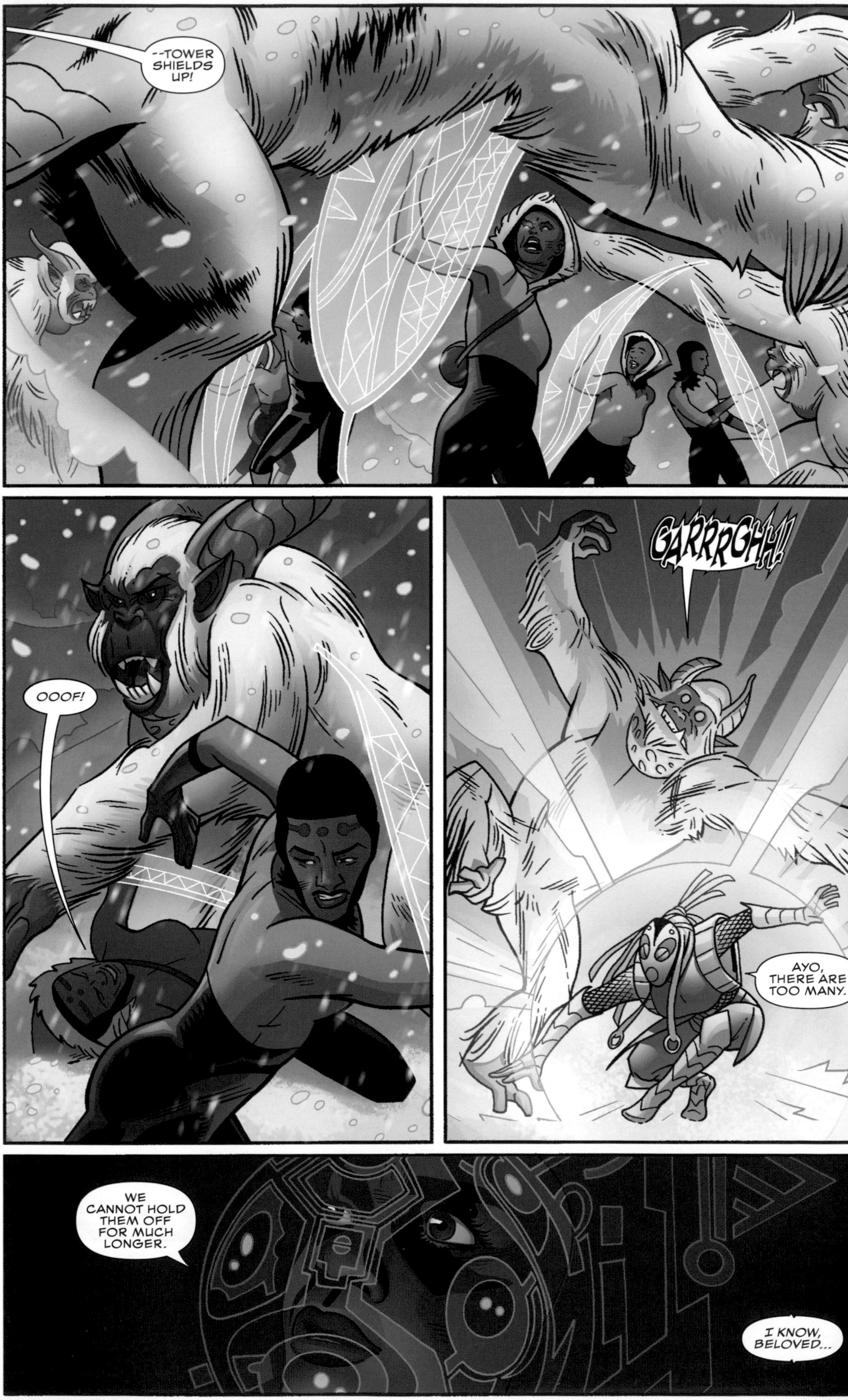
--TOWER SHIELDS UP!
OOOF!
GARRRGHH!
AYO, THERE ARE TOO MANY.
WE CANNOT HOLD THEM OFF FOR MUCH LONGER.
I KNOW, BELOVED...

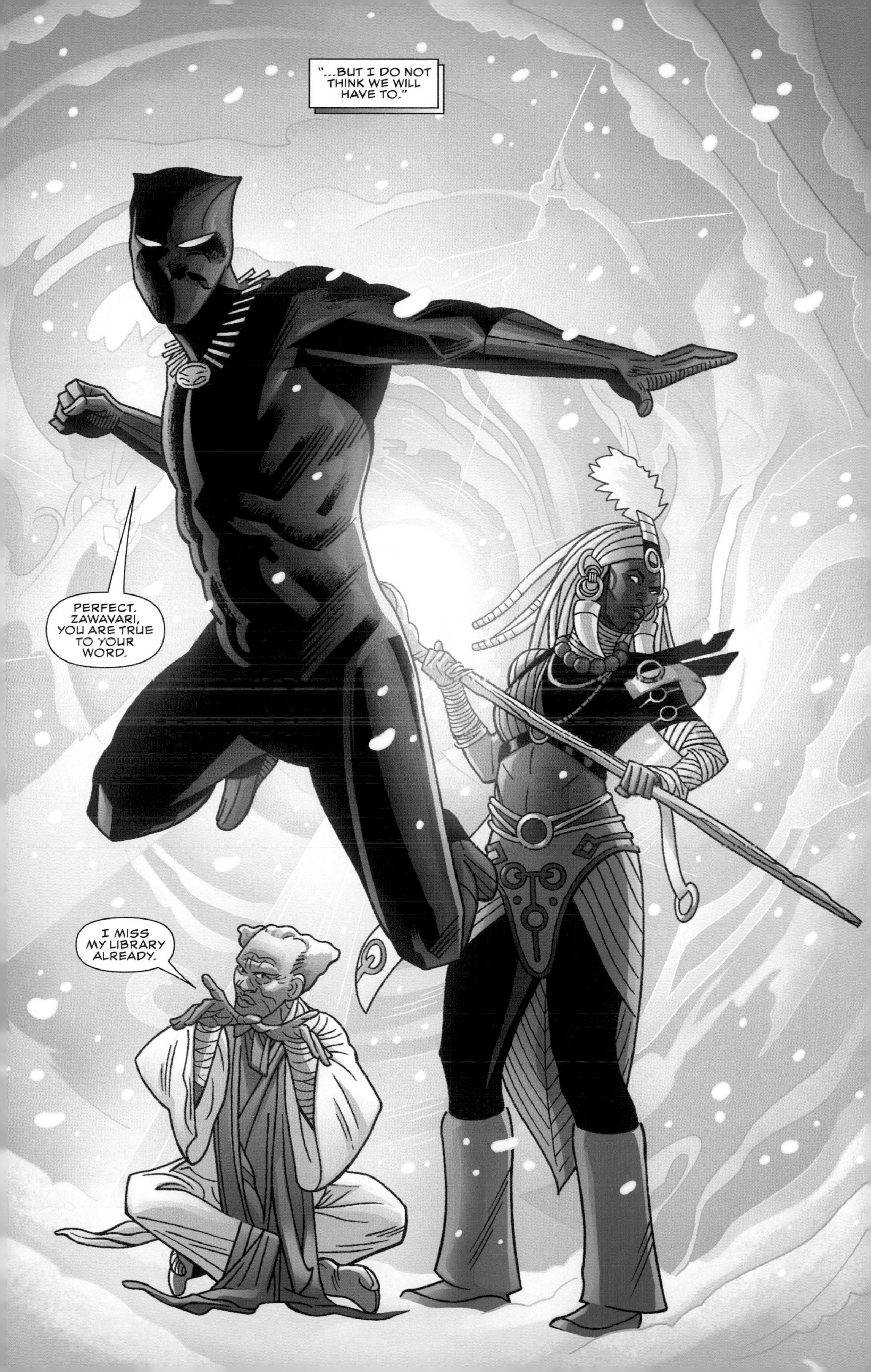
"...BUT I DO NOT THINK WE WILL HAVE TO."
PERFECT. ZAWAVARI, YOU ARE TRUE TO YOUR WORD.
I MISS MY LIBRARY ALREADY.

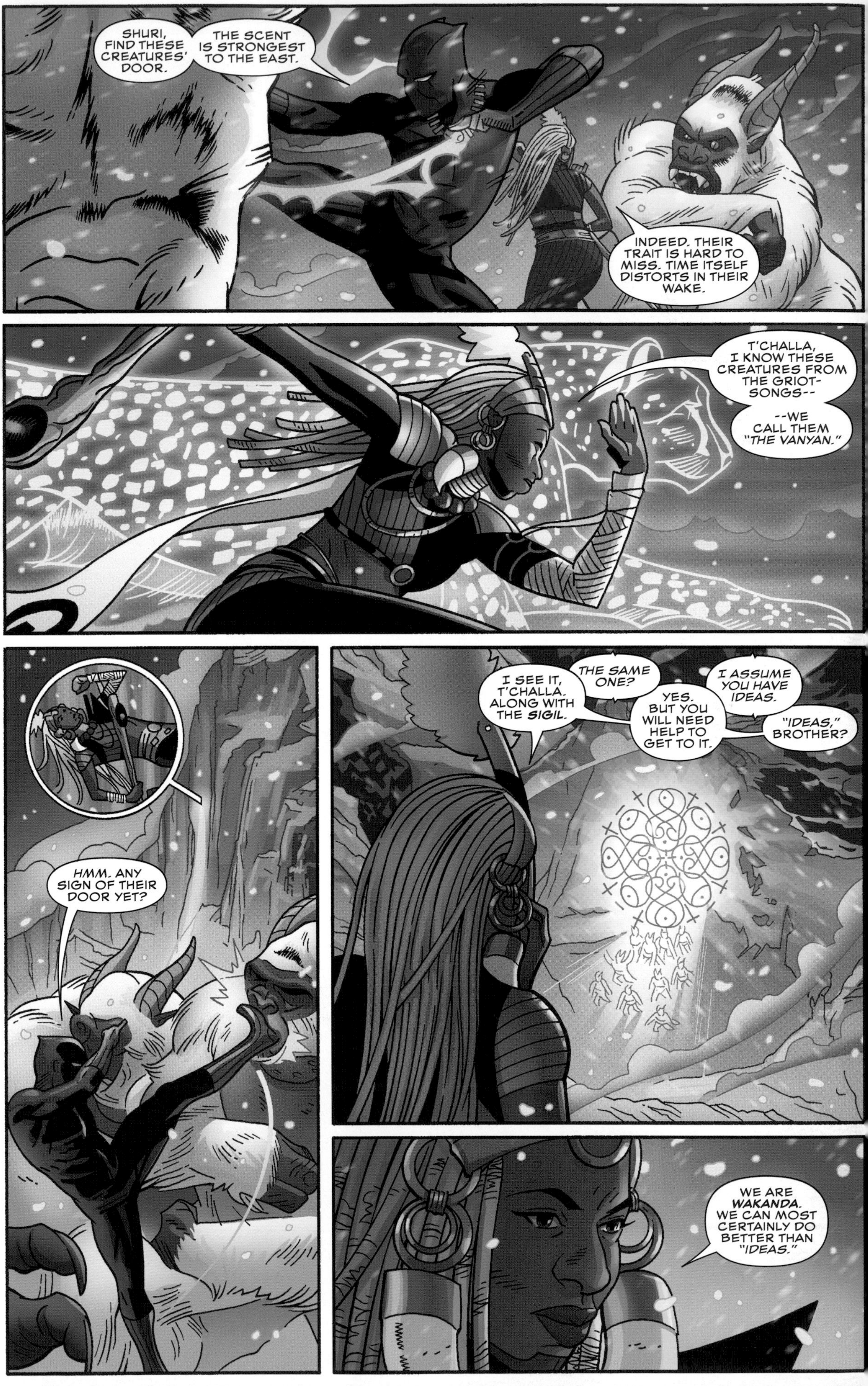
SHURI, FIND THESE CREATURES' DOOR.
THE SCENT IS STRONGEST TO THE EAST.
INDEED. THEIR TRAIT IS HARD TO MISS. TIME ITSELF DISTORTS IN THEIR WAKE.
T'CHALLA, I KNOW THESE CREATURES FROM THE GRIOT-SONGS--
--WE CALL THEM "THE VANYAN."
HMM. ANY SIGN OF THEIR DOOR YET?
I SEE IT, T'CHALLA. ALONG WITH THE SIGIL.
THE SAME ONE?
YES. BUT YOU WILL NEED HELP TO GET TO IT.
I ASSUME YOU HAVE IDEAS.
"IDEAS," BROTHER?
WE ARE WAKANDA. WE CAN MOST CERTAINLY DO BETTER THAN "IDEAS."

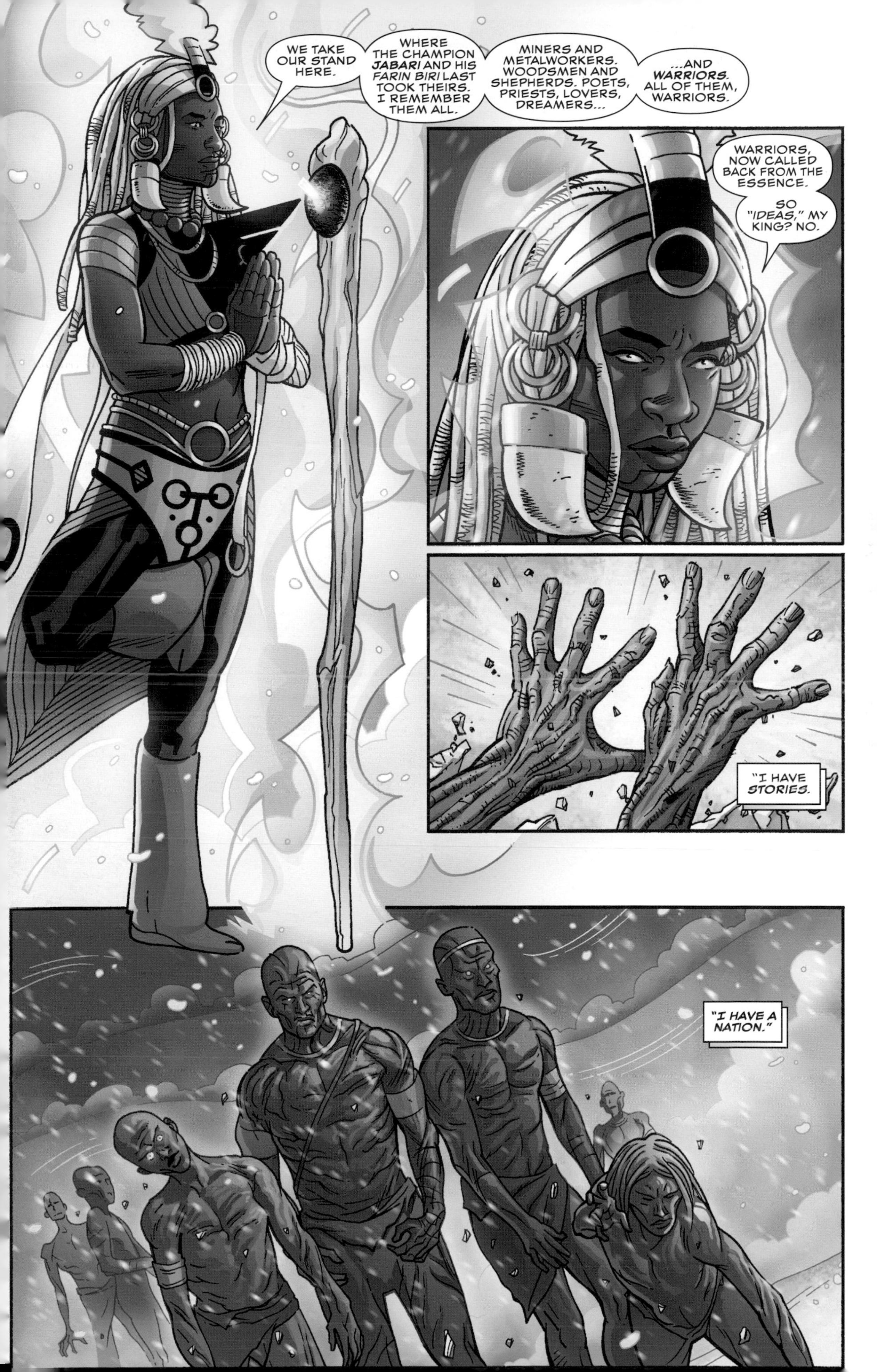
WE TAKE OUR STAND HERE.
WHERE THE CHAMPION JABARI AND HIS FARIN BIRI LAST TOOK THEIRS. I REMEMBER THEM ALL.
MINERS AND METALWORKERS. WOODSMEN AND SHEPHERDS. POETS, PRIESTS, LOVERS, DREAMERS...
...AND WARRIORS. ALL OF THEM, WARRIORS.
WARRIORS, NOW CALLED BACK FROM THE ESSENCE.
SO "IDEAS," MY KING? NO.
"I HAVE STORIES.
"I HAVE A NATION."

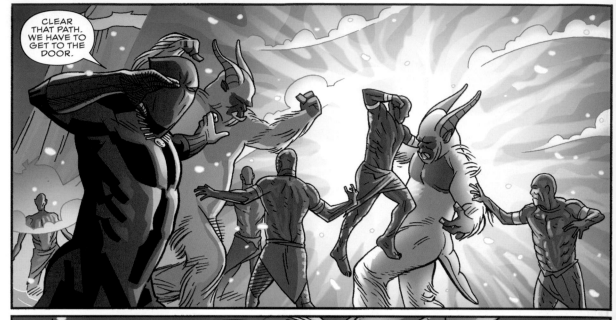

CLEAR THAT PATH. WE HAVE TO GET TO THE DOOR.

AYO, PROTECT SHURI WHILE SHE IS SPELL-CASTING.

I DO NOT KNOW IF WE ARE READY TO TAKE ORDERS FROM YOU AGAIN, T'CHALLA.

THUNK

AND *I* DO NOT KNOW IF I AM READY TO GIVE THEM TO YOU.

DO AS I ASK, NOT BECAUSE I ORDER IT, BUT BECAUSE YOU KNOW IT TO BE CORRECT.

DAMN THAT MAN. ALWAYS WITH THE MIND GAMES.

AND WHERE ARE *WE* GOING, T'CHALLA?

TO THE SOURCE OF THIS PLAGUE, ANEKA--

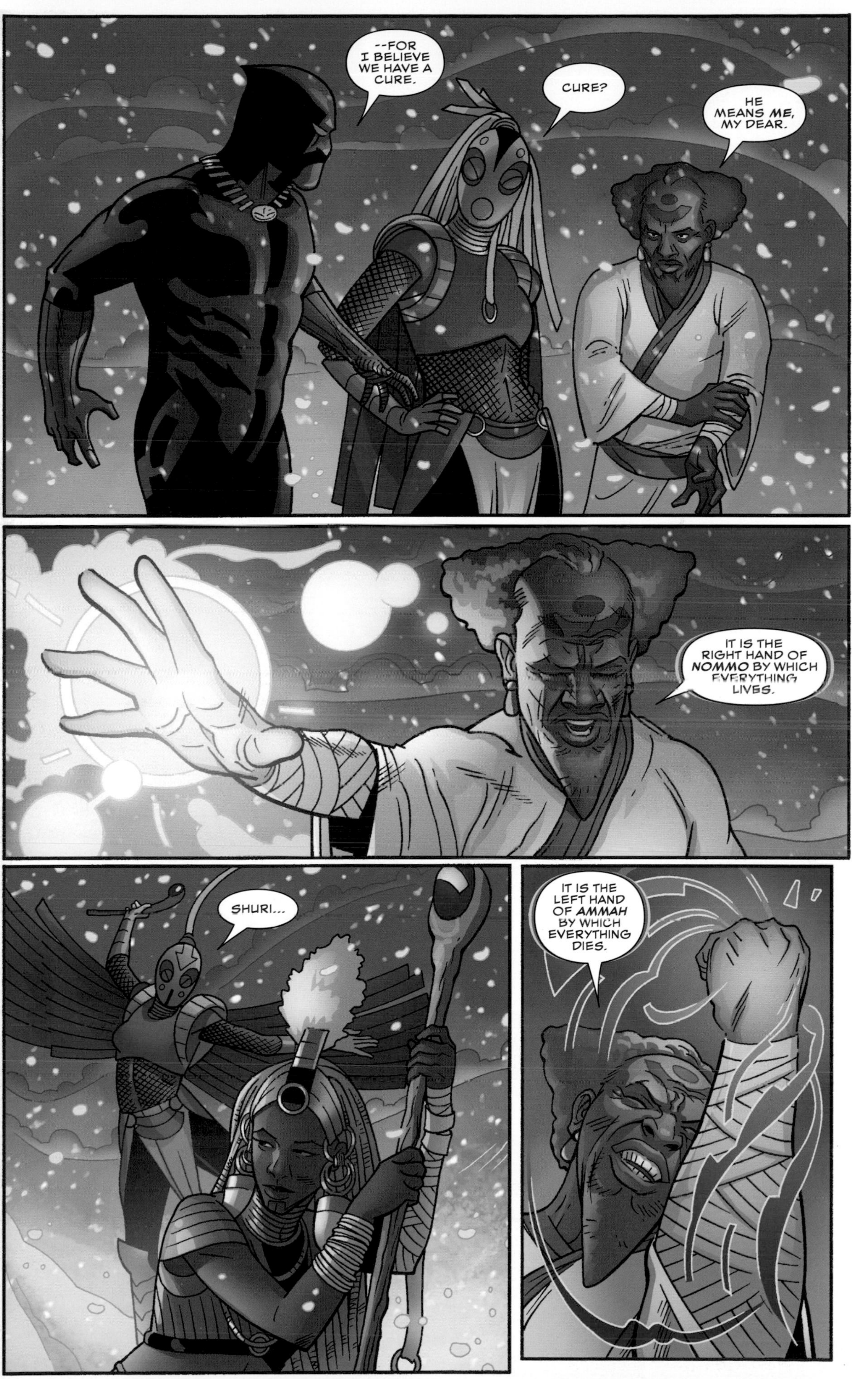
--FOR I BELIEVE WE HAVE A CURE.
CURE?
HE MEANS ME, MY DEAR.
IT IS THE RIGHT HAND OF NOMMO BY WHICH EVERYTHING LIVES.
SHURI...
IT IS THE LEFT HAND OF AMMAH BY WHICH EVERYTHING DIES.

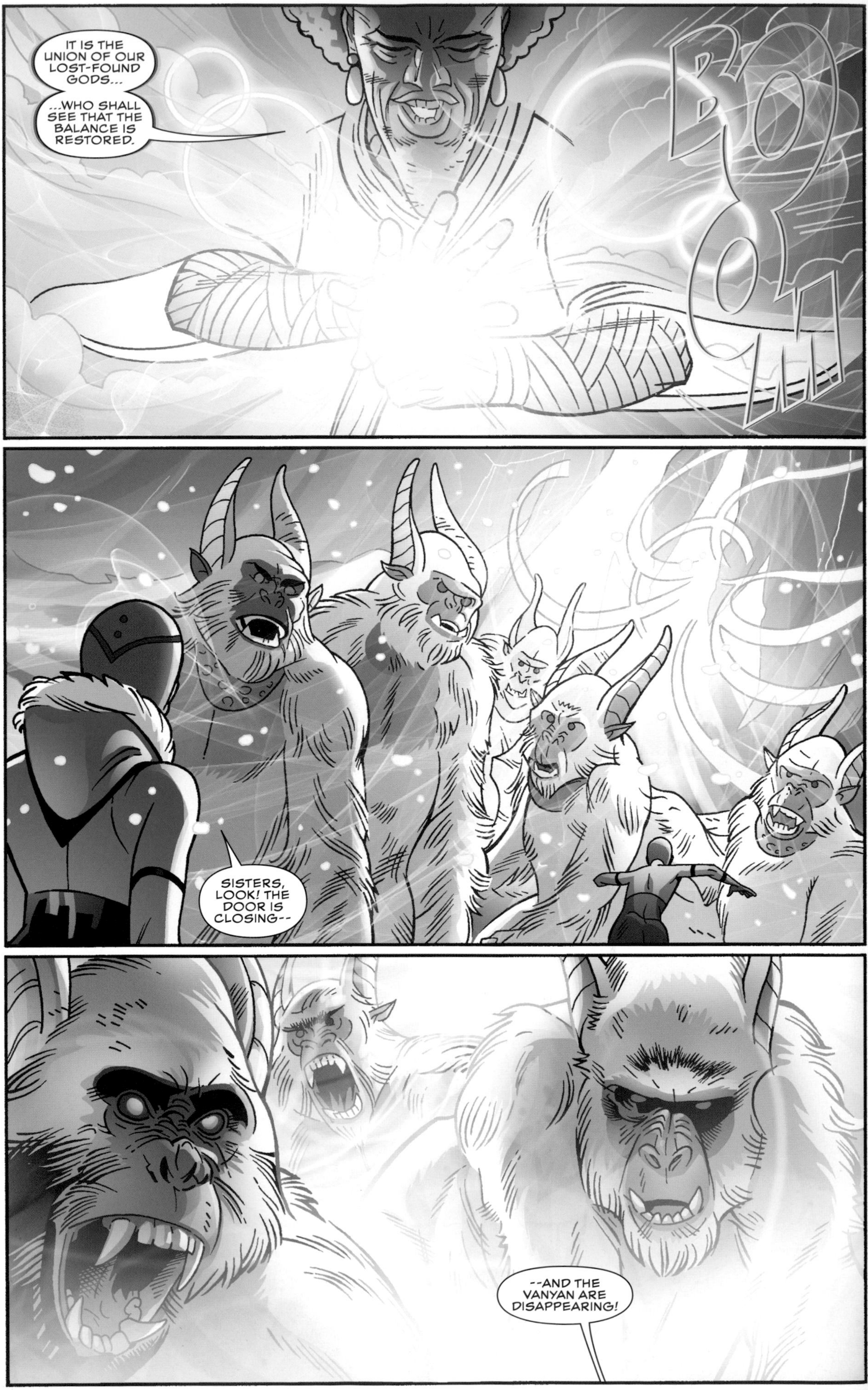
IT IS THE UNION OF OUR LOST-FOUND GODS...
...WHO SHALL SEE THAT THE BALANCE IS RESTORED.
BOOM
SISTERS, LOOK! THE DOOR IS CLOSING--
--AND THE VANYAN ARE DISAPPEARING!

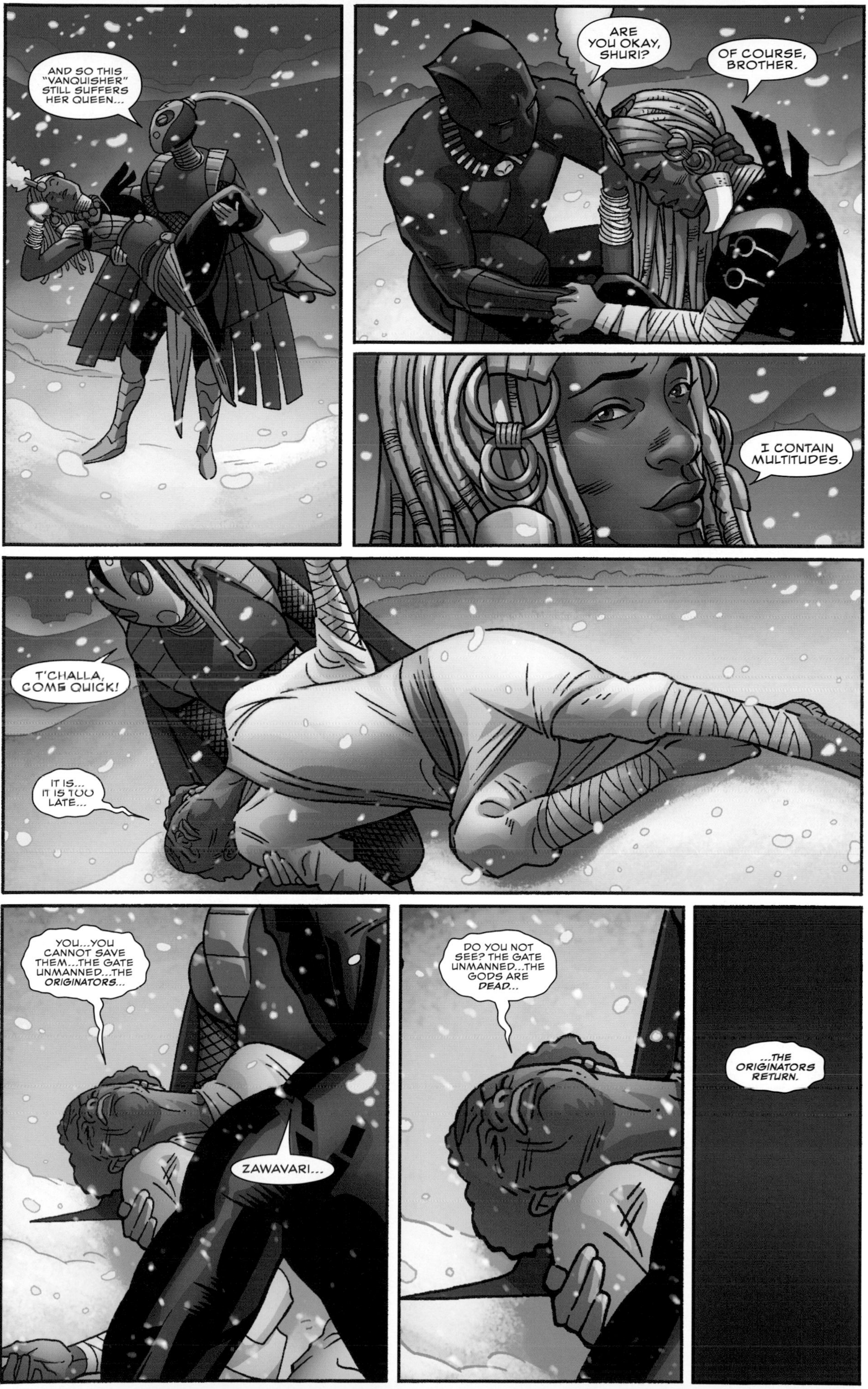
AND SO THIS "VANQUISHER" STILL SUFFERS HER QUEEN...
ARE YOU OKAY, SHURI?
OF COURSE, BROTHER.
I CONTAIN MULTITUDES.
T'CHALLA, COME QUICK!
IT IS... IT IS TOO LATE...
YOU...YOU CANNOT SAVE THEM...THE GATE UNMANNED...THE *ORIGINATORS*...
ZAWAVARI...
DO YOU NOT SEE? THE GATE UNMANNED...THE GODS ARE *DEAD*...
...THE ORIGINATORS RETURN.

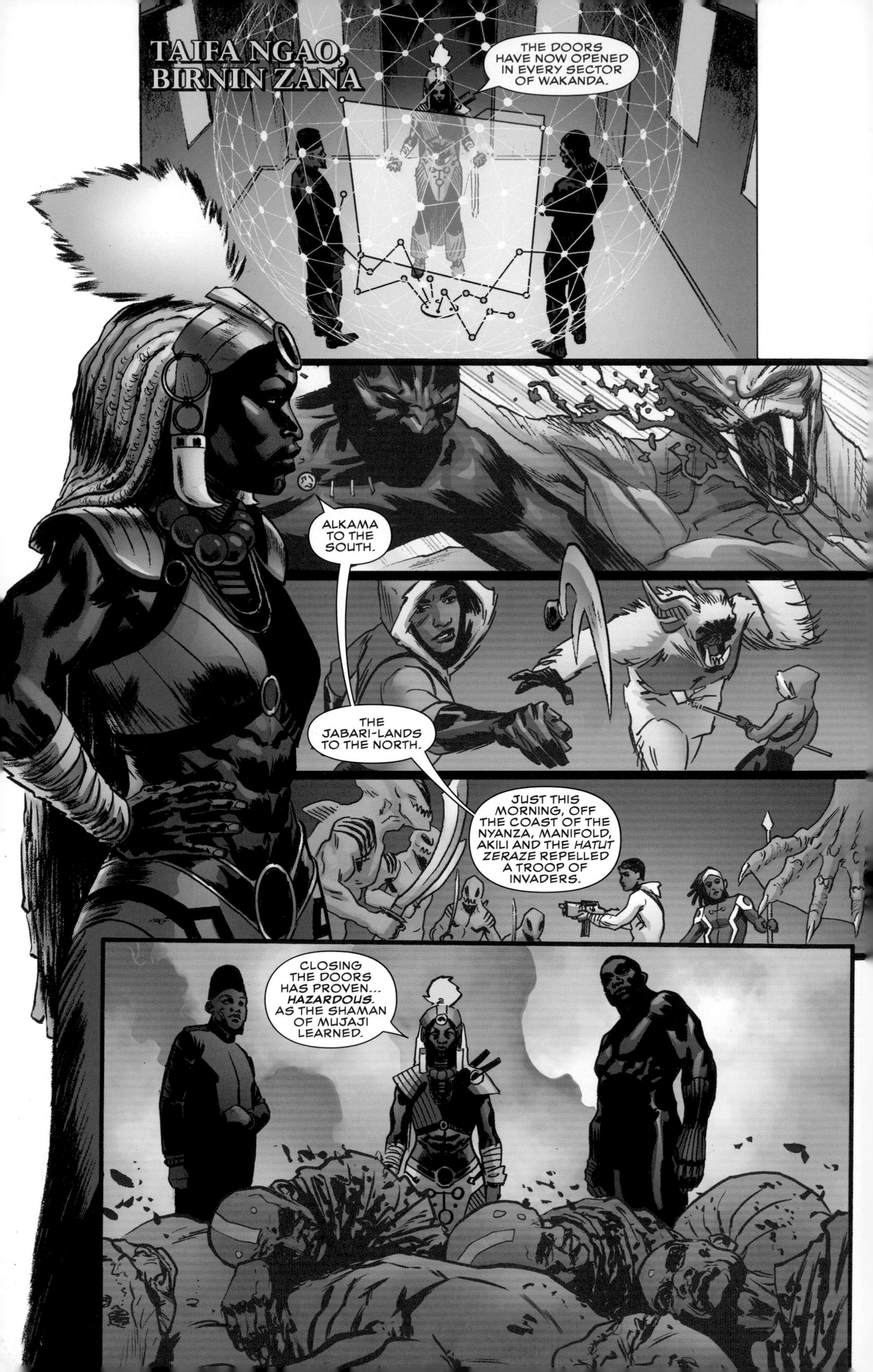
TAIFA NGAO, BIRNIN ZANA
THE DOORS HAVE NOW OPENED IN EVERY SECTOR OF WAKANDA.
ALKAMA TO THE SOUTH.
THE JABARI-LANDS TO THE NORTH.
JUST THIS MORNING, OFF THE COAST OF THE NYANZA, MANIFOLD, AKILI AND THE HATUT ZERAZE REPELLED A TROOP OF INVADERS.
CLOSING THE DOORS HAS PROVEN... HAZARDOUS. AS THE SHAMAN OF MUJAJI LEARNED.

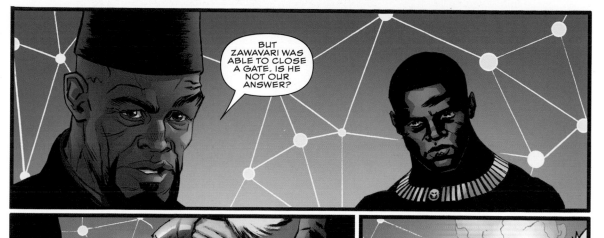

BUT ZAWAVARI WAS ABLE TO CLOSE A GATE. IS HE NOT OUR ANSWER?

ZAWAVARI HAS YET TO REGAIN CONSCIOUSNESS, HODARI.

OUR MEDICS THINK HE SUFFERED SOME SORT OF STROKE.

SO THE GOOD NEWS IS THAT WE *CAN* CLOSE THE GATES.

AND THE *BAD* NEWS IS THAT DOING SO RISKS DEATH.

SHURI, WHAT DID ZAWAVARI MEAN BY "THE GODS ARE DEAD"?

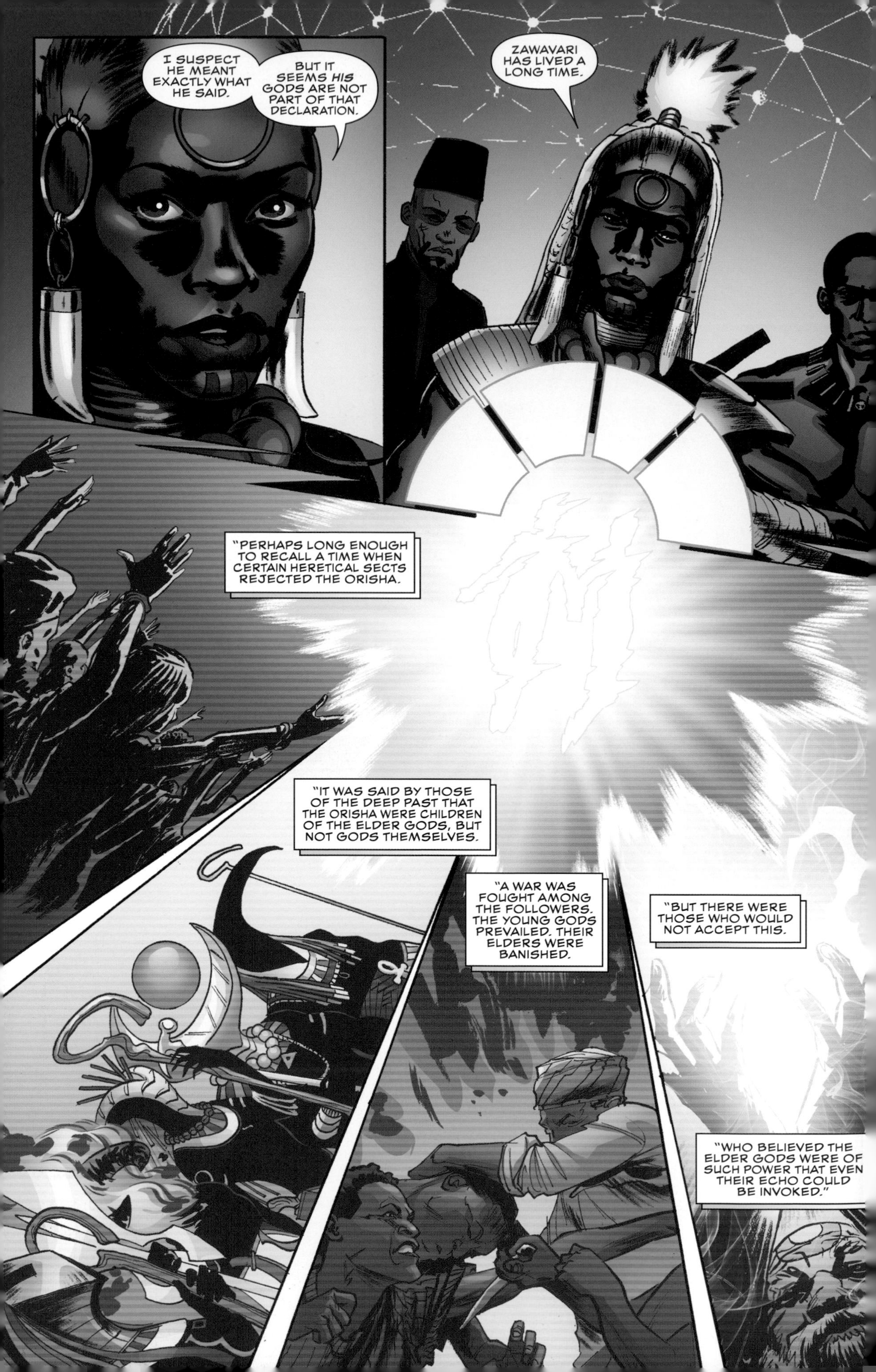
I SUSPECT HE MEANT EXACTLY WHAT HE SAID.
BUT IT SEEMS *HIS* GODS ARE NOT PART OF THAT DECLARATION.
ZAWAVARI HAS LIVED A LONG TIME.
"PERHAPS LONG ENOUGH TO RECALL A TIME WHEN CERTAIN HERETICAL SECTS REJECTED THE ORISHA.
"IT WAS SAID BY THOSE OF THE DEEP PAST THAT THE ORISHA WERE CHILDREN OF THE ELDER GODS, BUT NOT GODS THEMSELVES.
"A WAR WAS FOUGHT AMONG THE FOLLOWERS. THE YOUNG GODS PREVAILED. THEIR ELDERS WERE BANISHED.
"BUT THERE WERE THOSE WHO WOULD NOT ACCEPT THIS.
"WHO BELIEVED THE ELDER GODS WERE OF SUCH POWER THAT EVEN THEIR ECHO COULD BE INVOKED."

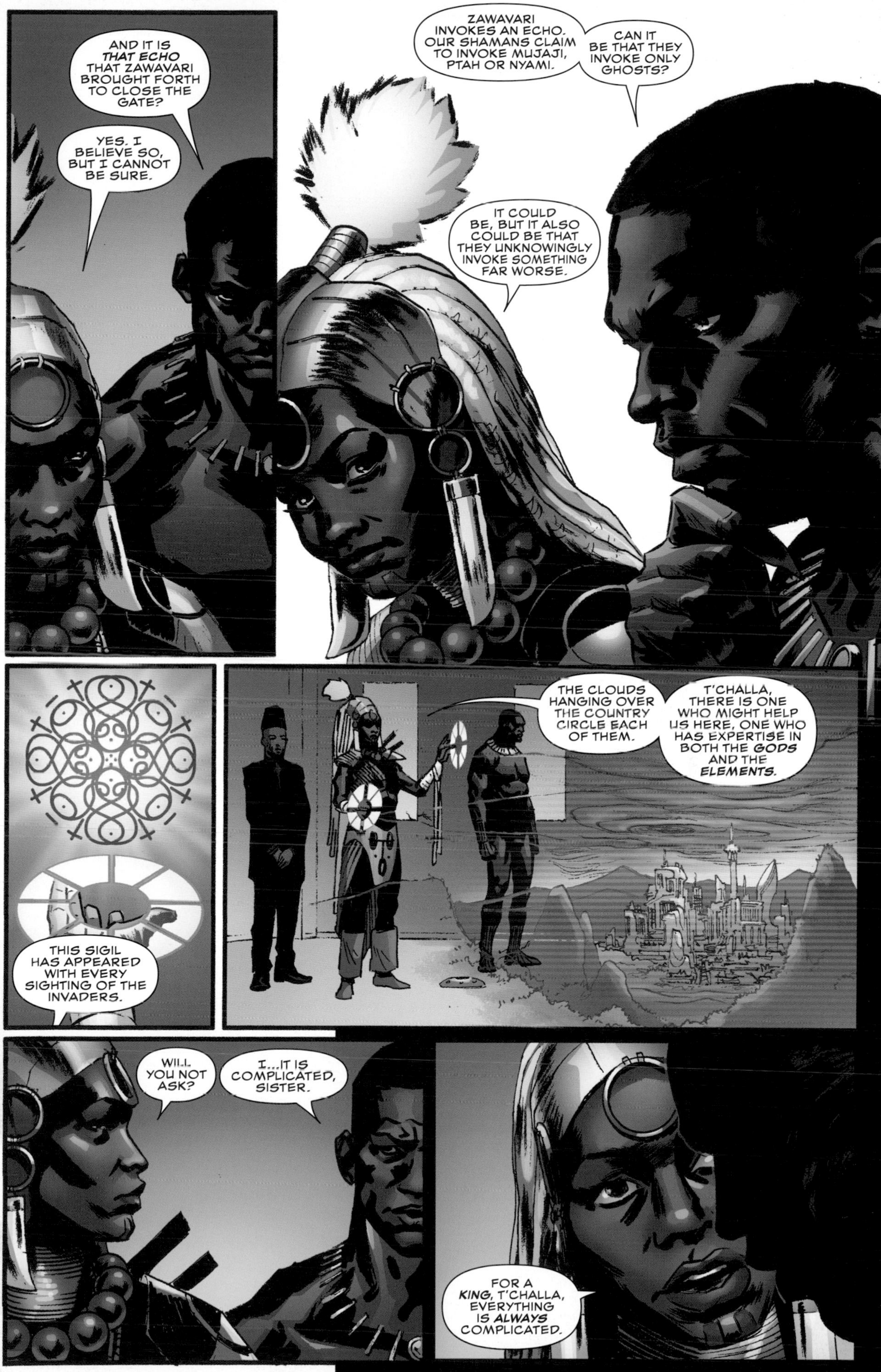

AND IT IS *THAT ECHO* THAT ZAWAVARI BROUGHT FORTH TO CLOSE THE GATE?
YES. I BELIEVE SO, BUT I CANNOT BE SURE.
ZAWAVARI INVOKES AN ECHO. OUR SHAMANS CLAIM TO INVOKE MUJAJI, PTAH OR NYAMI.
CAN IT BE THAT THEY INVOKE ONLY GHOSTS?
IT COULD BE, BUT IT ALSO COULD BE THAT THEY UNKNOWINGLY INVOKE SOMETHING FAR WORSE.
THIS SIGIL HAS APPEARED WITH EVERY SIGHTING OF THE INVADERS.
THE CLOUDS HANGING OVER THE COUNTRY CIRCLE EACH OF THEM.
T'CHALLA, THERE IS ONE WHO MIGHT HELP US HERE, ONE WHO HAS EXPERTISE IN BOTH THE *GODS* AND THE *ELEMENTS.*
WILL YOU NOT ASK?
I...IT IS COMPLICATED, SISTER.
FOR A *KING*, T'CHALLA, EVERYTHING IS *ALWAYS* COMPLICATED.

THIS WAS SUPPOSED TO BE FUN.

NO ROYAL DUTIES.

THE VILLAGE OF KANANNA-MDOGO

NO AFFAIRS OF STATE.

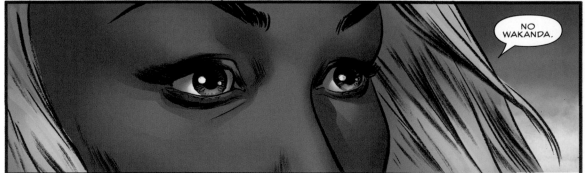

NO WAKANDA.

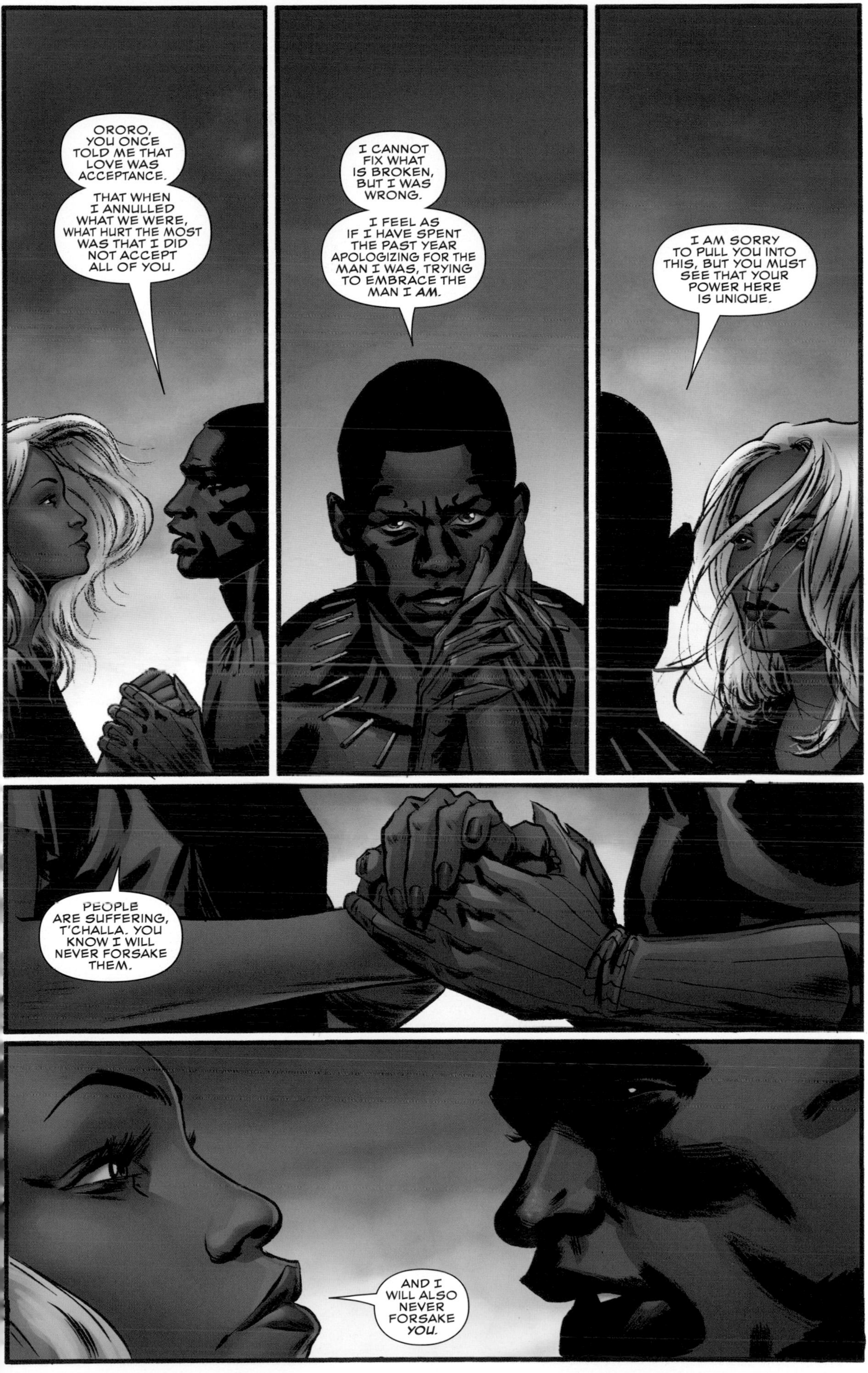
ORORO, YOU ONCE TOLD ME THAT LOVE WAS ACCEPTANCE.
THAT WHEN I ANNULLED WHAT WE WERE, WHAT HURT THE MOST WAS THAT I DID NOT ACCEPT ALL OF YOU.
I CANNOT FIX WHAT IS BROKEN, BUT I WAS WRONG.
I FEEL AS IF I HAVE SPENT THE PAST YEAR APOLOGIZING FOR THE MAN I WAS, TRYING TO EMBRACE THE MAN I *AM*.
I AM SORRY TO PULL YOU INTO THIS, BUT YOU MUST SEE THAT YOUR POWER HERE IS UNIQUE.
PEOPLE ARE SUFFERING, T'CHALLA. YOU KNOW I WILL NEVER FORSAKE THEM.
AND I WILL ALSO NEVER FORSAKE *YOU*.

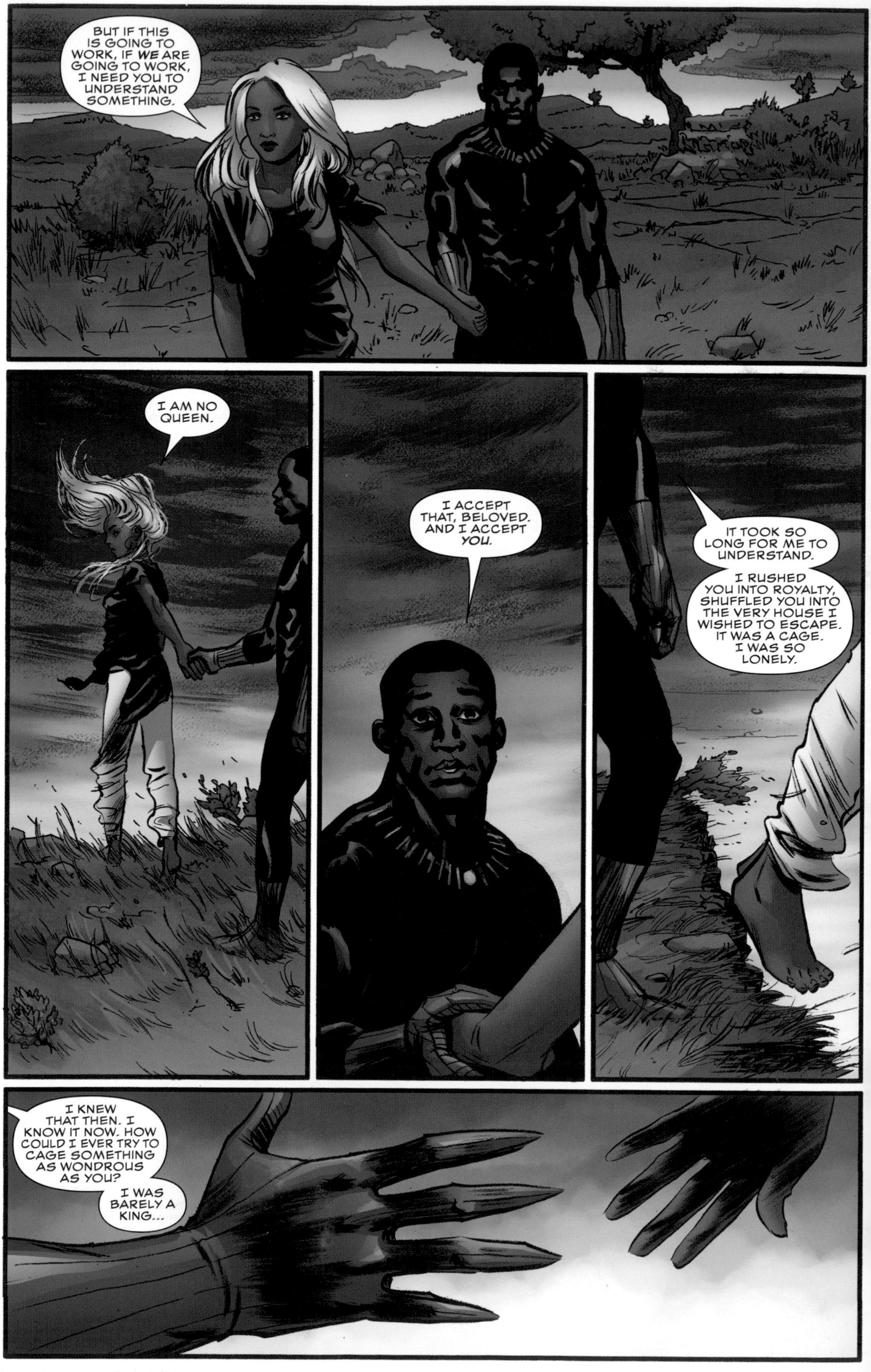
BUT IF THIS IS GOING TO WORK, IF WE ARE GOING TO WORK, I NEED YOU TO UNDERSTAND SOMETHING.
I AM NO QUEEN.
I ACCEPT THAT, BELOVED. AND I ACCEPT YOU.
IT TOOK SO LONG FOR ME TO UNDERSTAND.
I RUSHED YOU INTO ROYALTY, SHUFFLED YOU INTO THE VERY HOUSE I WISHED TO ESCAPE. IT WAS A CAGE. I WAS SO LONELY.
I KNEW THAT THEN. I KNOW IT NOW. HOW COULD I EVER TRY TO CAGE SOMETHING AS WONDROUS AS YOU?
I WAS BARELY A KING...

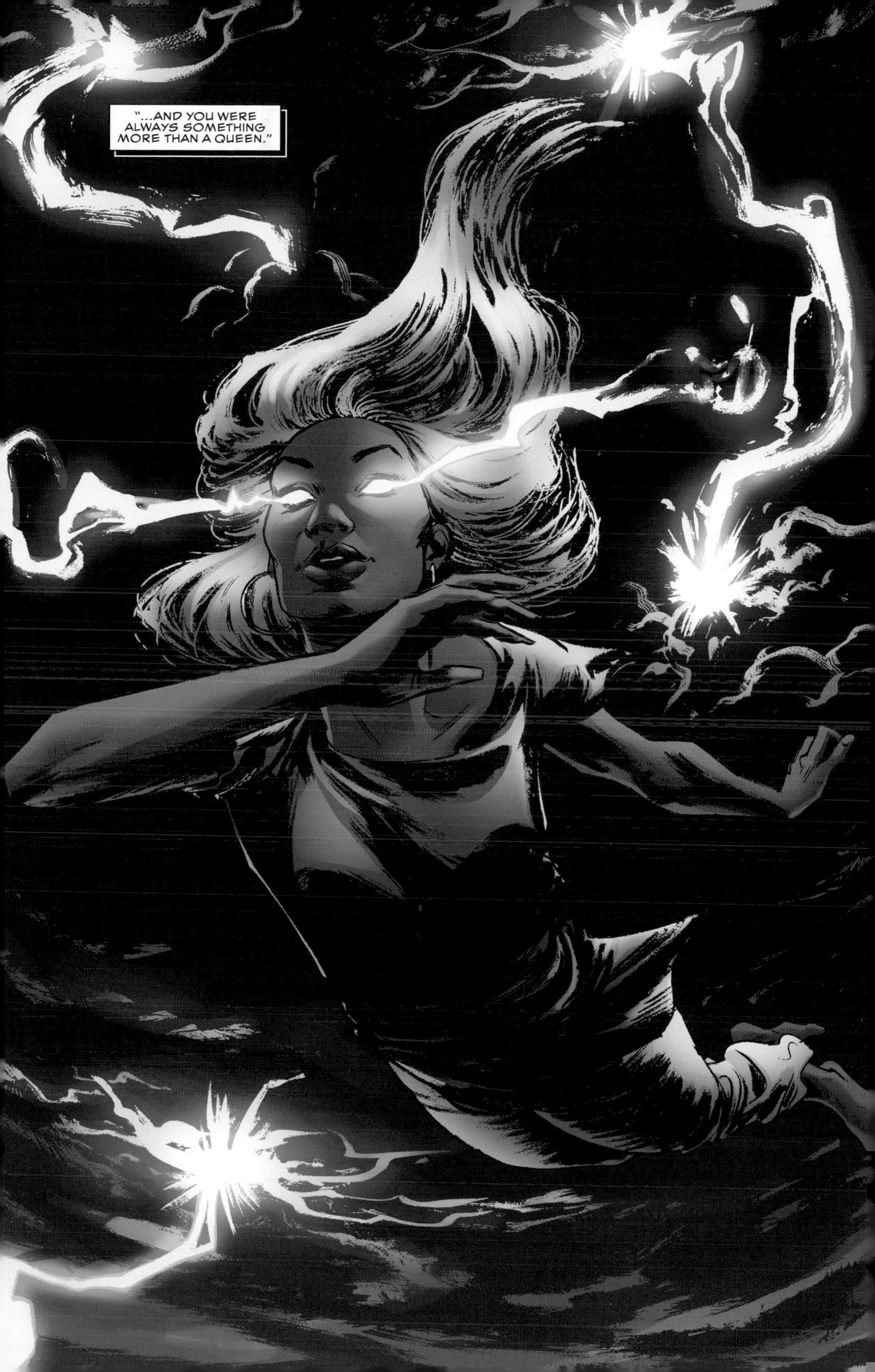
"...AND YOU WERE ALWAYS SOMETHING MORE THAN A QUEEN."

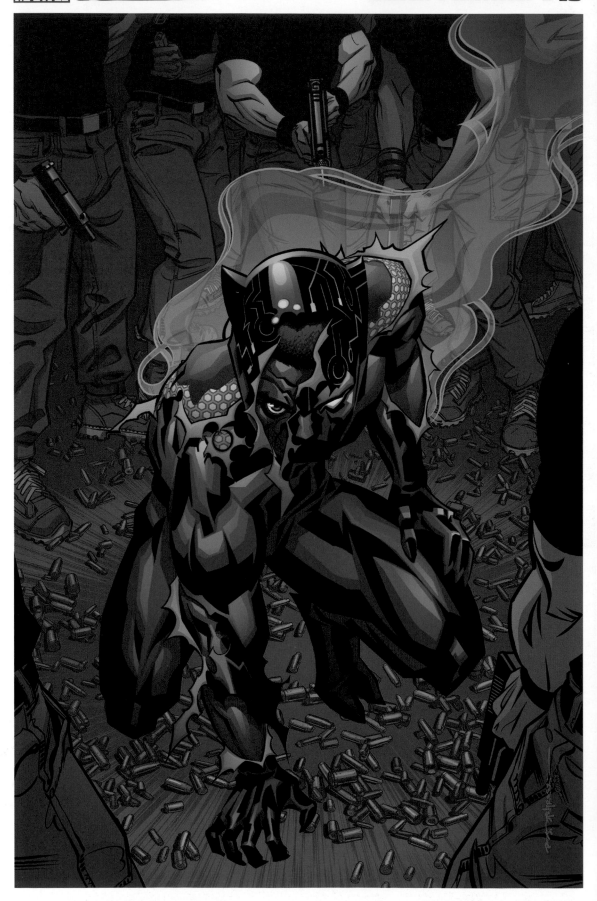

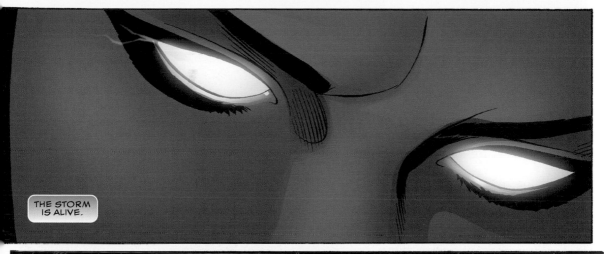

THE STORM IS ALIVE.

THE RAIN IN YOUR FACE IS HER MUSING.

THE THUNDER, HER FOOTSTEPS.

AND THE WIND IN YOUR HAIR IS NOT SIMPLY THE WIND...

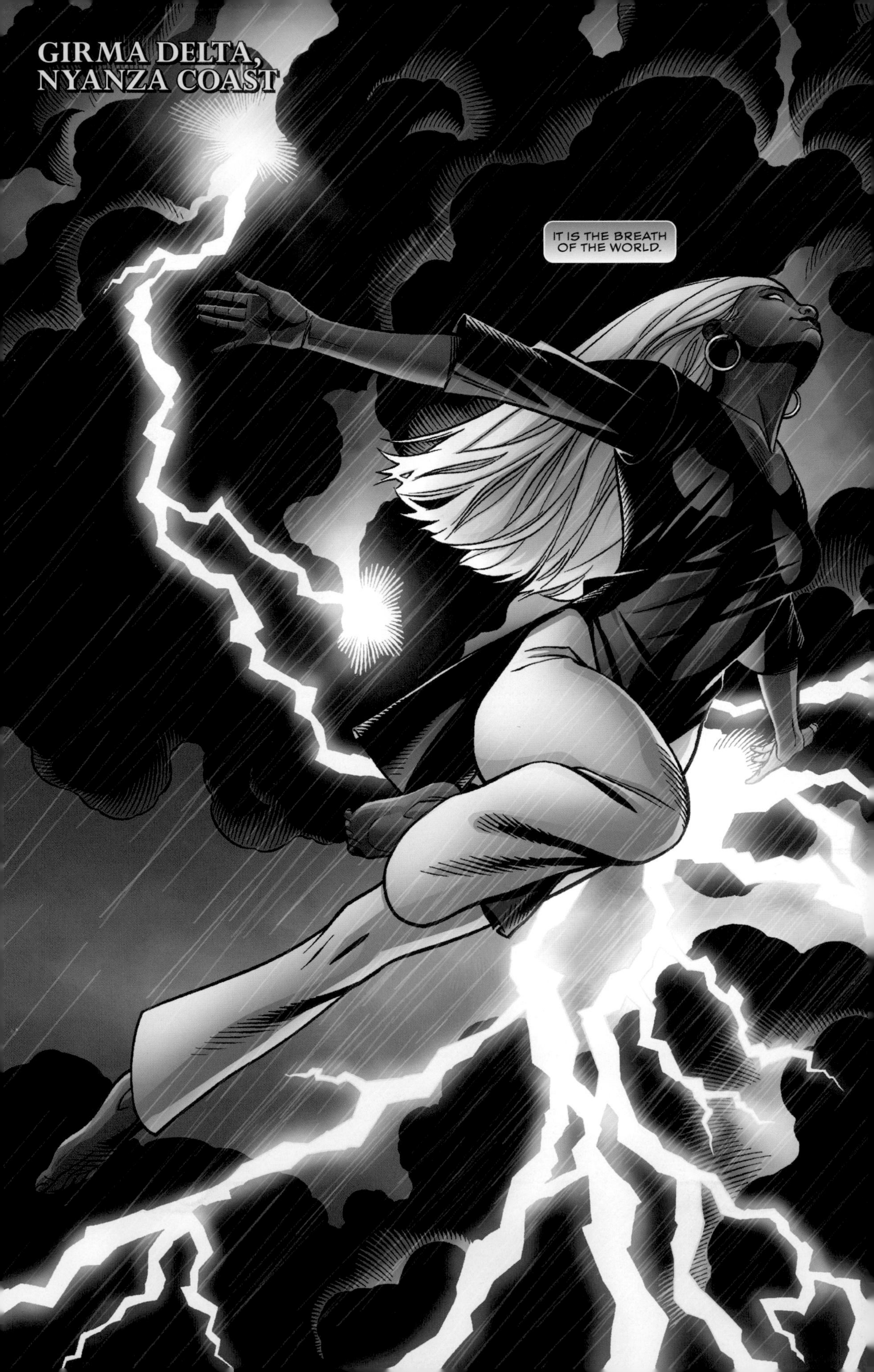
GIRMA DELTA,
NYANZA COAST
IT IS THE BREATH OF THE WORLD.

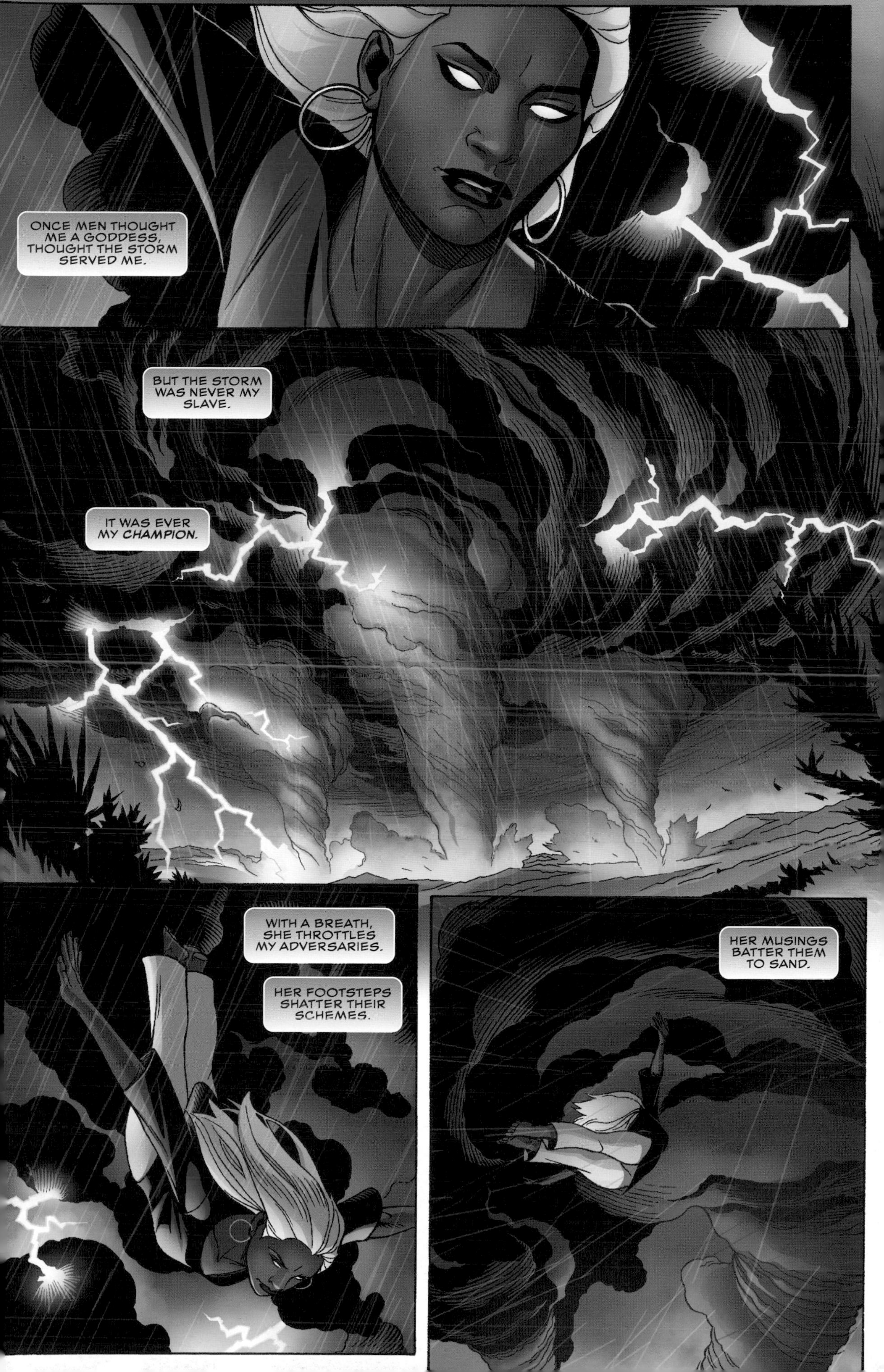
ONCE MEN THOUGHT ME A GODDESS, THOUGHT THE STORM SERVED ME.
BUT THE STORM WAS NEVER MY SLAVE.
IT WAS EVER MY *CHAMPION*.
WITH A BREATH, SHE THROTTLES MY ADVERSARIES.
HER FOOTSTEPS SHATTER THEIR SCHEMES.
HER MUSINGS BATTER THEM TO SAND.

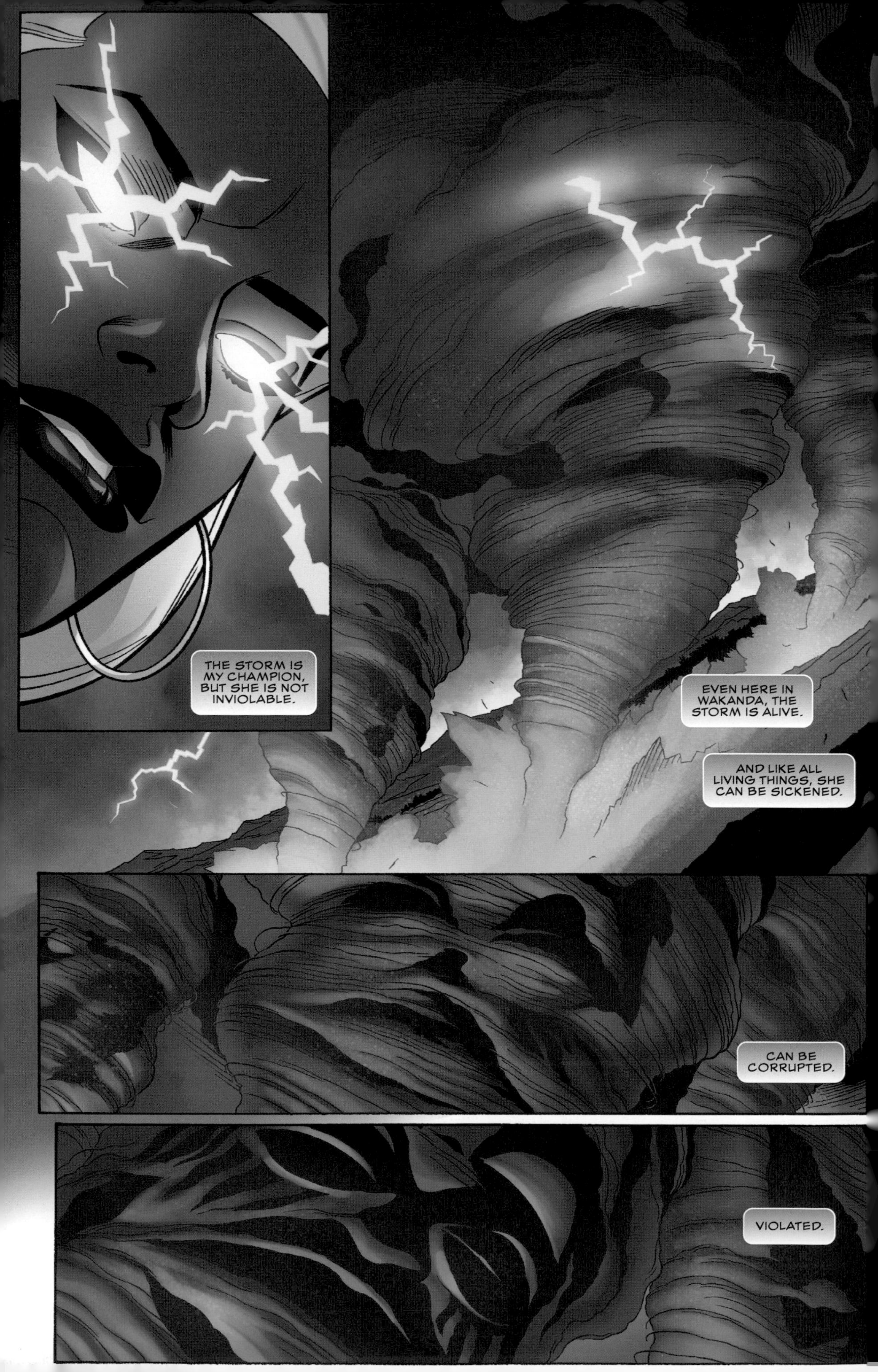
THE STORM IS MY CHAMPION, BUT SHE IS NOT INVIOLABLE.
EVEN HERE IN WAKANDA, THE STORM IS ALIVE.
AND LIKE ALL LIVING THINGS, SHE CAN BE SICKENED.
CAN BE CORRUPTED.
VIOLATED.

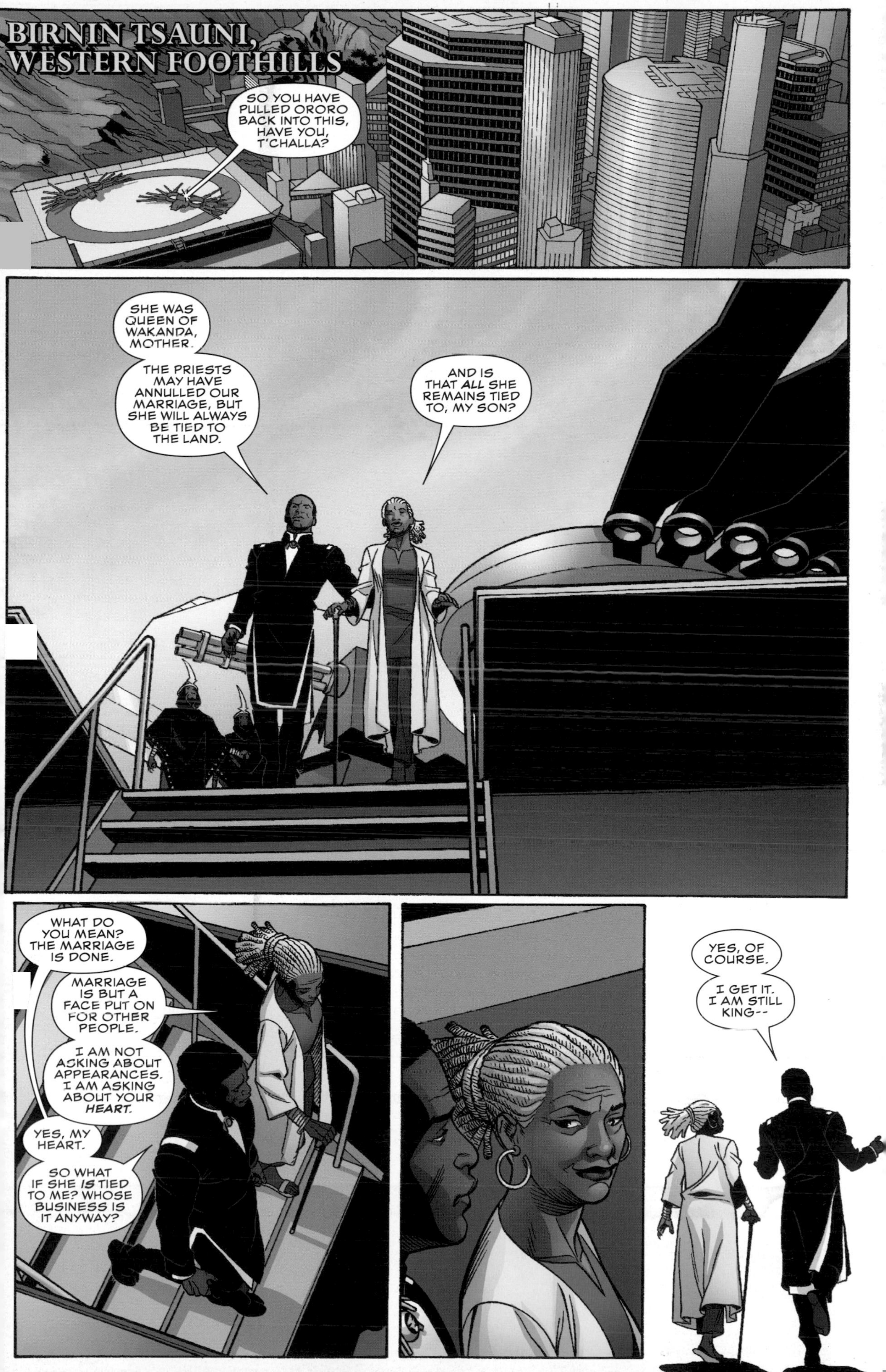
BIRNIN TSAUNI, WESTERN FOOTHILLS
SO YOU HAVE PULLED ORORO BACK INTO THIS, HAVE YOU, T'CHALLA?
SHE WAS QUEEN OF WAKANDA, MOTHER.
THE PRIESTS MAY HAVE ANNULLED OUR MARRIAGE, BUT SHE WILL ALWAYS BE TIED TO THE LAND.
AND IS THAT *ALL* SHE REMAINS TIED TO, MY SON?
WHAT DO YOU MEAN? THE MARRIAGE IS DONE.
MARRIAGE IS BUT A FACE PUT ON FOR OTHER PEOPLE.
I AM NOT ASKING ABOUT APPEARANCES. I AM ASKING ABOUT YOUR *HEART.*
YES, MY HEART.
SO WHAT IF SHE *IS* TIED TO ME? WHOSE BUSINESS IS IT ANYWAY?
YES, OF COURSE.
I GET IT. I AM STILL KING--

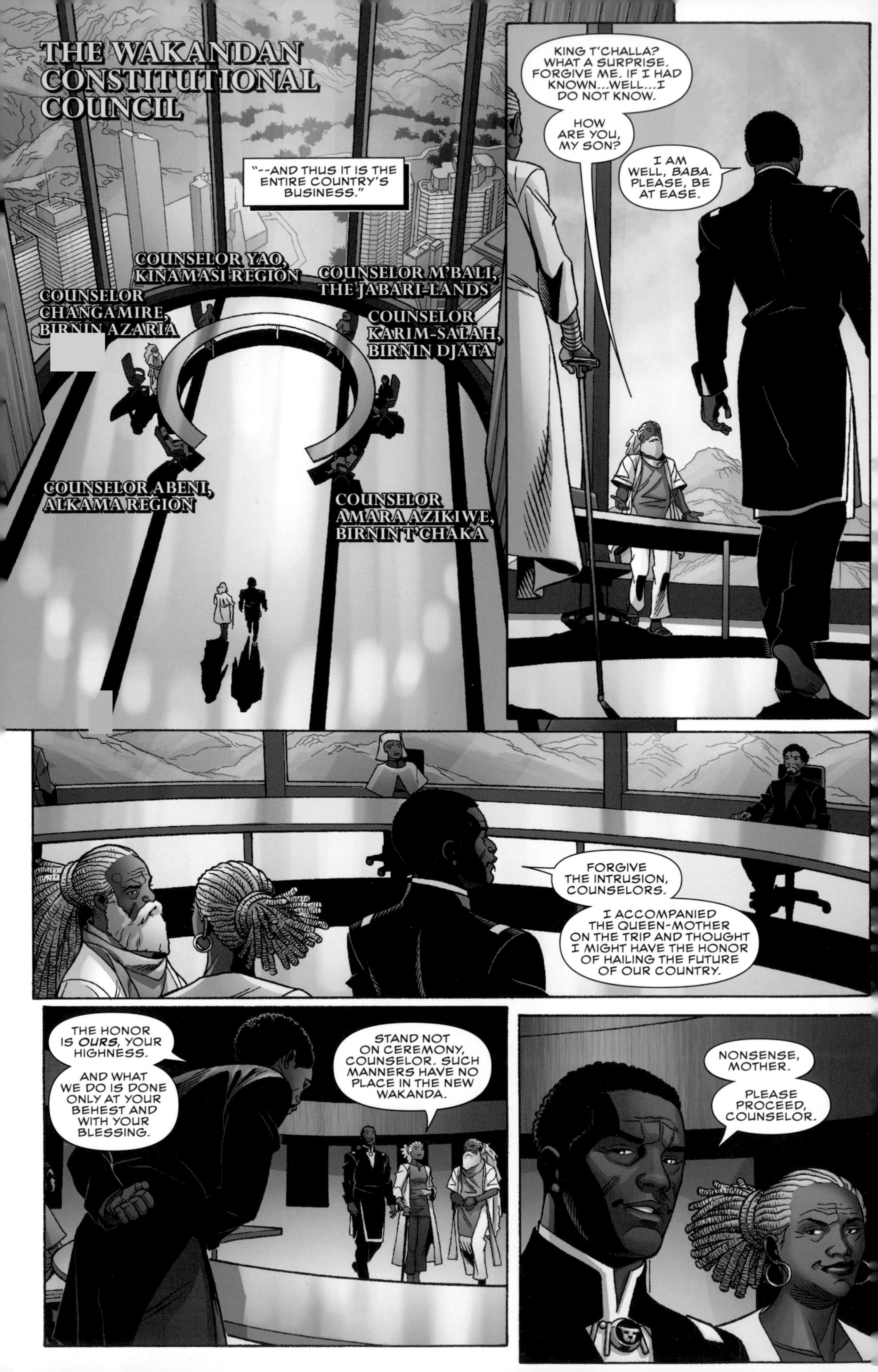
THE WAKANDAN CONSTITUTIONAL COUNCIL
"--AND THUS IT IS THE ENTIRE COUNTRY'S BUSINESS."
COUNSELOR YAO, KINAMASI REGION
COUNSELOR M'BALI, THE JABARI-LANDS
COUNSELOR CHANGAMIRE, BIRNIN AZARIA
COUNSELOR KARIM-SALAH, BIRNIN DJATA
COUNSELOR ABENI, ALKAMA REGION
COUNSELOR AMARA AZIKIWE, BIRNIN T'CHAKA
KING T'CHALLA? WHAT A SURPRISE. FORGIVE ME. IF I HAD KNOWN...WELL...I DO NOT KNOW.
HOW ARE YOU, MY SON?
I AM WELL, BABA. PLEASE, BE AT EASE.
FORGIVE THE INTRUSION, COUNSELORS.
I ACCOMPANIED THE QUEEN-MOTHER ON THE TRIP AND THOUGHT I MIGHT HAVE THE HONOR OF HAILING THE FUTURE OF OUR COUNTRY.
THE HONOR IS OURS, YOUR HIGHNESS.
AND WHAT WE DO IS DONE ONLY AT YOUR BEHEST AND WITH YOUR BLESSING.
STAND NOT ON CEREMONY, COUNSELOR. SUCH MANNERS HAVE NO PLACE IN THE NEW WAKANDA.
NONSENSE, MOTHER.
PLEASE PROCEED, COUNSELOR.

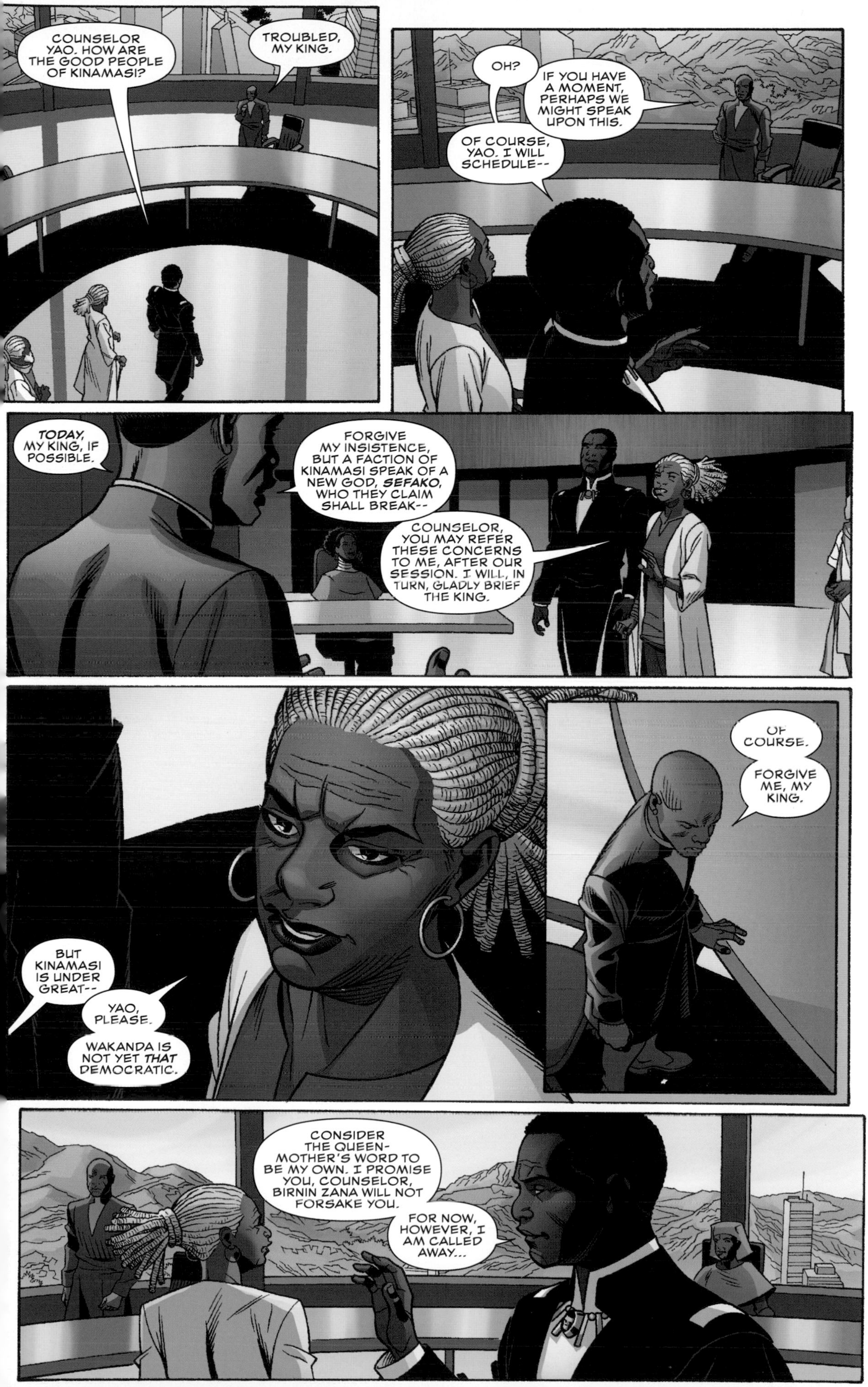
COUNSELOR YAO. HOW ARE THE GOOD PEOPLE OF KINAMASI?
TROUBLED, MY KING.
OH?
IF YOU HAVE A MOMENT, PERHAPS WE MIGHT SPEAK UPON THIS.
OF COURSE, YAO. I WILL SCHEDULE--
TODAY, MY KING, IF POSSIBLE.
FORGIVE MY INSISTENCE, BUT A FACTION OF KINAMASI SPEAK OF A NEW GOD, *SEFAKO,* WHO THEY CLAIM SHALL BREAK--
COUNSELOR, YOU MAY REFER THESE CONCERNS TO ME, AFTER OUR SESSION. I WILL, IN TURN, GLADLY BRIEF THE KING.
BUT KINAMASI IS UNDER GREAT--
YAO, PLEASE.
WAKANDA IS NOT YET *THAT* DEMOCRATIC.
OF COURSE.
FORGIVE ME, MY KING.
CONSIDER THE QUEEN-MOTHER'S WORD TO BE MY OWN. I PROMISE YOU, COUNSELOR, BIRNIN ZANA WILL NOT FORSAKE YOU.
FOR NOW, HOWEVER, I AM CALLED AWAY...

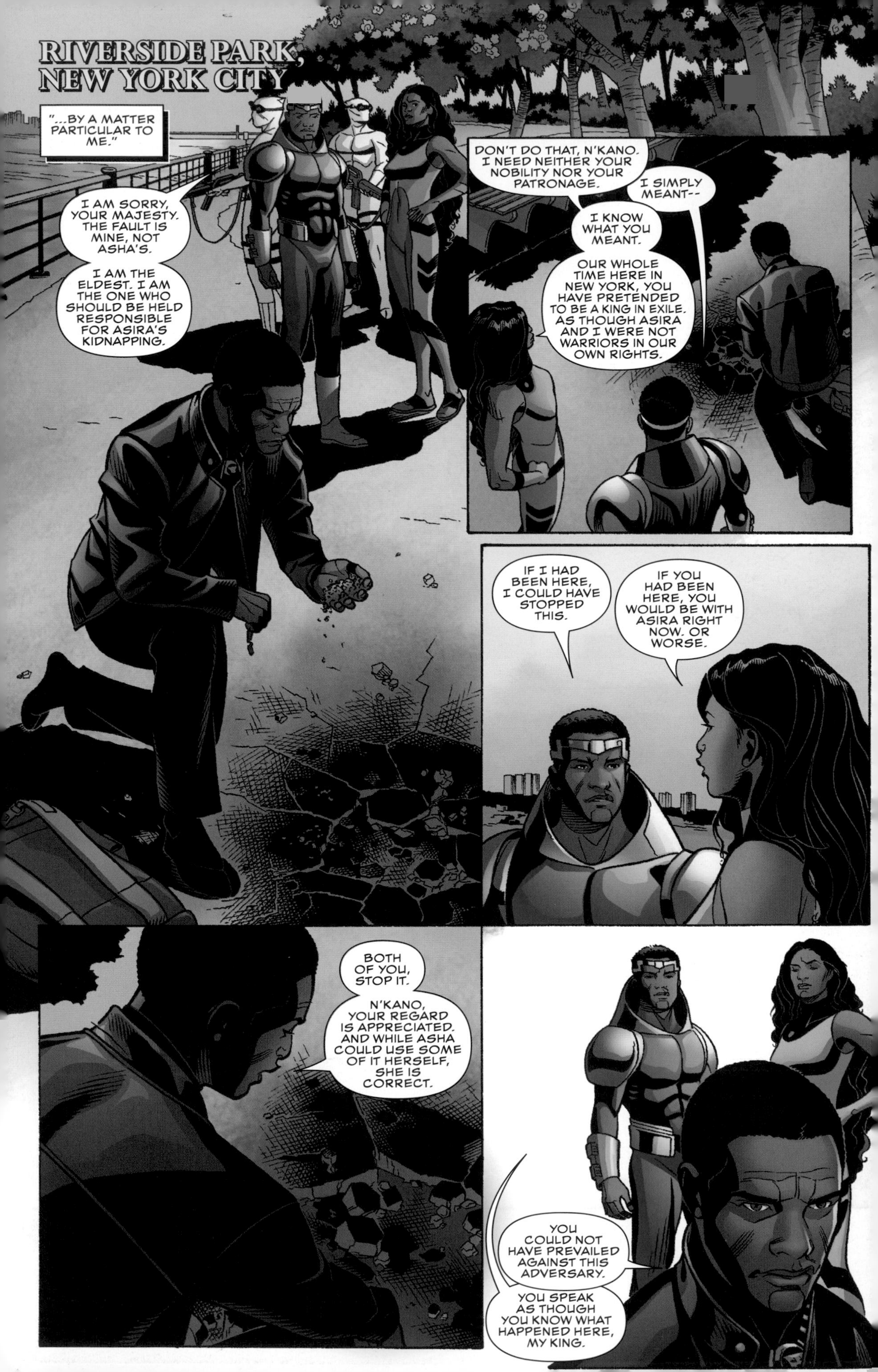
RIVERSIDE PARK, NEW YORK CITY
"...BY A MATTER PARTICULAR TO ME."
I AM SORRY, YOUR MAJESTY. THE FAULT IS MINE, NOT ASHA'S.
I AM THE ELDEST. I AM THE ONE WHO SHOULD BE HELD RESPONSIBLE FOR ASIRA'S KIDNAPPING.
DON'T DO THAT, N'KANO. I NEED NEITHER YOUR NOBILITY NOR YOUR PATRONAGE.
I SIMPLY MEANT--
I KNOW WHAT YOU MEANT.
OUR WHOLE TIME HERE IN NEW YORK, YOU HAVE PRETENDED TO BE A KING IN EXILE. AS THOUGH ASIRA AND I WERE NOT WARRIORS IN OUR OWN RIGHTS.
IF I HAD BEEN HERE, I COULD HAVE STOPPED THIS.
IF YOU HAD BEEN HERE, YOU WOULD BE WITH ASIRA RIGHT NOW. OR WORSE.
BOTH OF YOU, STOP IT.
N'KANO, YOUR REGARD IS APPRECIATED. AND WHILE ASHA COULD USE SOME OF IT HERSELF, SHE IS CORRECT.
YOU COULD NOT HAVE PREVAILED AGAINST THIS ADVERSARY.
YOU SPEAK AS THOUGH YOU KNOW WHAT HAPPENED HERE, MY KING.

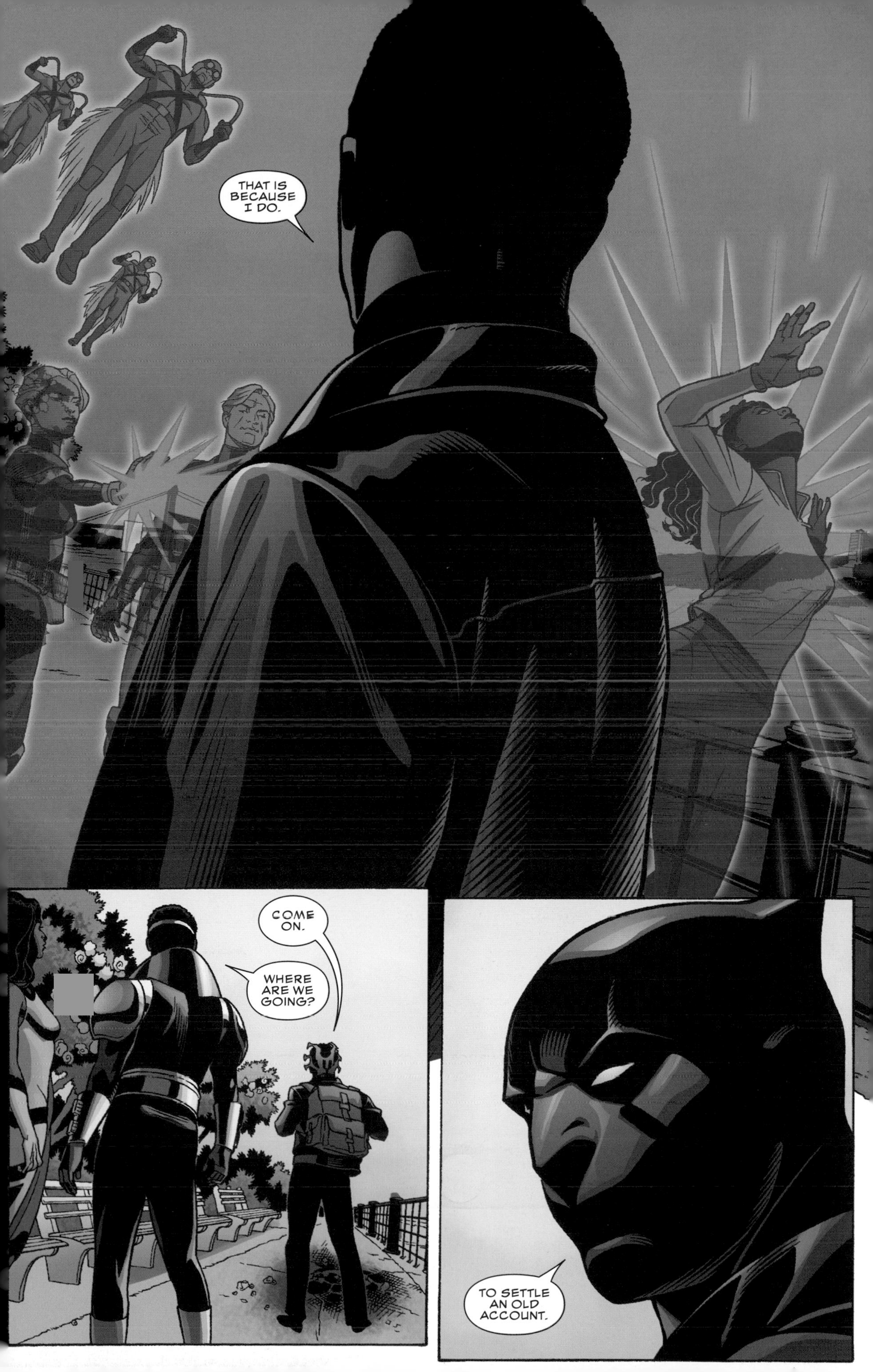
THAT IS BECAUSE I DO.
COME ON.
WHERE ARE WE GOING?
TO SETTLE AN OLD ACCOUNT.

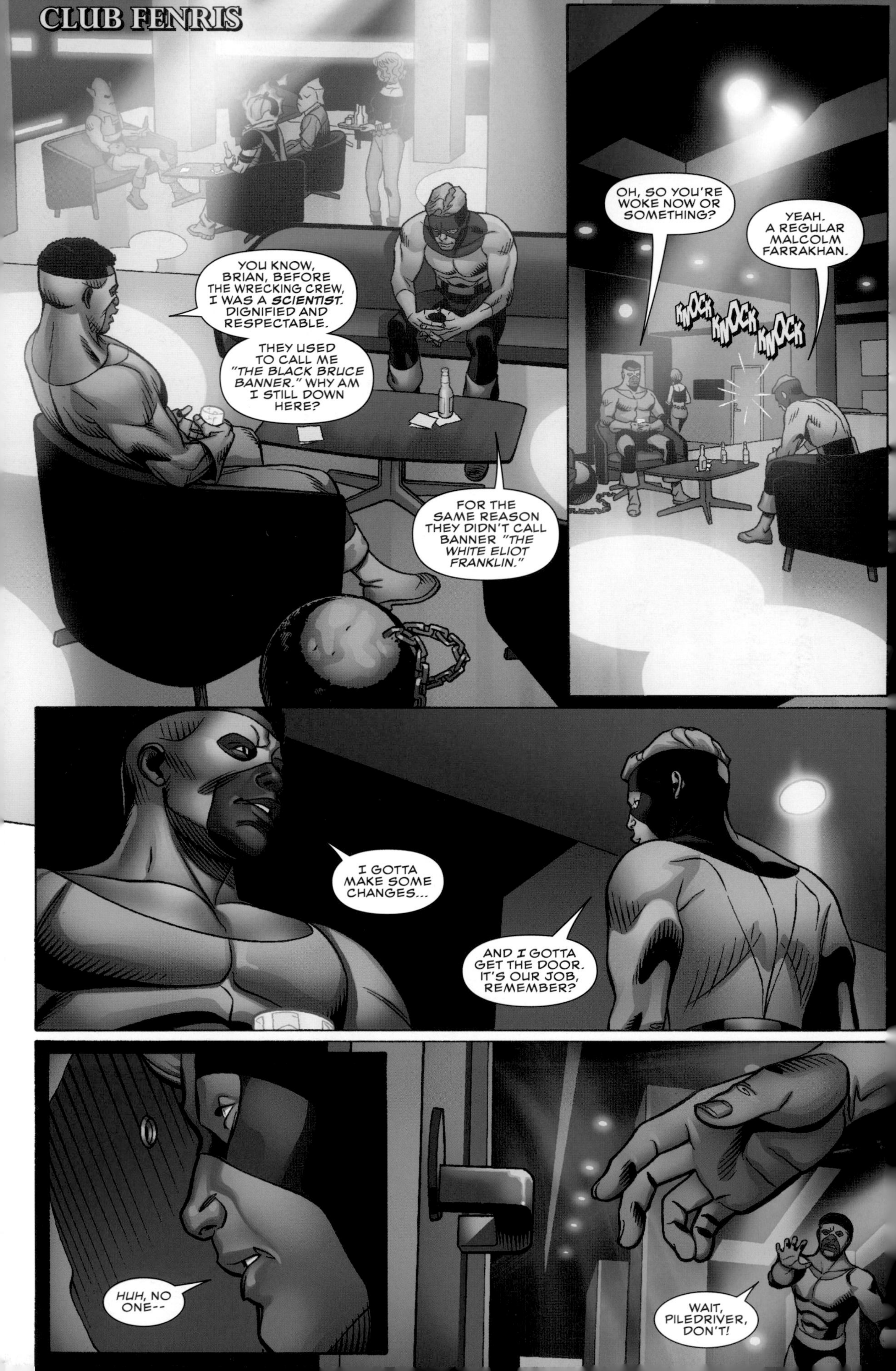
CLUB FENRIS
YOU KNOW, BRIAN, BEFORE THE WRECKING CREW, I WAS A SCIENTIST. DIGNIFIED AND RESPECTABLE.
THEY USED TO CALL ME "THE BLACK BRUCE BANNER." WHY AM I STILL DOWN HERE?
FOR THE SAME REASON THEY DIDN'T CALL BANNER "THE WHITE ELIOT FRANKLIN."
OH, SO YOU'RE WOKE NOW OR SOMETHING?
YEAH. A REGULAR MALCOLM FARRAKHAN.
KNOCK KNOCK KNOCK
I GOTTA MAKE SOME CHANGES...
AND I GOTTA GET THE DOOR. IT'S OUR JOB, REMEMBER?
HUH, NO ONE--
WAIT, PILEDRIVER, DON'T!

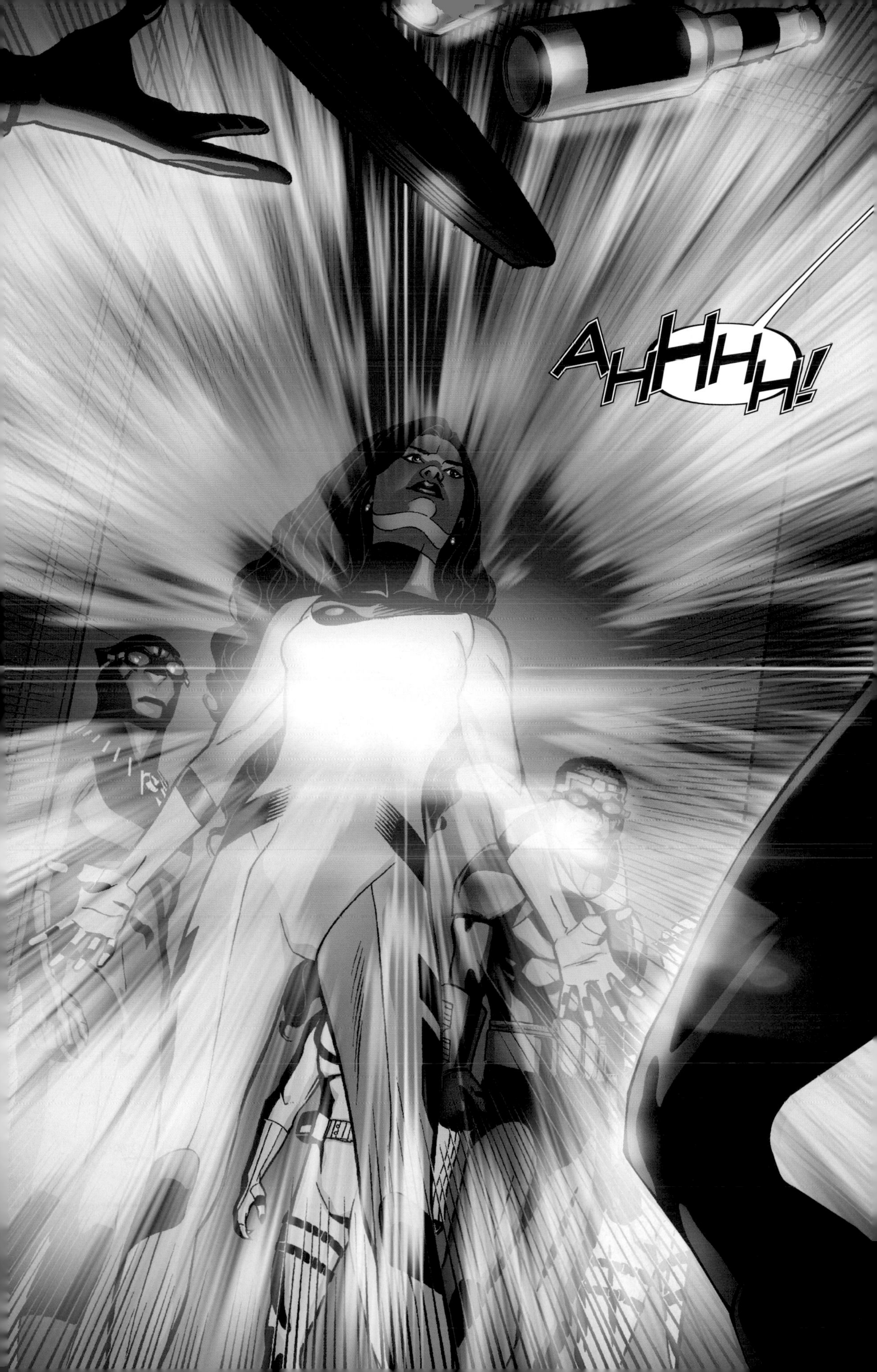
AHHHH!

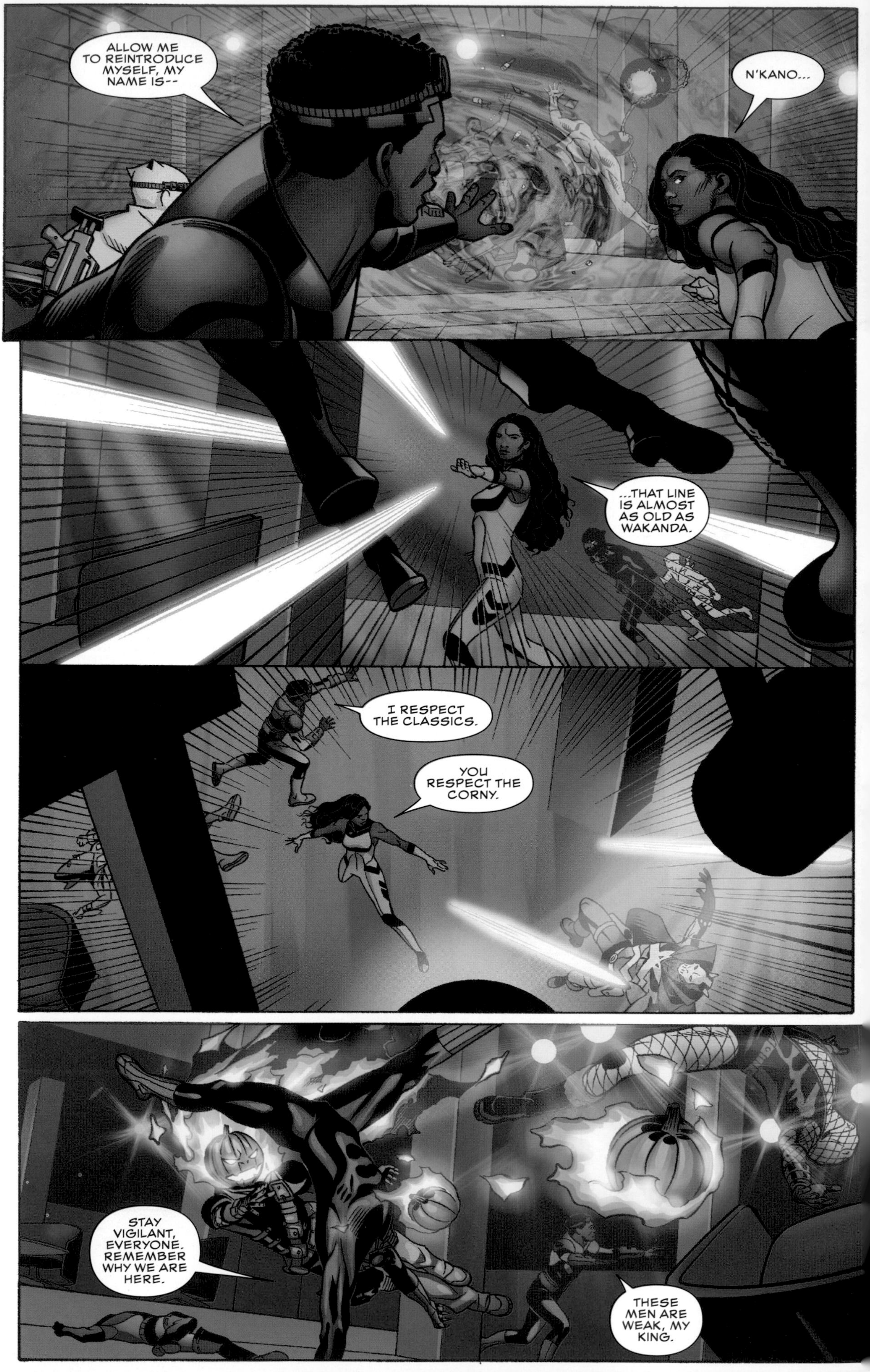
ALLOW ME TO REINTRODUCE MYSELF, MY NAME IS--
N'KANO...
...THAT LINE IS ALMOST AS OLD AS WAKANDA.
I RESPECT THE CLASSICS.
YOU RESPECT THE CORNY.
STAY VIGILANT, EVERYONE. REMEMBER WHY WE ARE HERE.
THESE MEN ARE WEAK, MY KING.

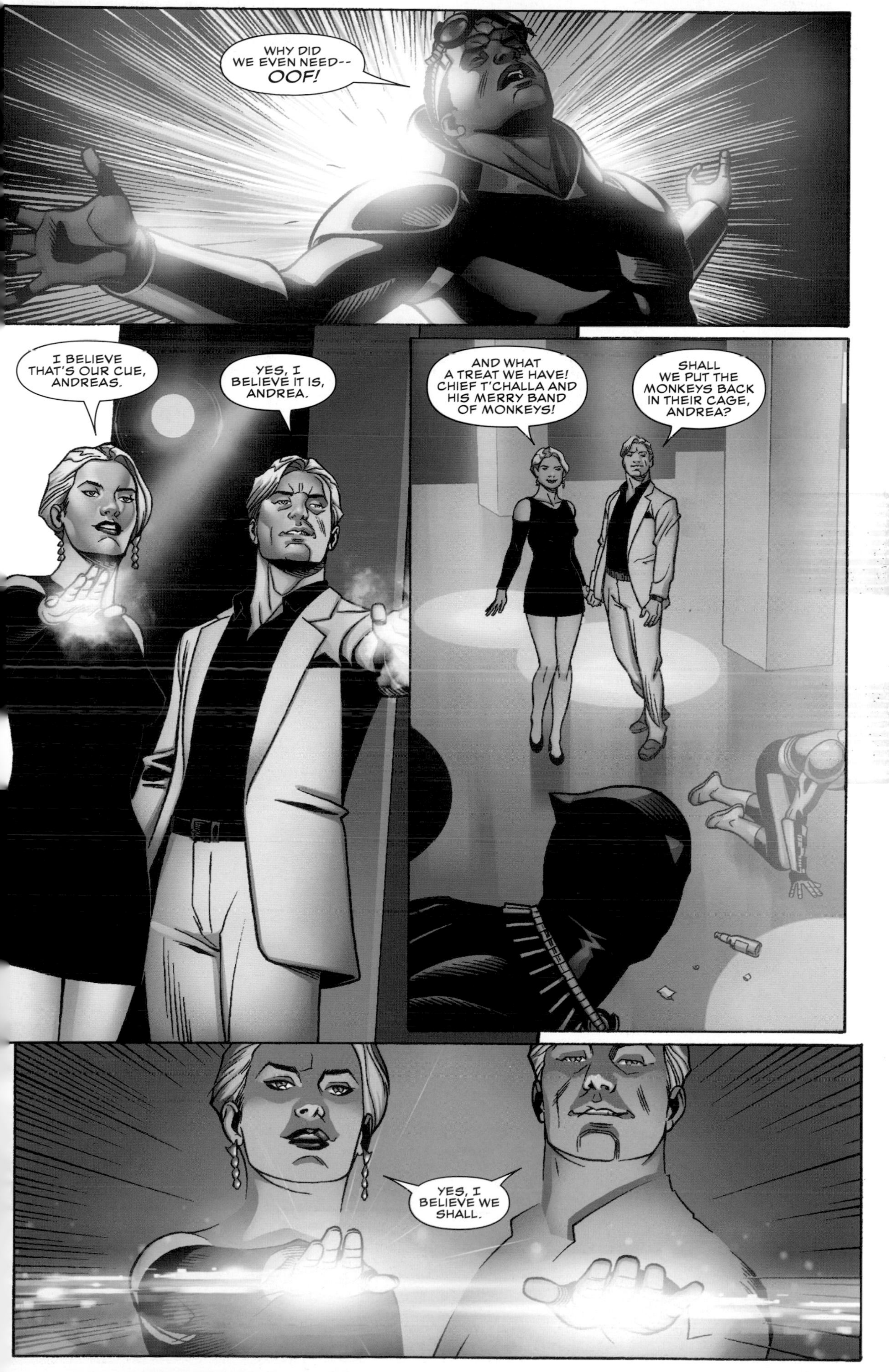
WHY DID WE EVEN NEED-- OOF!
I BELIEVE THAT'S OUR CUE, ANDREAS.
YES, I BELIEVE IT IS, ANDREA.
AND WHAT A TREAT WE HAVE! CHIEF T'CHALLA AND HIS MERRY BAND OF MONKEYS!
SHALL WE PUT THE MONKEYS BACK IN THEIR CAGE, ANDREA?
YES, I BELIEVE WE SHALL.

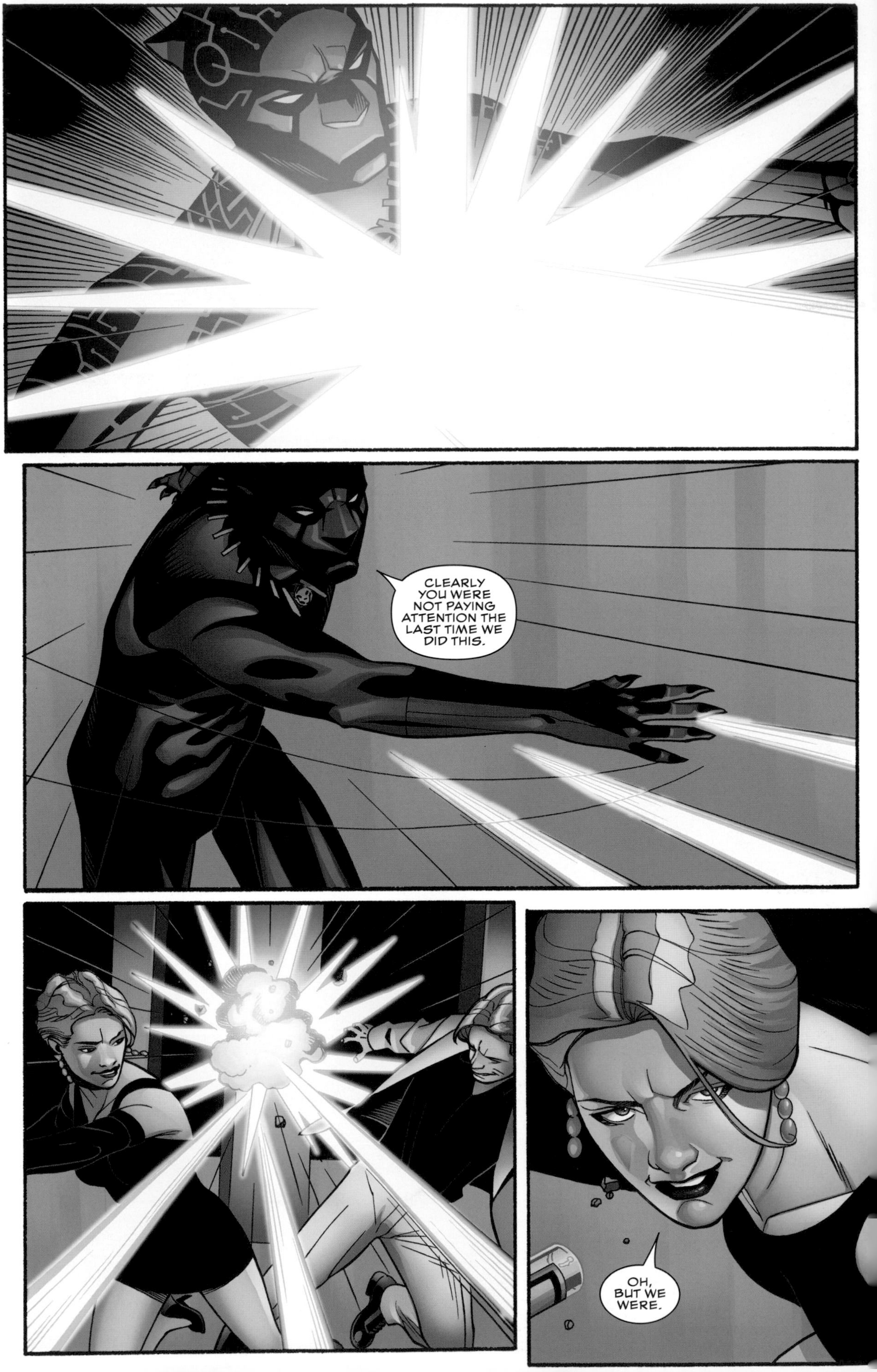
CLEARLY YOU WERE NOT PAYING ATTENTION THE LAST TIME WE DID THIS.
OH, BUT WE WERE.

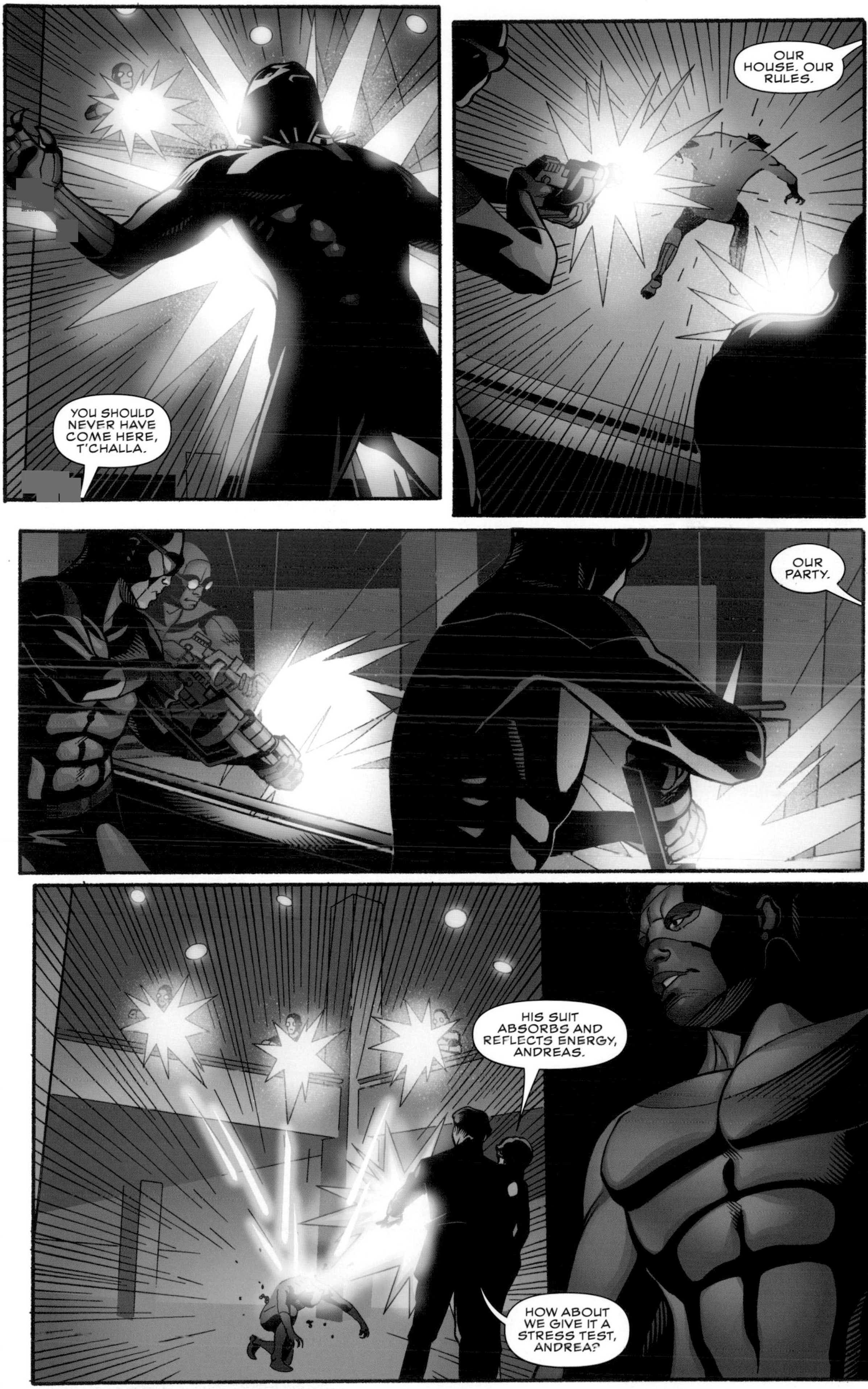
YOU SHOULD NEVER HAVE COME HERE, T'CHALLA.
OUR HOUSE. OUR RULES.
OUR PARTY.
HIS SUIT ABSORBS AND REFLECTS ENERGY, ANDREAS.
HOW ABOUT WE GIVE IT A STRESS TEST, ANDREA?

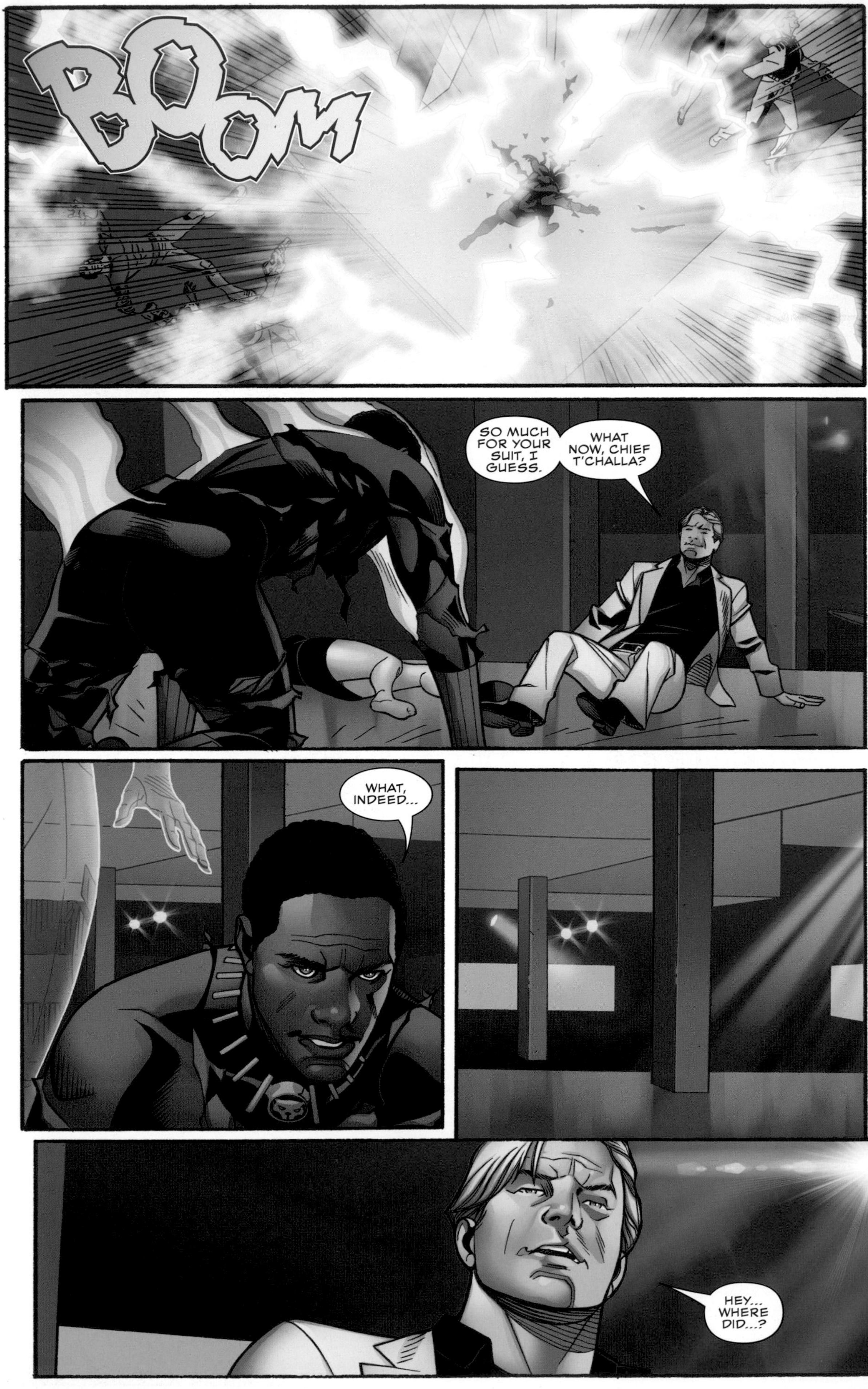
BOOM
SO MUCH FOR YOUR SUIT, I GUESS.
WHAT NOW, CHIEF T'CHALLA?
WHAT, INDEED...
HEY... WHERE DID...?

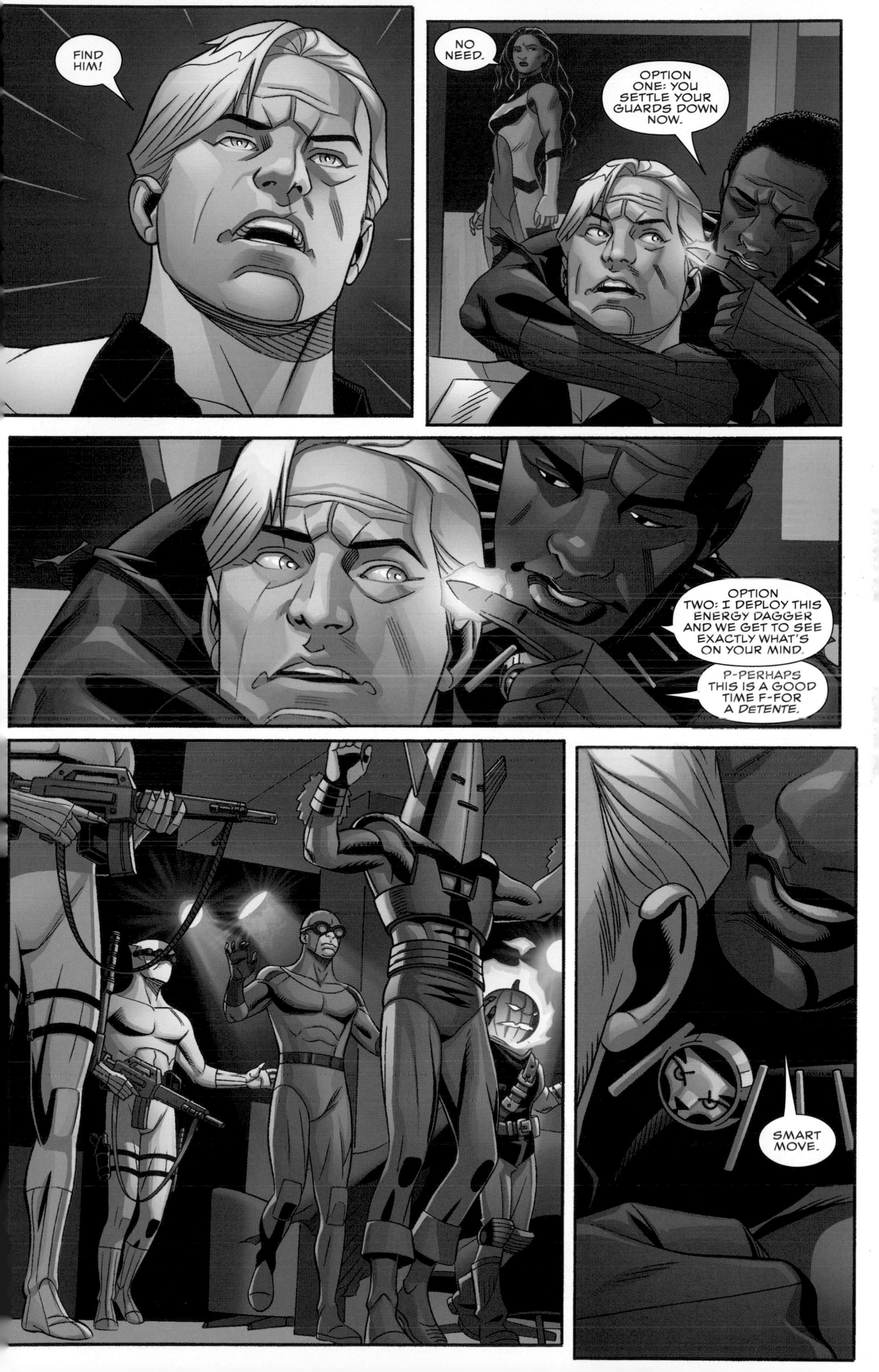
FIND HIM!
NO NEED.
OPTION ONE: YOU SETTLE YOUR GUARDS DOWN NOW.
OPTION TWO: I DEPLOY THIS ENERGY DAGGER AND WE GET TO SEE EXACTLY WHAT'S ON YOUR MIND.
P-PERHAPS THIS IS A GOOD TIME F-FOR A *DETENTE*.
SMART MOVE.

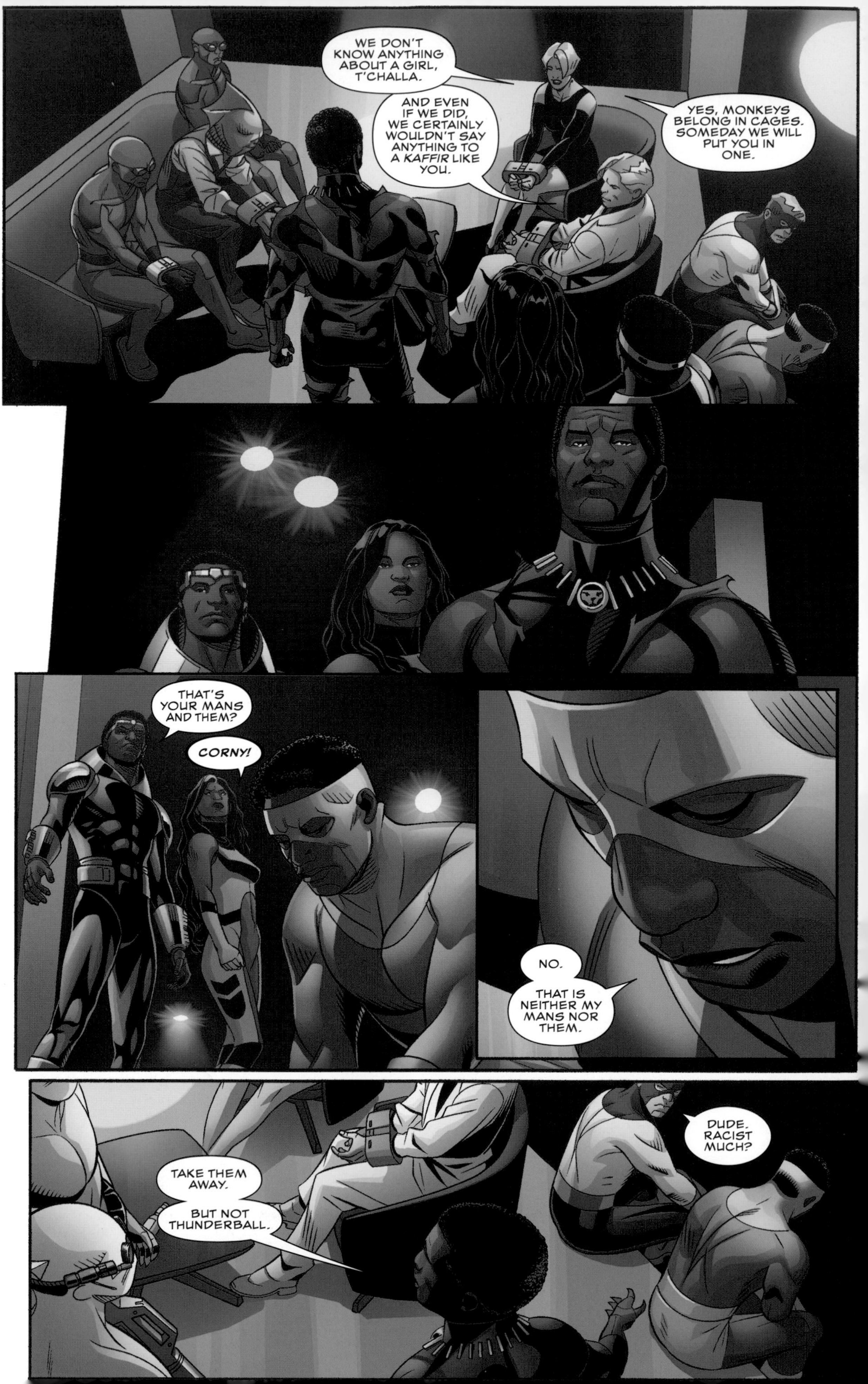
WE DON'T KNOW ANYTHING ABOUT A GIRL, T'CHALLA.
AND EVEN IF WE DID, WE CERTAINLY WOULDN'T SAY ANYTHING TO A *KAFFIR* LIKE YOU.
YES, MONKEYS BELONG IN CAGES. SOMEDAY WE WILL PUT YOU IN ONE.
THAT'S YOUR MANS AND THEM?
CORNY!
NO.
THAT IS NEITHER MY MANS NOR THEM.
TAKE THEM AWAY.
BUT NOT THUNDERBALL.
DUDE. RACIST MUCH?

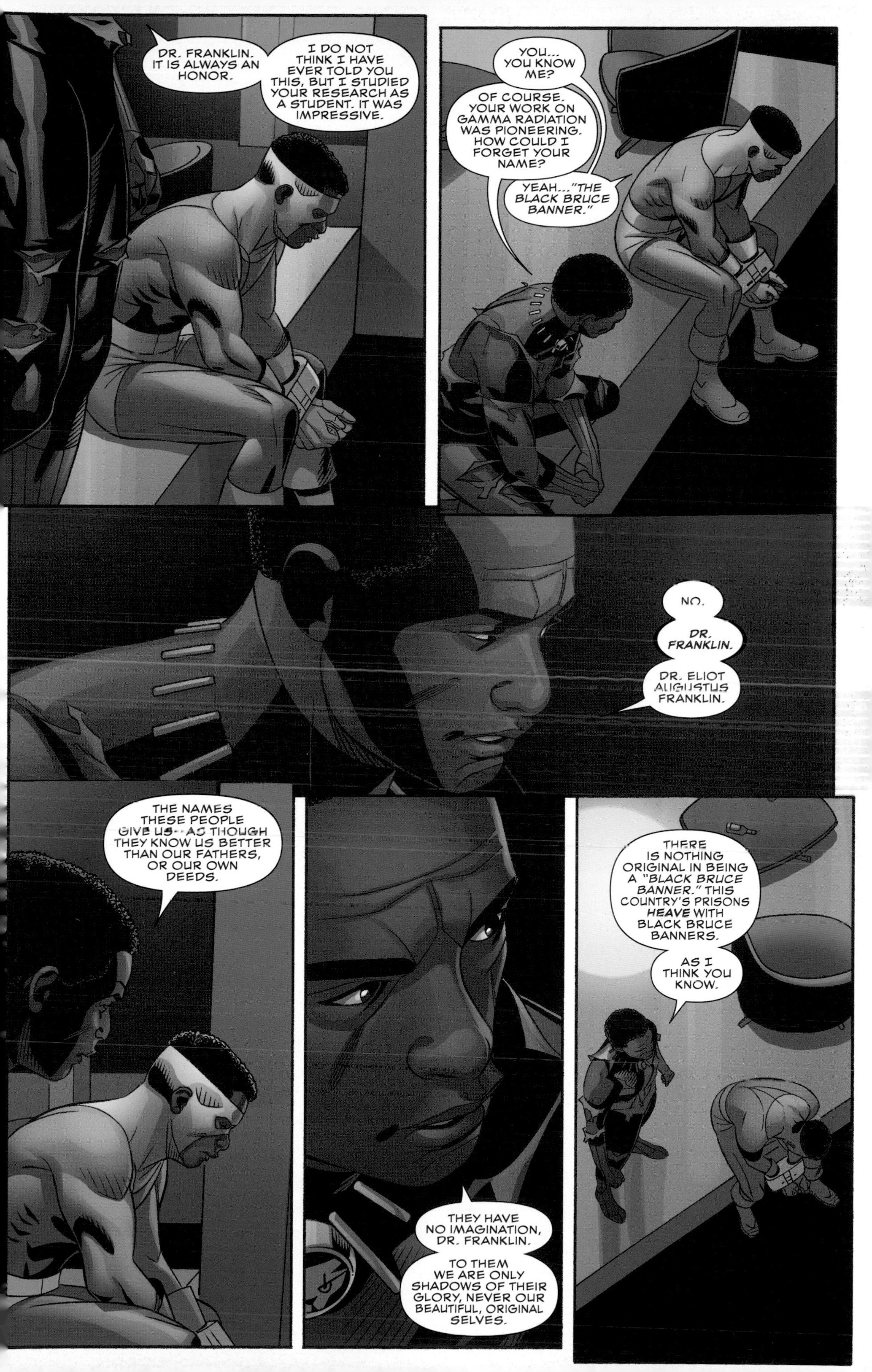
DR. FRANKLIN. IT IS ALWAYS AN HONOR.
I DO NOT THINK I HAVE EVER TOLD YOU THIS, BUT I STUDIED YOUR RESEARCH AS A STUDENT. IT WAS IMPRESSIVE.
YOU... YOU KNOW ME?
OF COURSE. YOUR WORK ON GAMMA RADIATION WAS PIONEERING. HOW COULD I FORGET YOUR NAME?
YEAH..."THE BLACK BRUCE BANNER."
NO.
DR. FRANKLIN.
DR. ELIOT AUGUSTUS FRANKLIN.
THE NAMES THESE PEOPLE GIVE US--AS THOUGH THEY KNOW US BETTER THAN OUR FATHERS, OR OUR OWN DEEDS.
THEY HAVE NO IMAGINATION, DR. FRANKLIN.
TO THEM WE ARE ONLY SHADOWS OF THEIR GLORY, NEVER OUR BEAUTIFUL, ORIGINAL SELVES.
THERE IS NOTHING ORIGINAL IN BEING A "BLACK BRUCE BANNER." THIS COUNTRY'S PRISONS HEAVE WITH BLACK BRUCE BANNERS.
AS I THINK YOU KNOW.

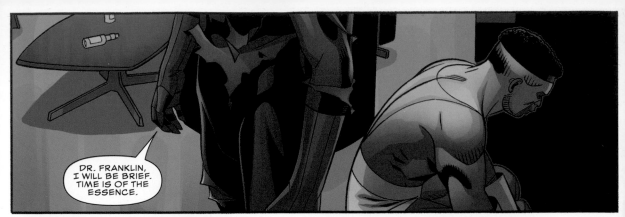

DR. FRANKLIN, I WILL BE BRIEF. TIME IS OF THE ESSENCE.

THE GIRL.

YES, THE GIRL.

THESE PEOPLE WHO EMPLOY YOU, THESE PEOPLE WHO MOCK US, TO WHOM WE ARE ONLY SHADOWS, THEY TOOK HER AND...

WELL, DR. FRANKLIN, I BELIEVE THAT YOU ARE A BRILLIANT MAN.

BUT MORE, I BELIEVE YOU WERE A GOOD MAN ONCE. AND THAT YOU MIGHT WELL BE ONE AGAIN.

YOU DO NOT HAVE TO ANSWER TO WHATEVER THEY CALL YOU, DR. FRANKLIN.

IT IS NOT TOO LATE TO RECOVER YOUR OWN NAME.

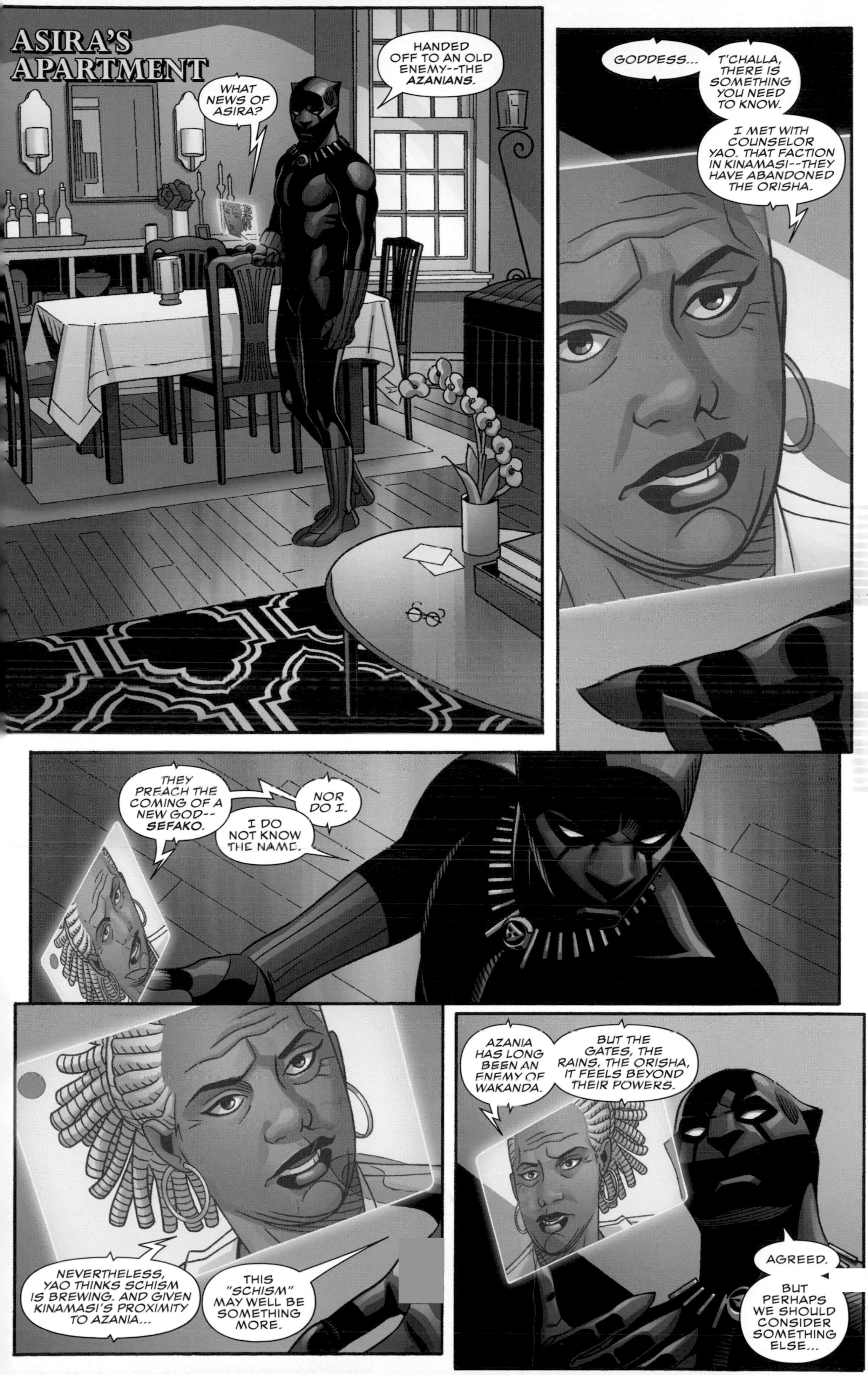
ASIRA'S APARTMENT
WHAT NEWS OF ASIRA?
HANDED OFF TO AN OLD ENEMY--THE AZANIANS.
GODDESS...
T'CHALLA, THERE IS SOMETHING YOU NEED TO KNOW.
I MET WITH COUNSELOR YAO. THAT FACTION IN KINAMASI--THEY HAVE ABANDONED THE ORISHA.
THEY PREACH THE COMING OF A NEW GOD--SEFAKO.
NOR DO I.
I DO NOT KNOW THE NAME.
NEVERTHELESS, YAO THINKS SCHISM IS BREWING. AND GIVEN KINAMASI'S PROXIMITY TO AZANIA...
THIS "SCHISM" MAY WELL BE SOMETHING MORE.
AZANIA HAS LONG BEEN AN ENEMY OF WAKANDA.
BUT THE GATES, THE RAINS, THE ORISHA, IT FEELS BEYOND THEIR POWERS.
AGREED.
BUT PERHAPS WE SHOULD CONSIDER SOMETHING ELSE...

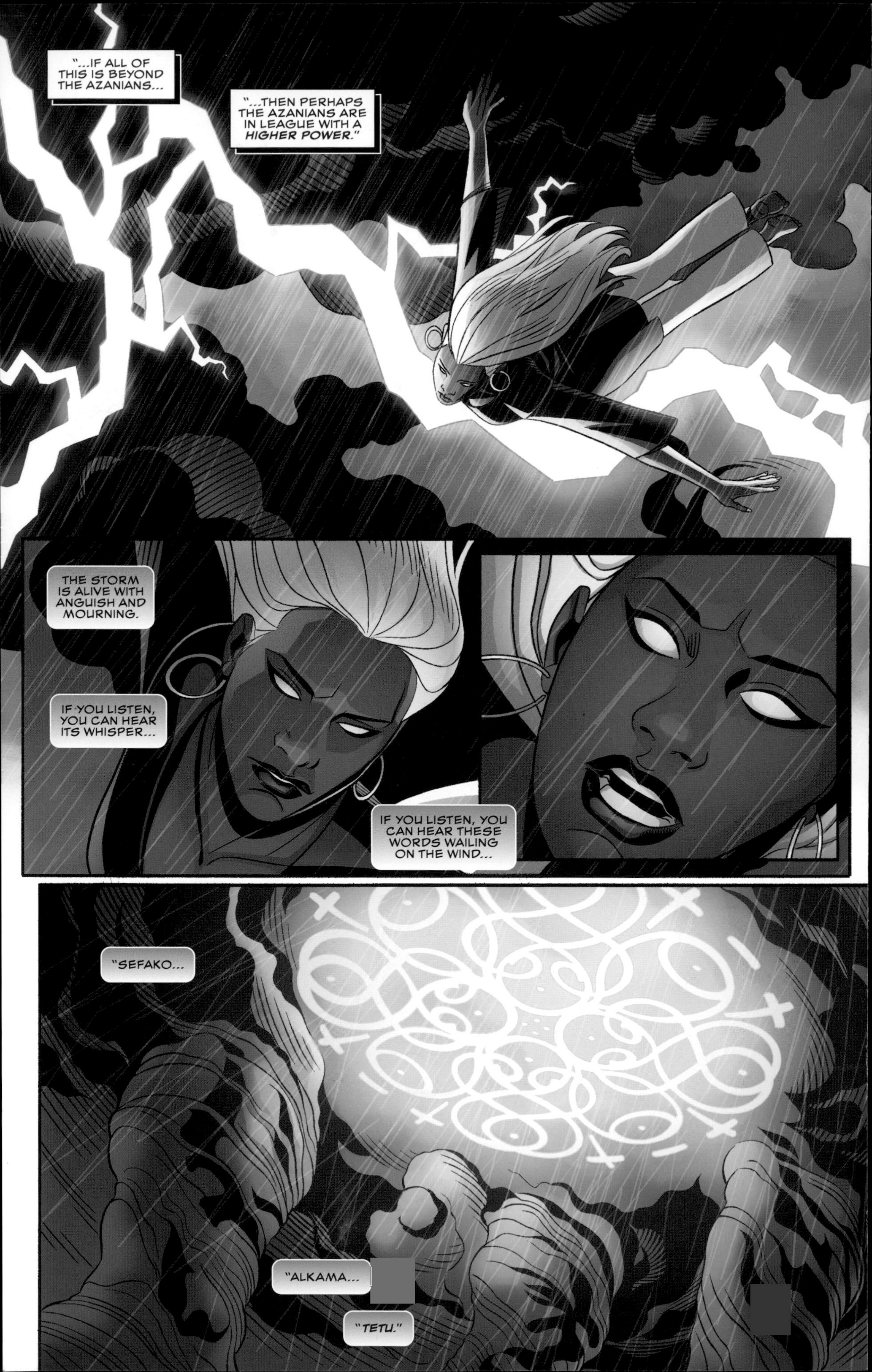
"...IF ALL OF THIS IS BEYOND THE AZANIANS...
"...THEN PERHAPS THE AZANIANS ARE IN LEAGUE WITH A HIGHER POWER."
THE STORM IS ALIVE WITH ANGUISH AND MOURNING.
IF YOU LISTEN, YOU CAN HEAR ITS WHISPER...
IF YOU LISTEN, YOU CAN HEAR THESE WORDS WAILING ON THE WIND...
"SEFAKO...
"ALKAMA...
"TETU."

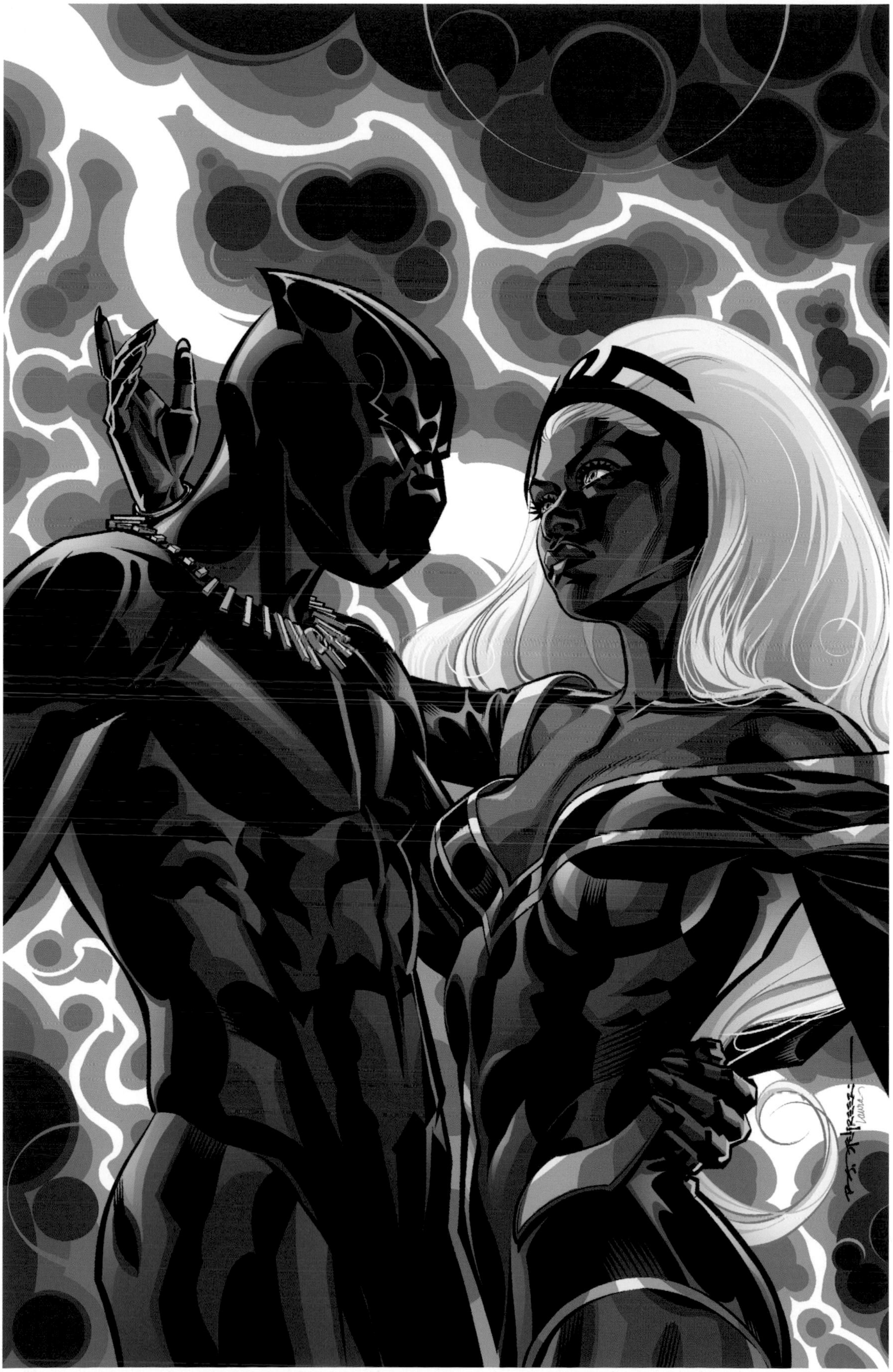

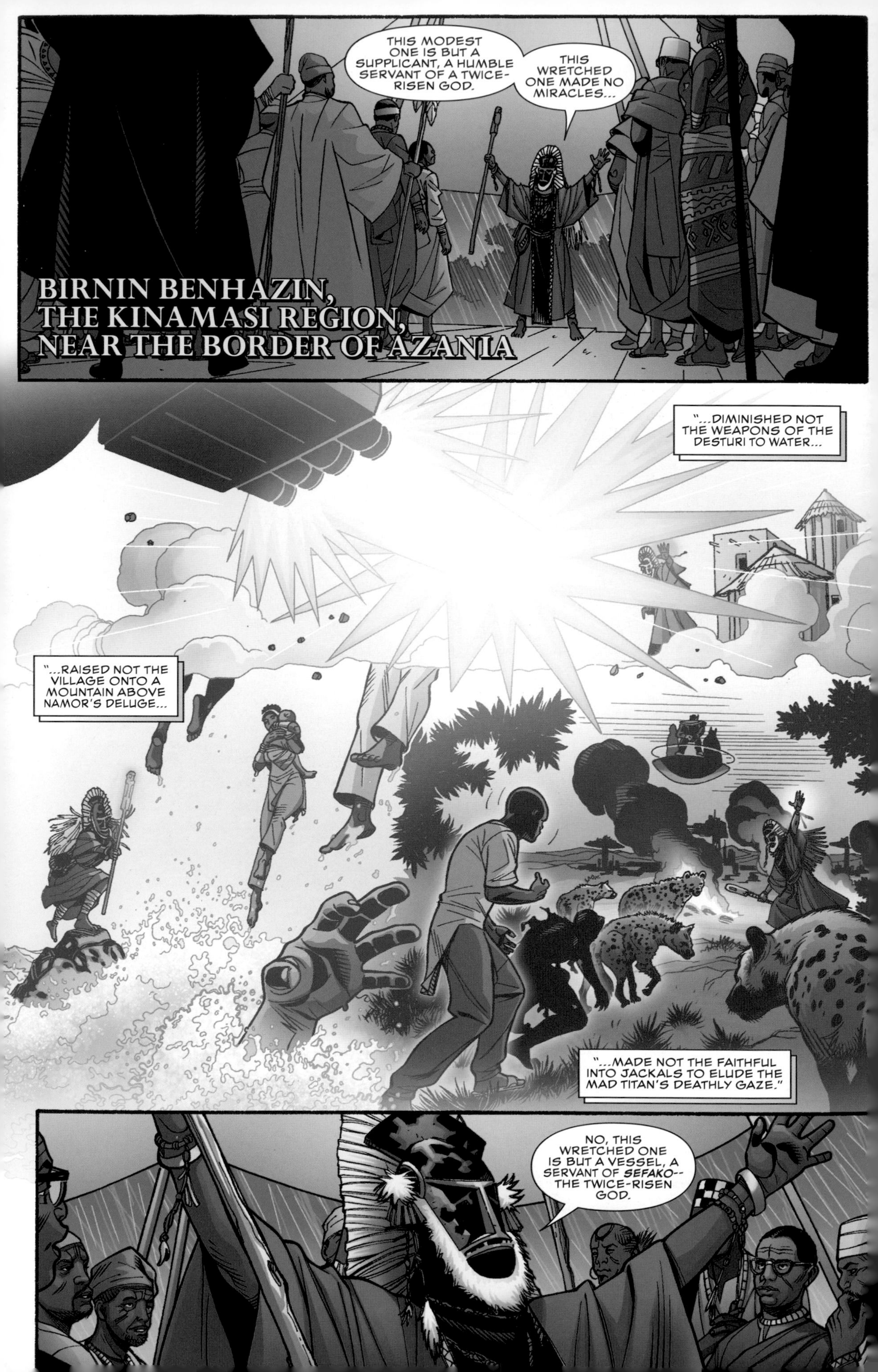
THIS MODEST ONE IS BUT A SUPPLICANT, A HUMBLE SERVANT OF A TWICE-RISEN GOD.
THIS WRETCHED ONE MADE NO MIRACLES...
BIRNIN BENHAZIN, THE KINAMASI REGION, NEAR THE BORDER OF AZANIA
"...DIMINISHED NOT THE WEAPONS OF THE DESTURI TO WATER...
"...RAISED NOT THE VILLAGE ONTO A MOUNTAIN ABOVE NAMOR'S DELUGE...
"...MADE NOT THE FAITHFUL INTO JACKALS TO ELUDE THE MAD TITAN'S DEATHLY GAZE."
NO, THIS WRETCHED ONE IS BUT A VESSEL, A SERVANT OF SEFAKO-- THE TWICE-RISEN GOD.

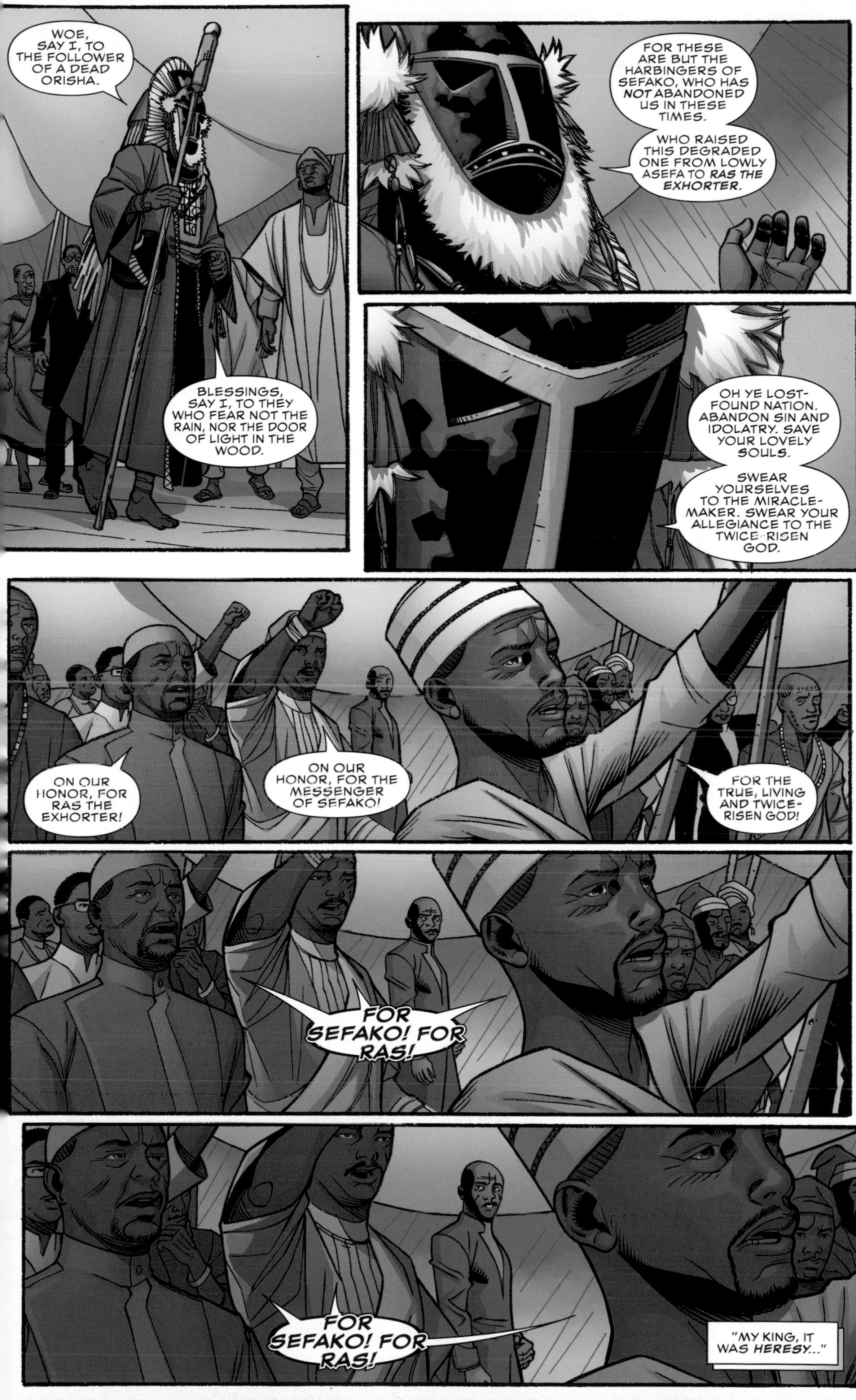
WOE, SAY I, TO THE FOLLOWER OF A DEAD ORISHA.
BLESSINGS, SAY I, TO THEY WHO FEAR NOT THE RAIN, NOR THE DOOR OF LIGHT IN THE WOOD.
FOR THESE ARE BUT THE HARBINGERS OF SEFAKO, WHO HAS NOT ABANDONED US IN THESE TIMES.
WHO RAISED THIS DEGRADED ONE FROM LOWLY ASEFA TO RAS THE EXHORTER.
OH YE LOST-FOUND NATION. ABANDON SIN AND IDOLATRY. SAVE YOUR LOVELY SOULS.
SWEAR YOURSELVES TO THE MIRACLE-MAKER. SWEAR YOUR ALLEGIANCE TO THE TWICE-RISEN GOD.
ON OUR HONOR, FOR RAS THE EXHORTER!
ON OUR HONOR, FOR THE MESSENGER OF SEFAKO!
FOR THE TRUE, LIVING AND TWICE-RISEN GOD!
FOR SEFAKO! FOR RAS!
FOR SEFAKO! FOR RAS!
"MY KING, IT WAS HERESY..."

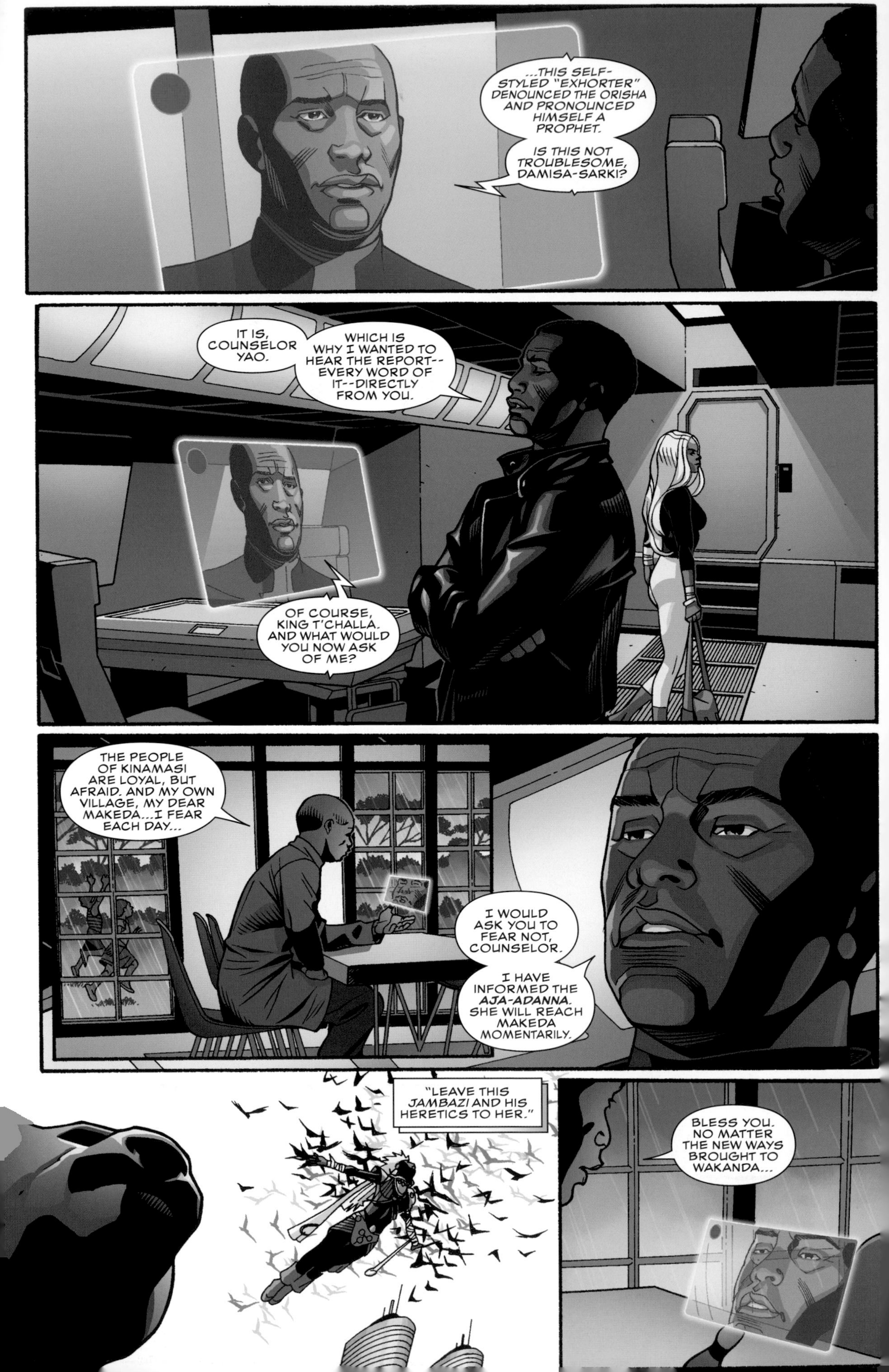
...THIS SELF-STYLED "EXHORTER" DENOUNCED THE ORISHA AND PRONOUNCED HIMSELF A PROPHET.
IS THIS NOT TROUBLESOME, DAMISA-SARKI?
IT IS, COUNSELOR YAO.
WHICH IS WHY I WANTED TO HEAR THE REPORT--EVERY WORD OF IT--DIRECTLY FROM YOU.
OF COURSE, KING T'CHALLA. AND WHAT WOULD YOU NOW ASK OF ME?
THE PEOPLE OF KINAMASI ARE LOYAL, BUT AFRAID. AND MY OWN VILLAGE, MY DEAR MAKEDA...I FEAR EACH DAY...
I WOULD ASK YOU TO FEAR NOT, COUNSELOR.
I HAVE INFORMED THE AJA-ADANNA. SHE WILL REACH MAKEDA MOMENTARILY.
"LEAVE THIS JAMBAZI AND HIS HERETICS TO HER."
BLESS YOU. NO MATTER THE NEW WAYS BROUGHT TO WAKANDA...

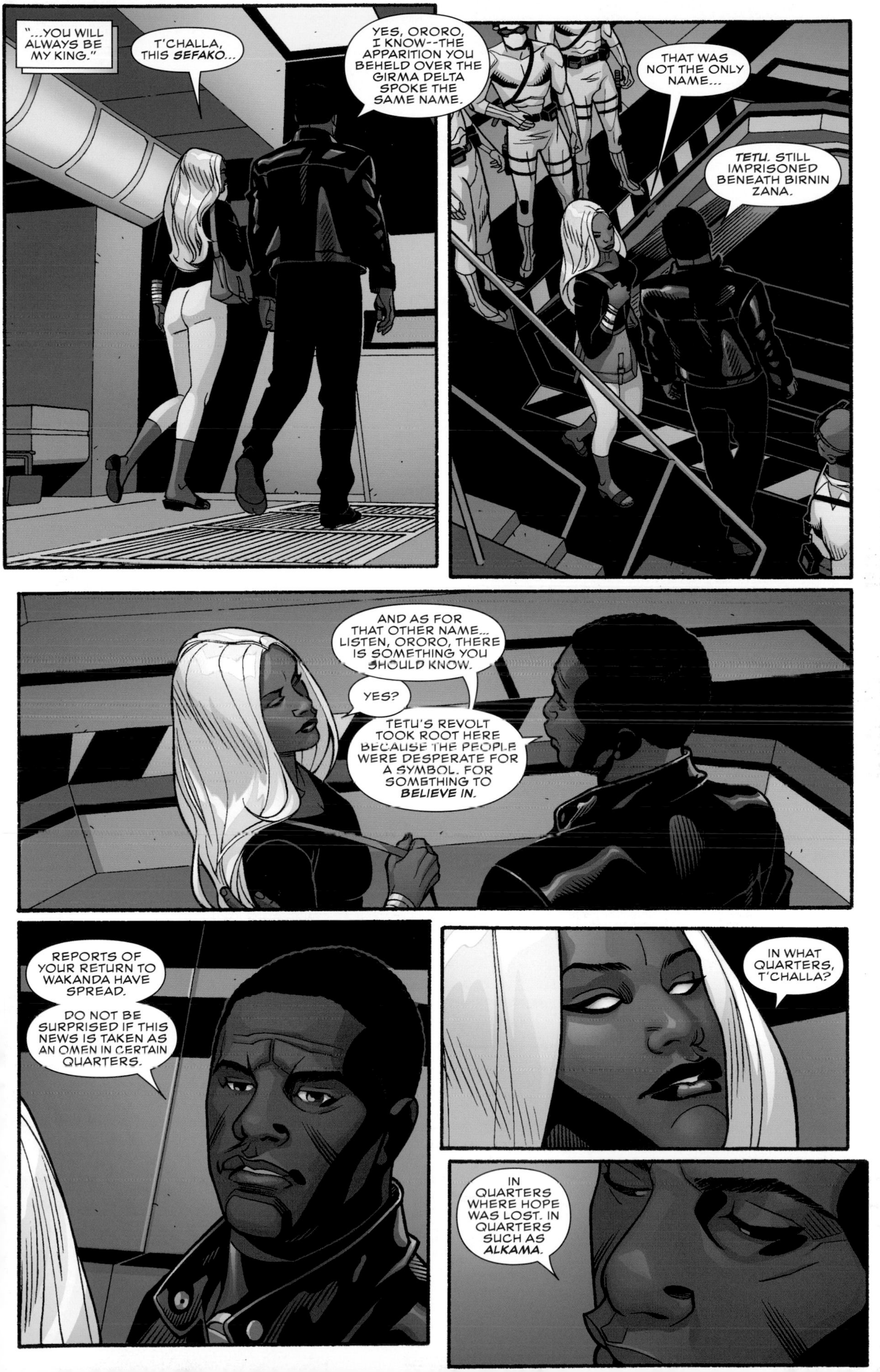
"...YOU WILL ALWAYS BE MY KING."
T'CHALLA, THIS SEFAKO...
YES, ORORO, I KNOW--THE APPARITION YOU BEHELD OVER THE GIRMA DELTA SPOKE THE SAME NAME.
THAT WAS NOT THE ONLY NAME...
TETU. STILL IMPRISONED BENEATH BIRNIN ZANA.
AND AS FOR THAT OTHER NAME... LISTEN, ORORO, THERE IS SOMETHING YOU SHOULD KNOW.
YES?
TETU'S REVOLT TOOK ROOT HERE BECAUSE THE PEOPLE WERE DESPERATE FOR A SYMBOL. FOR SOMETHING TO BELIEVE IN.
REPORTS OF YOUR RETURN TO WAKANDA HAVE SPREAD.
DO NOT BE SURPRISED IF THIS NEWS IS TAKEN AS AN OMEN IN CERTAIN QUARTERS.
IN WHAT QUARTERS, T'CHALLA?
IN QUARTERS WHERE HOPE WAS LOST. IN QUARTERS SUCH AS ALKAMA.

THE VILLAGE OF OBODO AGHA, ALKAMA FIELDS

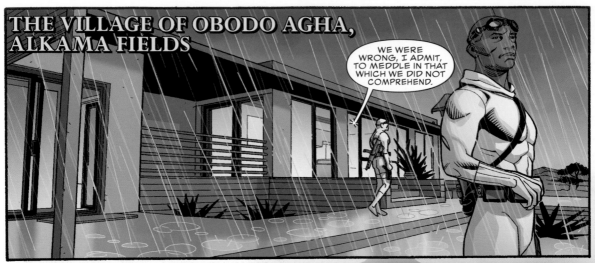

WE WERE WRONG, I ADMIT, TO MEDDLE IN THAT WHICH WE DID NOT COMPREHEND.

BUT THE DESTURI, NAMOR, THANOS...AND NO ORISHA?

THEN THE DROUGHT...THE HARVEST TURNED TO DUST IN OUR HANDS.

"TETU PROMISED A RESTORATION.

"AND WHEN THE RAINS CAME, WE SWORE OURSELVES TO HIM."

BUT NOW IT IS A DELUGE THAT DOES NOT END. AND I KNOW NOW THAT WE SWORE OURSELVES TO SOMETHING AWFUL AND UNSEEN.

THE DOOR OF LIGHT--HOW LONG HAS IT BEEN OPEN?

TWO WEEKS.

AND WHAT HAS COME THROUGH IT?

CREATURES OF MYTH AND LEGEND--THE ANANSI, PART MEN AND PART SPIDER.

DAMISA-SARKI, THEY TOOK MY DAUGHTER, MY ABENA! WE TRIED TO FIGHT THEM, BUT...WE ARE ORPHANS BEFORE OUR GODS.

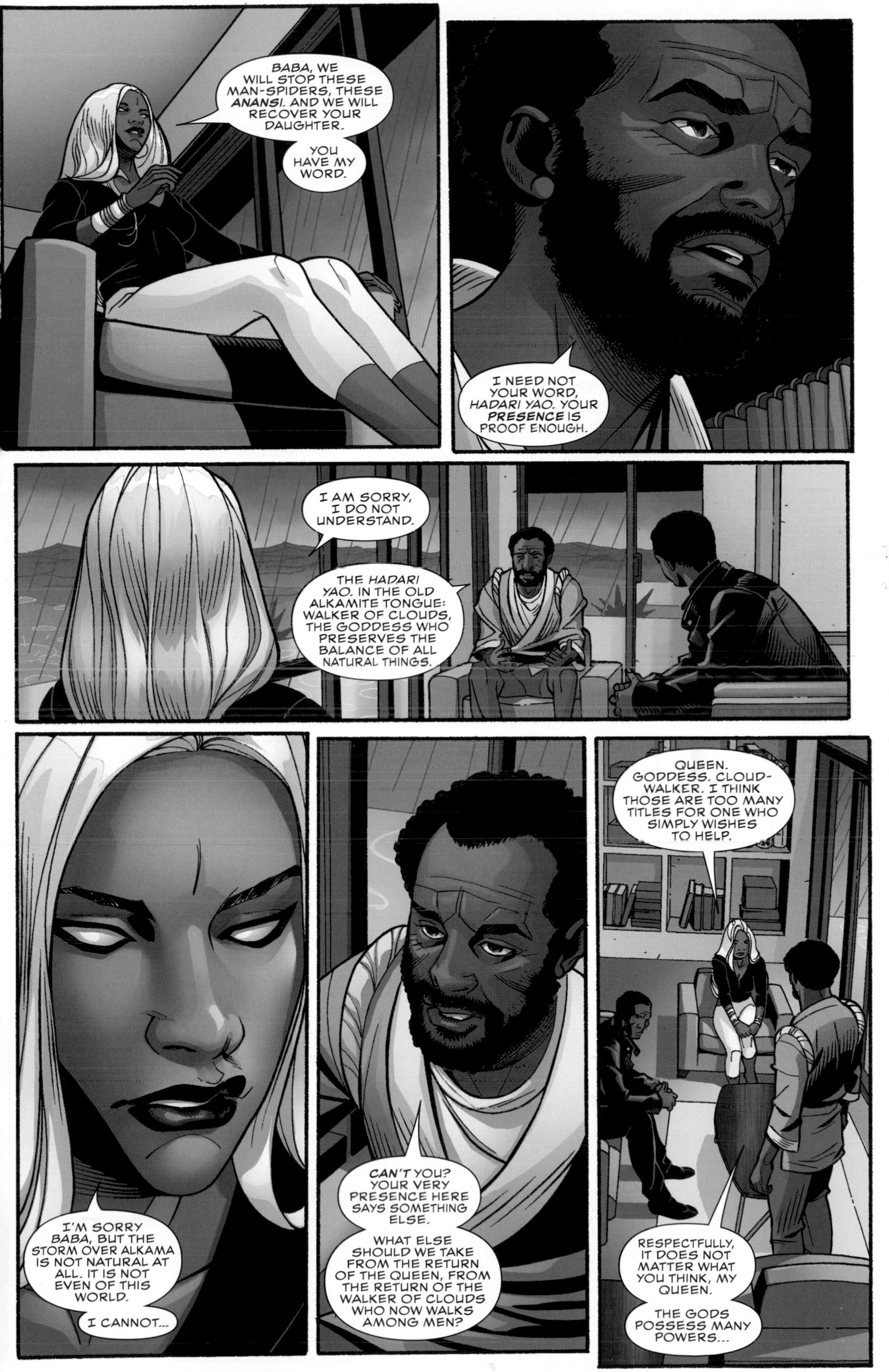
BABA, WE WILL STOP THESE MAN-SPIDERS, THESE ANANSI. AND WE WILL RECOVER YOUR DAUGHTER.
YOU HAVE MY WORD.
I NEED NOT YOUR WORD, HADARI YAO. YOUR PRESENCE IS PROOF ENOUGH.
I AM SORRY, I DO NOT UNDERSTAND.
THE HADARI YAO. IN THE OLD ALKAMITE TONGUE: WALKER OF CLOUDS, THE GODDESS WHO PRESERVES THE BALANCE OF ALL NATURAL THINGS.
I'M SORRY BABA, BUT THE STORM OVER ALKAMA IS NOT NATURAL AT ALL. IT IS NOT EVEN OF THIS WORLD.
I CANNOT...
CAN'T YOU? YOUR VERY PRESENCE HERE SAYS SOMETHING ELSE.
WHAT ELSE SHOULD WE TAKE FROM THE RETURN OF THE QUEEN, FROM THE RETURN OF THE WALKER OF CLOUDS WHO NOW WALKS AMONG MEN?
QUEEN. GODDESS. CLOUD-WALKER. I THINK THOSE ARE TOO MANY TITLES FOR ONE WHO SIMPLY WISHES TO HELP.
RESPECTFULLY, IT DOES NOT MATTER WHAT YOU THINK, MY QUEEN.
THE GODS POSSESS MANY POWERS...

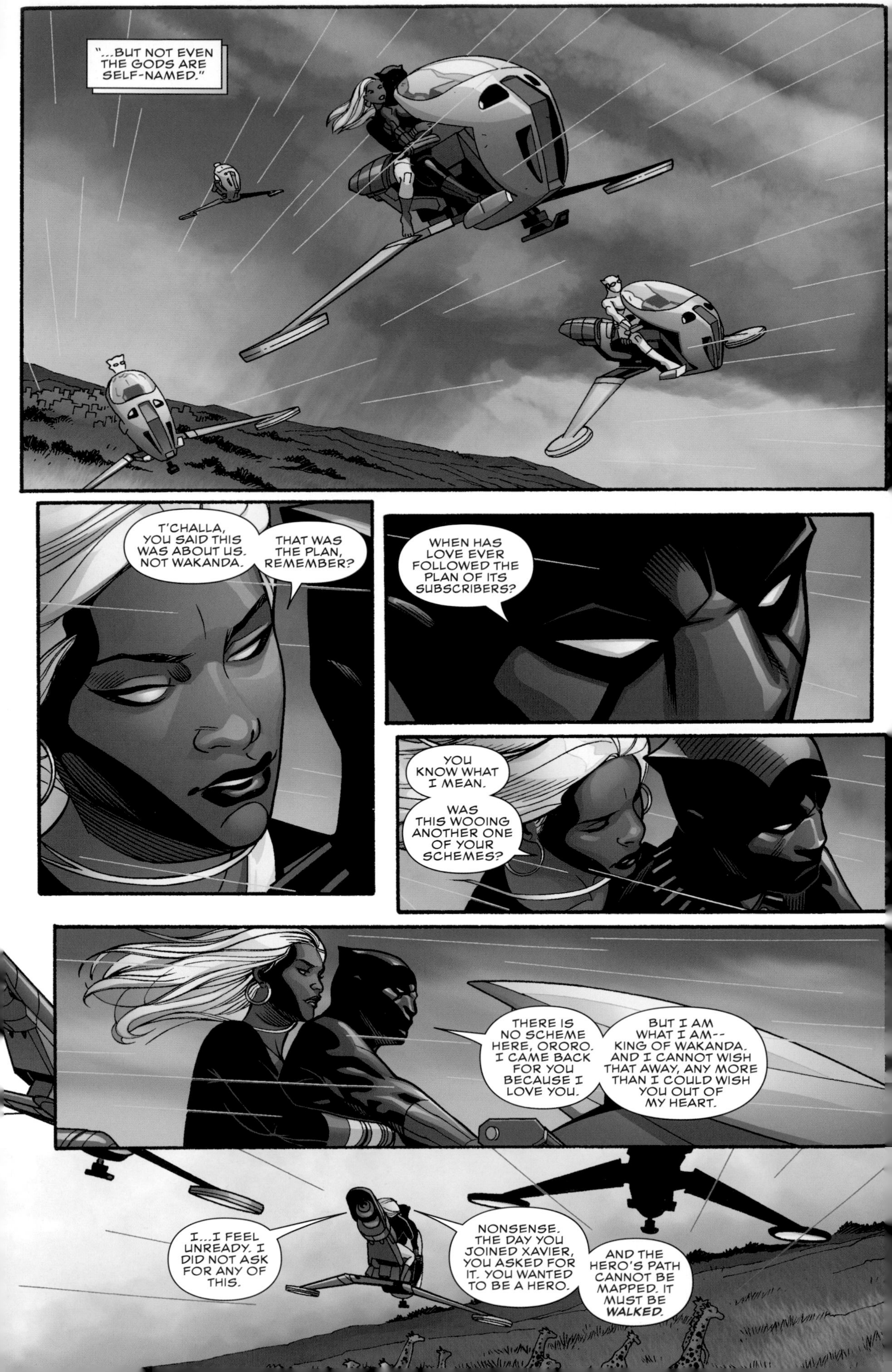
"...BUT NOT EVEN THE GODS ARE SELF-NAMED."
T'CHALLA, YOU SAID THIS WAS ABOUT US. NOT WAKANDA.
THAT WAS THE PLAN, REMEMBER?
WHEN HAS LOVE EVER FOLLOWED THE PLAN OF ITS SUBSCRIBERS?
YOU KNOW WHAT I MEAN.
WAS THIS WOOING ANOTHER ONE OF YOUR SCHEMES?
THERE IS NO SCHEME HERE, ORORO. I CAME BACK FOR YOU BECAUSE I LOVE YOU.
BUT I AM WHAT I AM-- KING OF WAKANDA. AND I CANNOT WISH THAT AWAY, ANY MORE THAN I COULD WISH YOU OUT OF MY HEART.
I...I FEEL UNREADY. I DID NOT ASK FOR ANY OF THIS.
NONSENSE. THE DAY YOU JOINED XAVIER, YOU ASKED FOR IT. YOU WANTED TO BE A HERO.
AND THE HERO'S PATH CANNOT BE MAPPED. IT MUST BE *WALKED*.

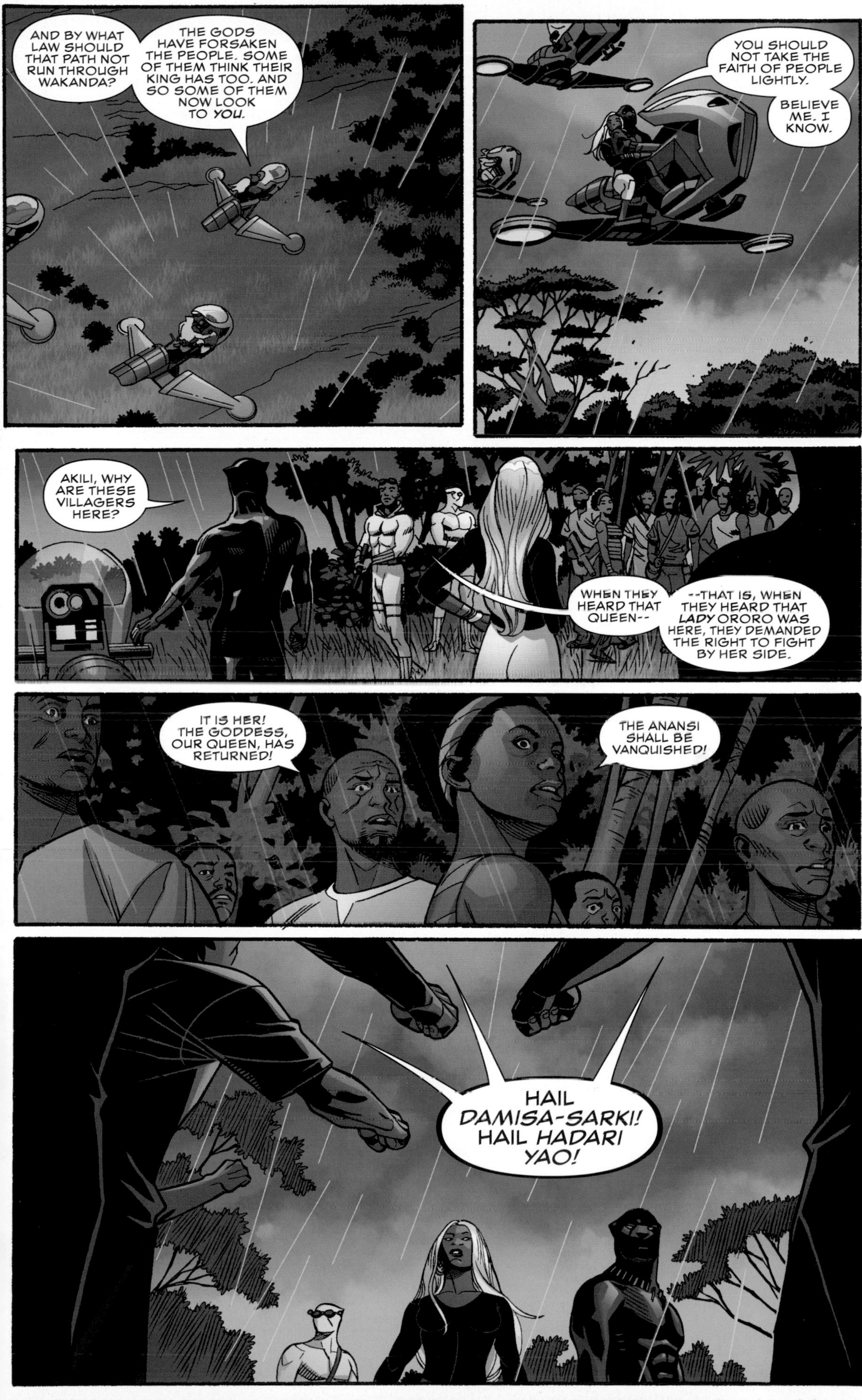
AND BY WHAT LAW SHOULD THAT PATH NOT RUN THROUGH WAKANDA?
THE GODS HAVE FORSAKEN THE PEOPLE. SOME OF THEM THINK THEIR KING HAS TOO. AND SO SOME OF THEM NOW LOOK TO *YOU*.
YOU SHOULD NOT TAKE THE FAITH OF PEOPLE LIGHTLY.
BELIEVE ME. I KNOW.
AKILI, WHY ARE THESE VILLAGERS HERE?
WHEN THEY HEARD THAT QUEEN--
--THAT IS, WHEN THEY HEARD THAT *LADY* ORORO WAS HERE, THEY DEMANDED THE RIGHT TO FIGHT BY HER SIDE.
IT IS HER! THE GODDESS, OUR QUEEN, HAS RETURNED!
THE ANANSI SHALL BE VANQUISHED!
HAIL *DAMISA-SARKI*! HAIL *HADARI YAO*!

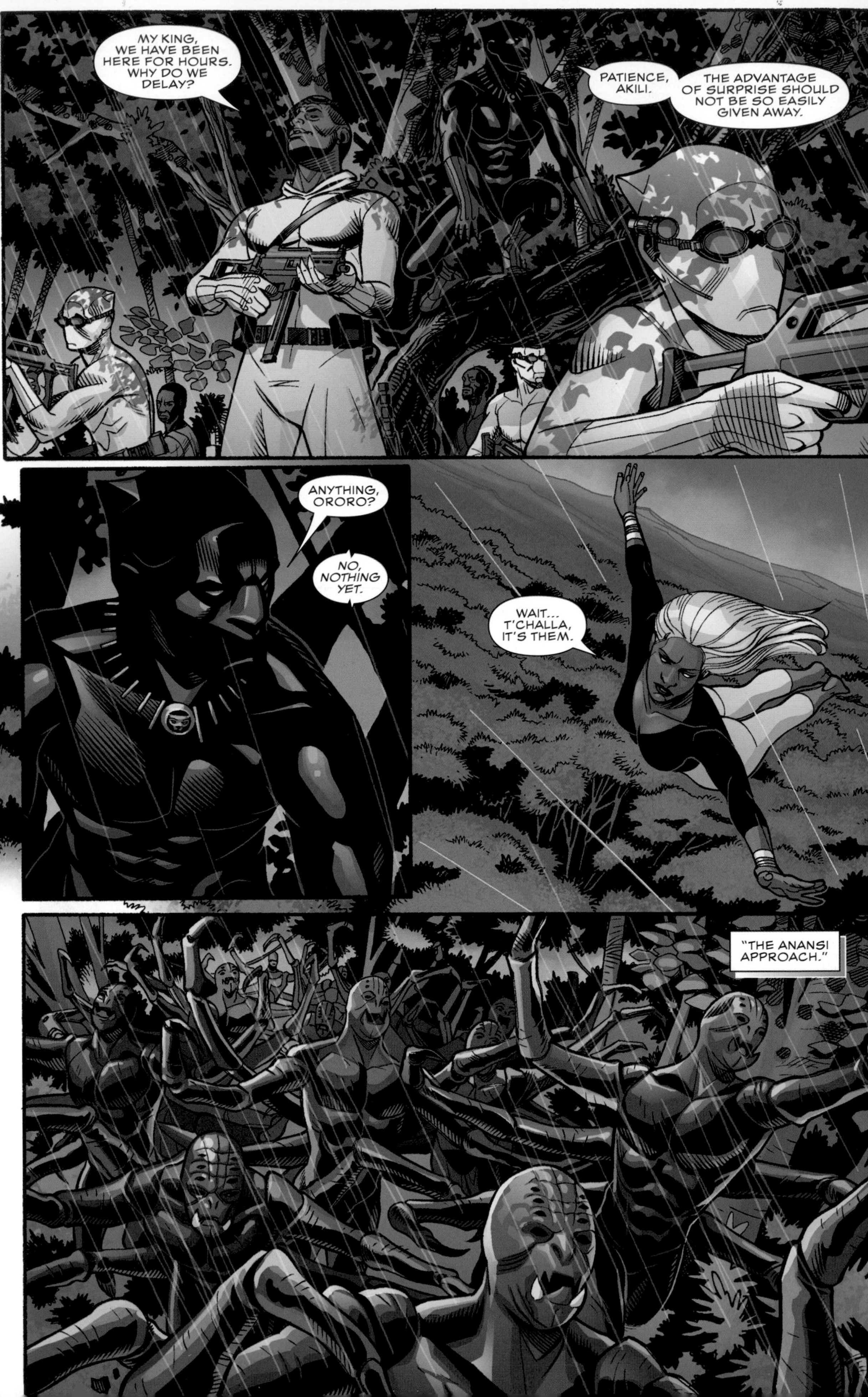
MY KING, WE HAVE BEEN HERE FOR HOURS. WHY DO WE DELAY?
PATIENCE, AKILI.
THE ADVANTAGE OF SURPRISE SHOULD NOT BE SO EASILY GIVEN AWAY.
ANYTHING, ORORO?
NO, NOTHING YET.
WAIT... T'CHALLA, IT'S THEM.
"THE ANANSI APPROACH."

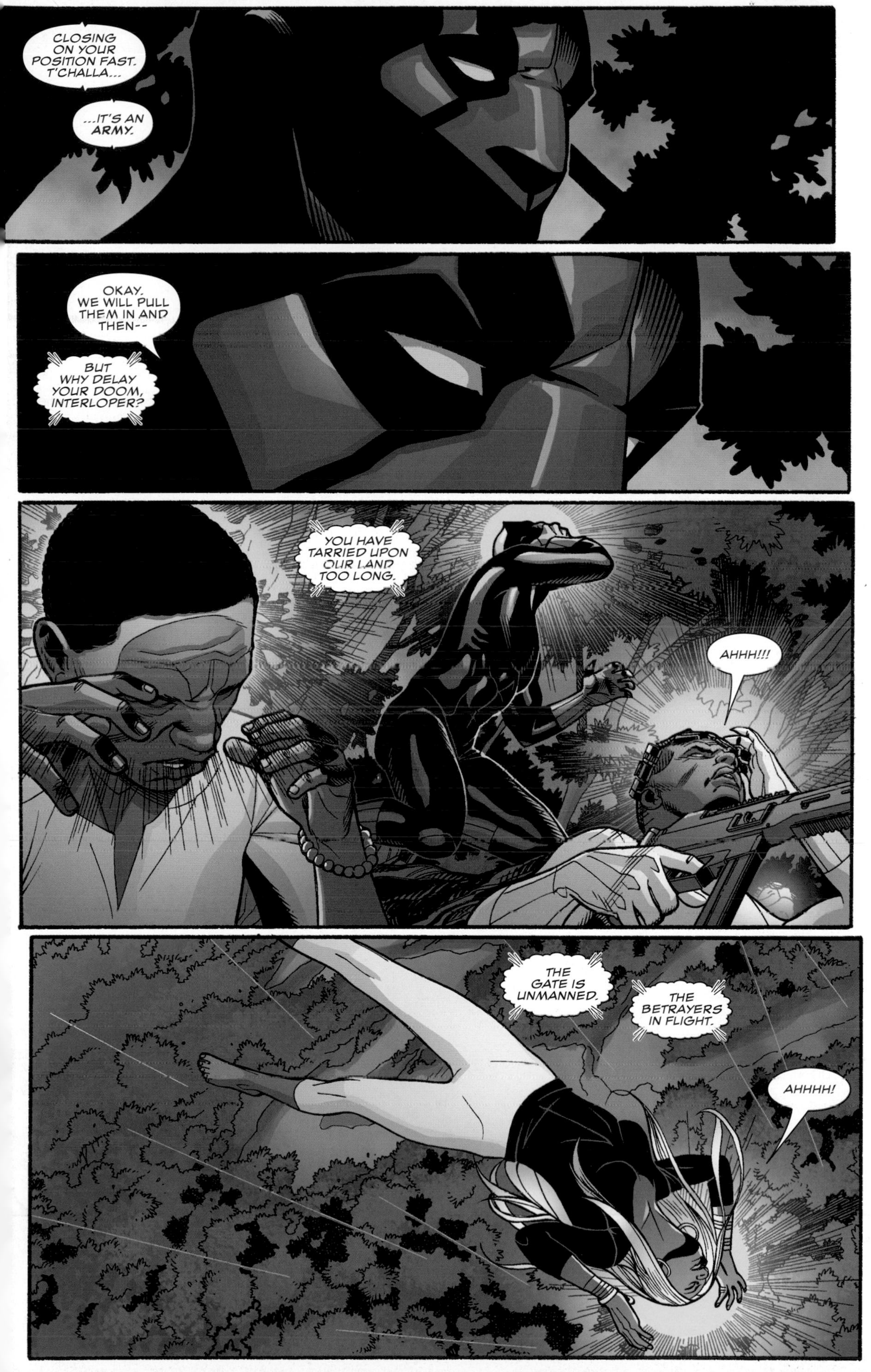
CLOSING ON YOUR POSITION FAST. T'CHALLA...
...IT'S AN ARMY.
OKAY. WE WILL PULL THEM IN AND THEN--
BUT WHY DELAY YOUR DOOM, INTERLOPER?
YOU HAVE TARRIED UPON OUR LAND TOO LONG.
AHHH!!!
THE GATE IS UNMANNED.
THE BETRAYERS IN FLIGHT.
AHHHH!

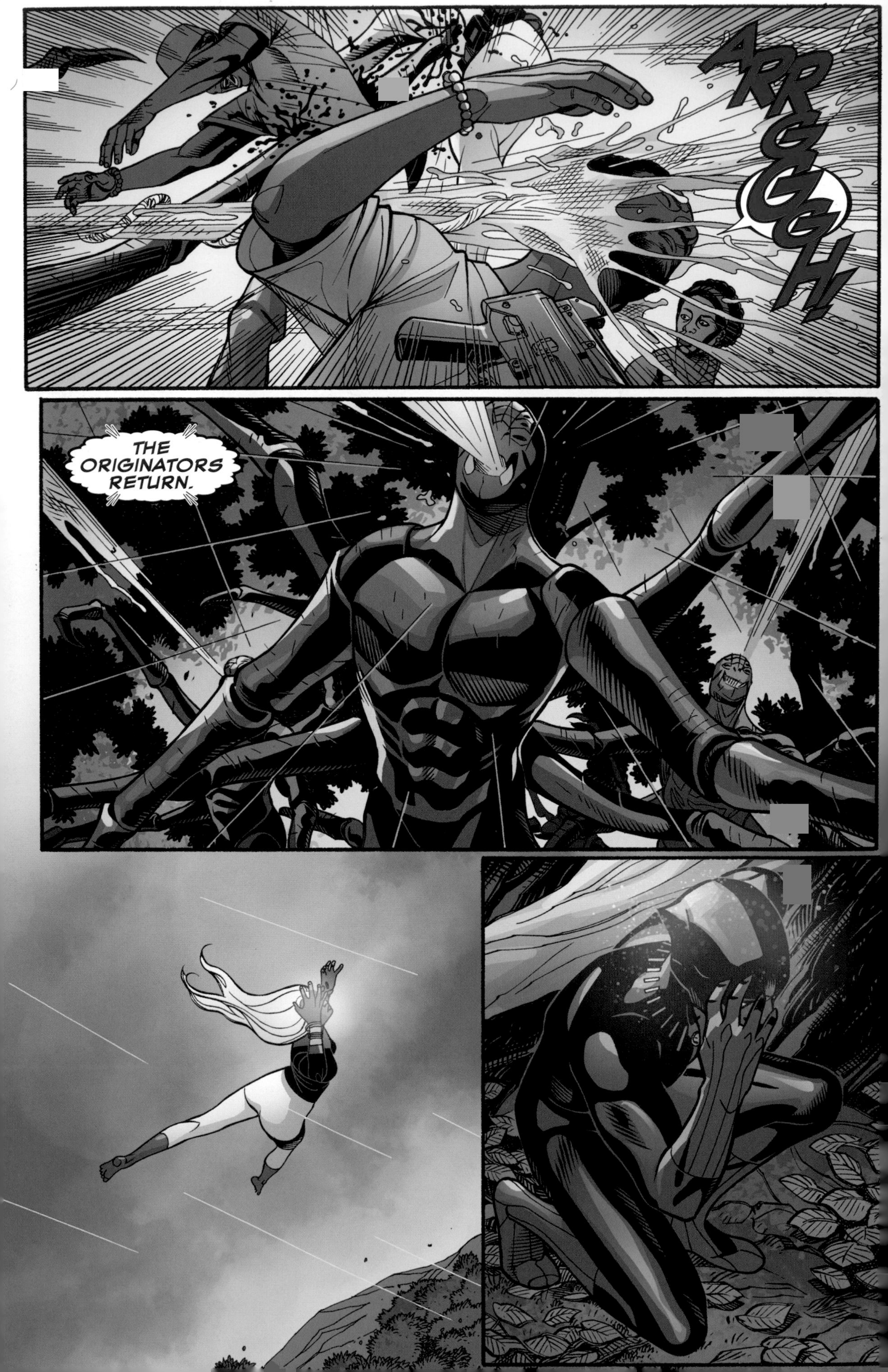
ARRGGGH!
THE ORIGINATORS RETURN.

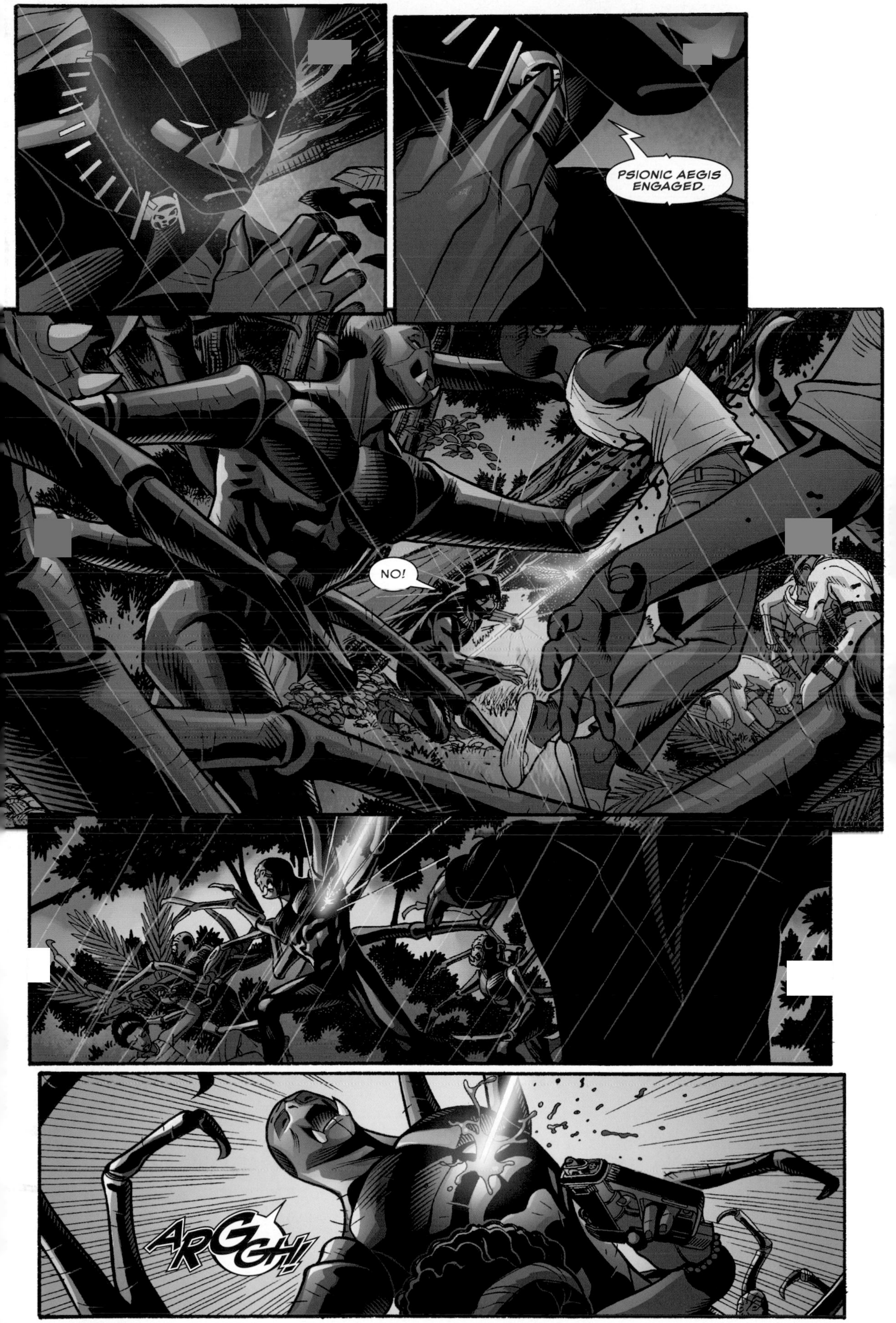
PSIONIC AEGIS ENGAGED.
NO!
ARGGH!

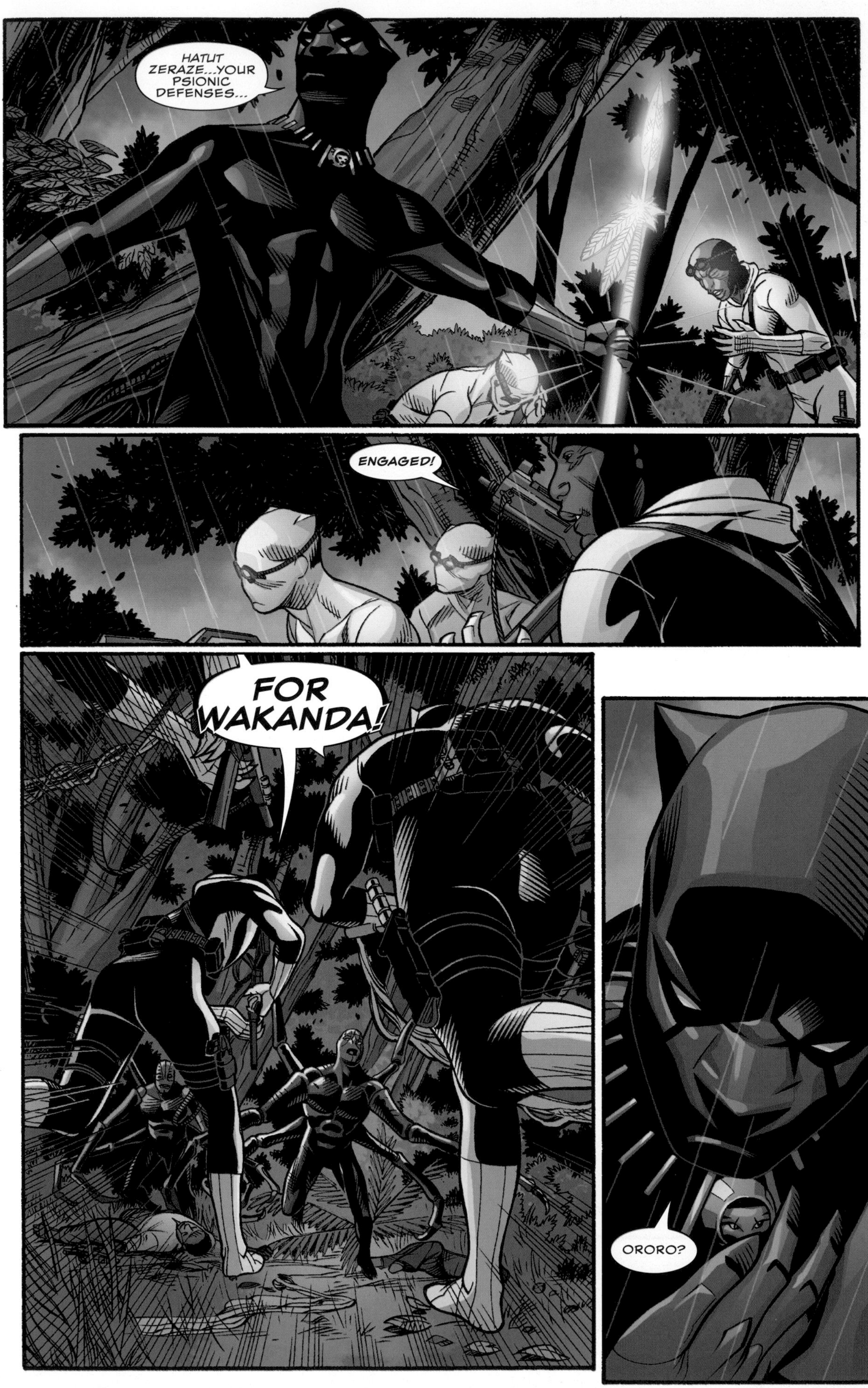
HATUT ZERAZE...YOUR PSIONIC DEFENSES...
ENGAGED!
FOR WAKANDA!
ORORO?

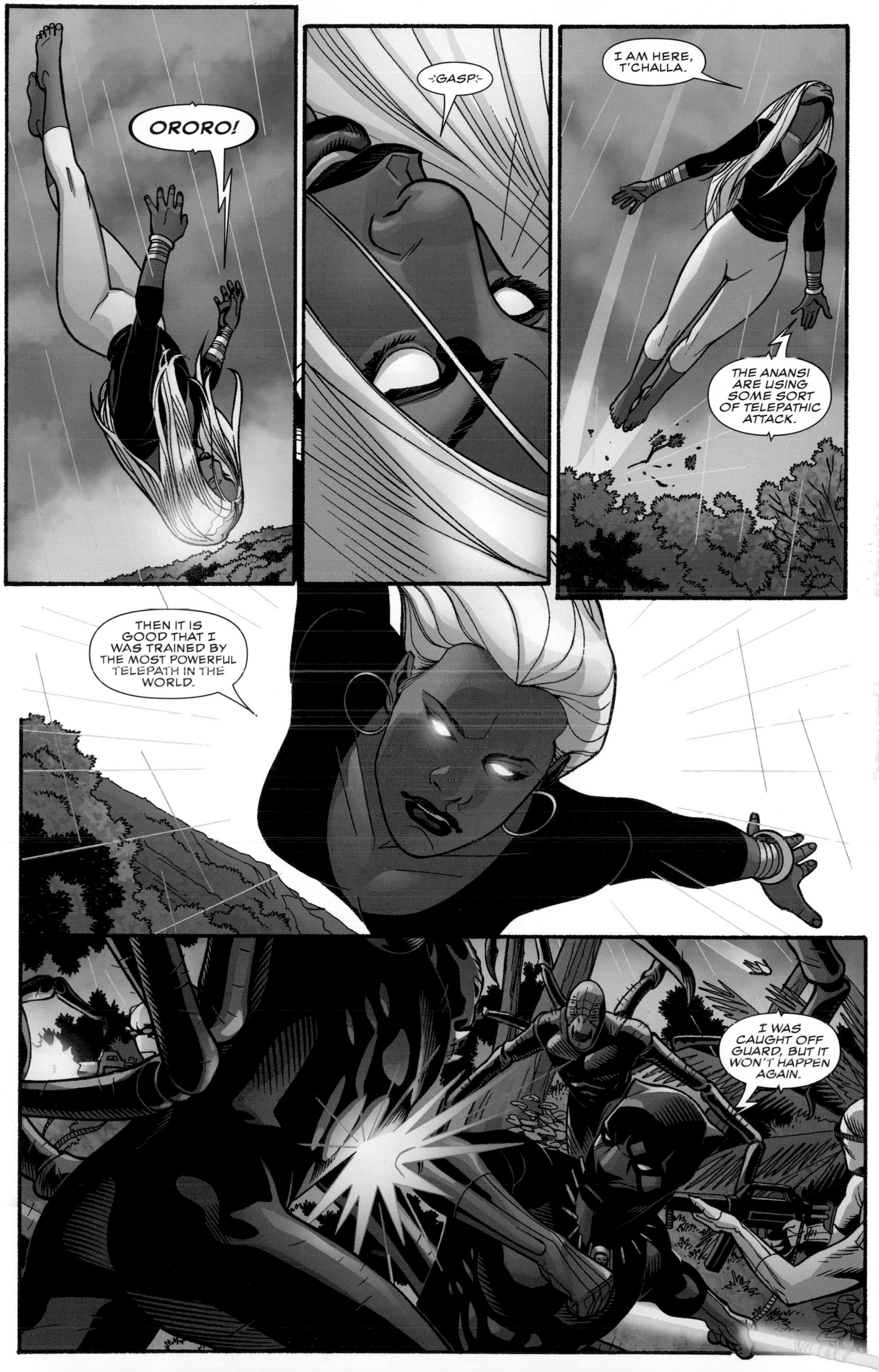
ORORO!
-GASP-
I AM HERE, T'CHALLA.
THE ANANSI ARE USING SOME SORT OF TELEPATHIC ATTACK.
THEN IT IS GOOD THAT I WAS TRAINED BY THE MOST POWERFUL TELEPATH IN THE WORLD.
I WAS CAUGHT OFF GUARD, BUT IT WON'T HAPPEN AGAIN.

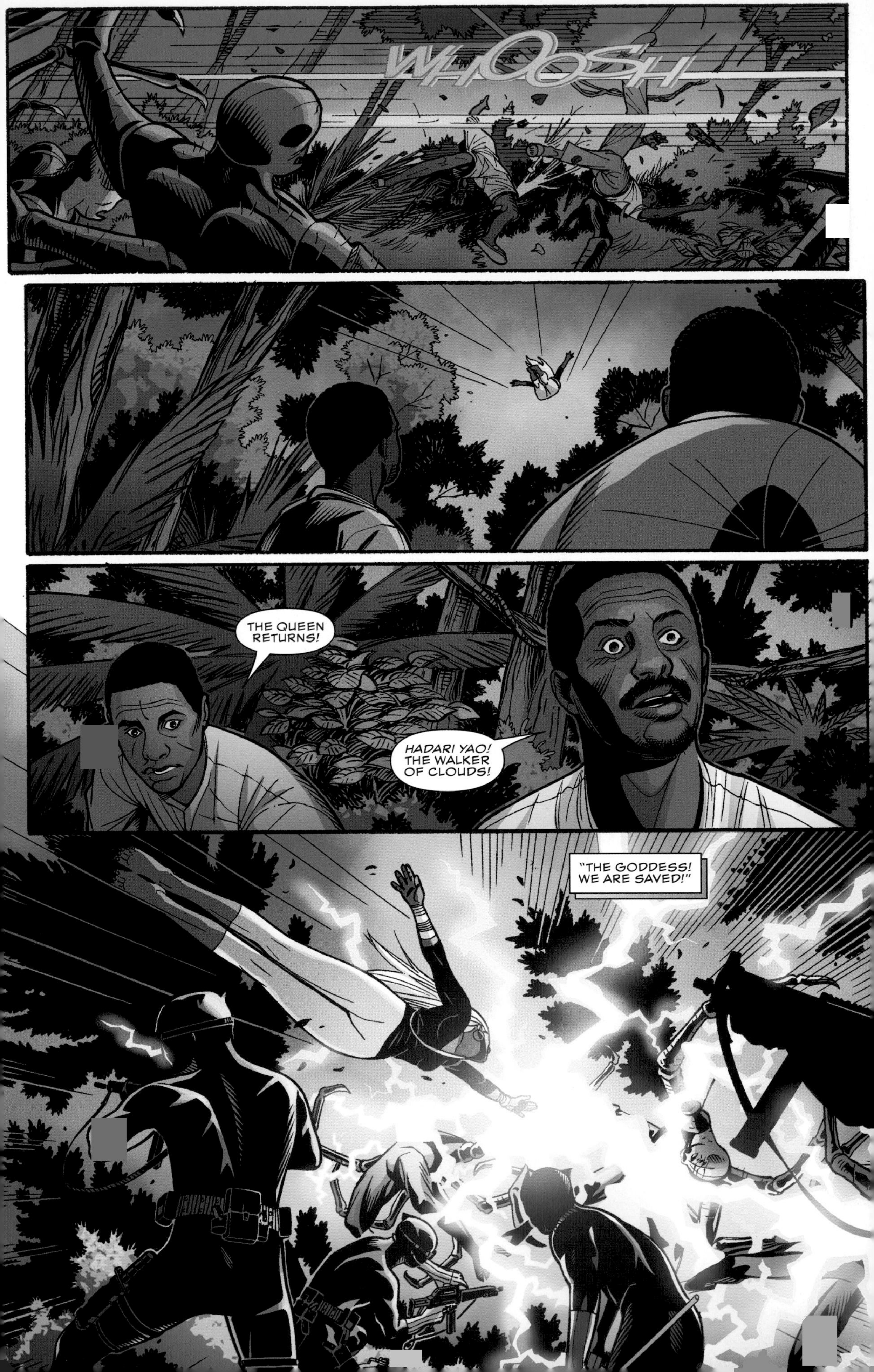
WHOOOSH
THE QUEEN RETURNS!
HADARI YAO! THE WALKER OF CLOUDS!
"THE GODDESS! WE ARE SAVED!"

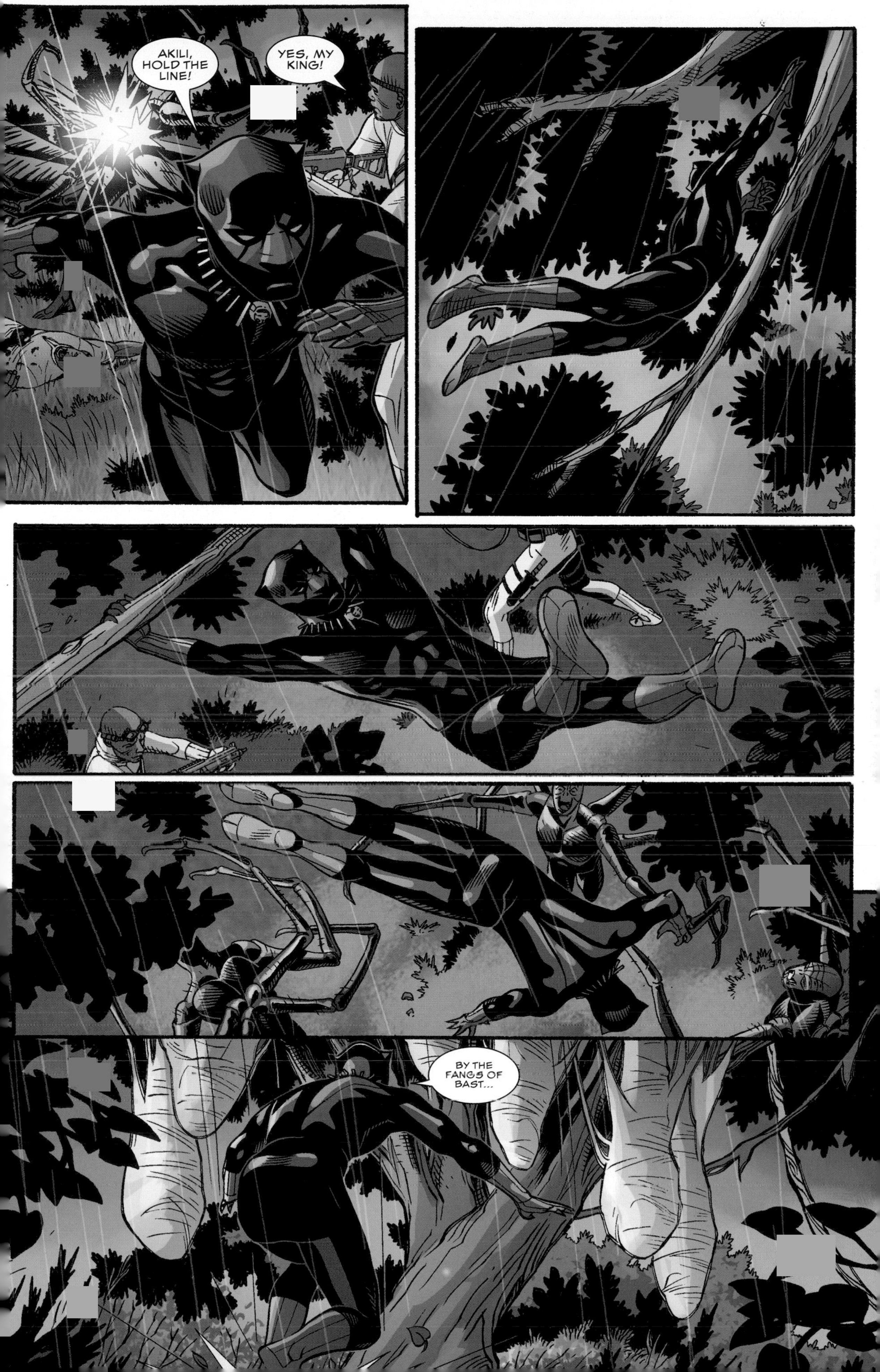
AKILI, HOLD THE LINE!
YES, MY KING!
BY THE FANGS OF BAST...

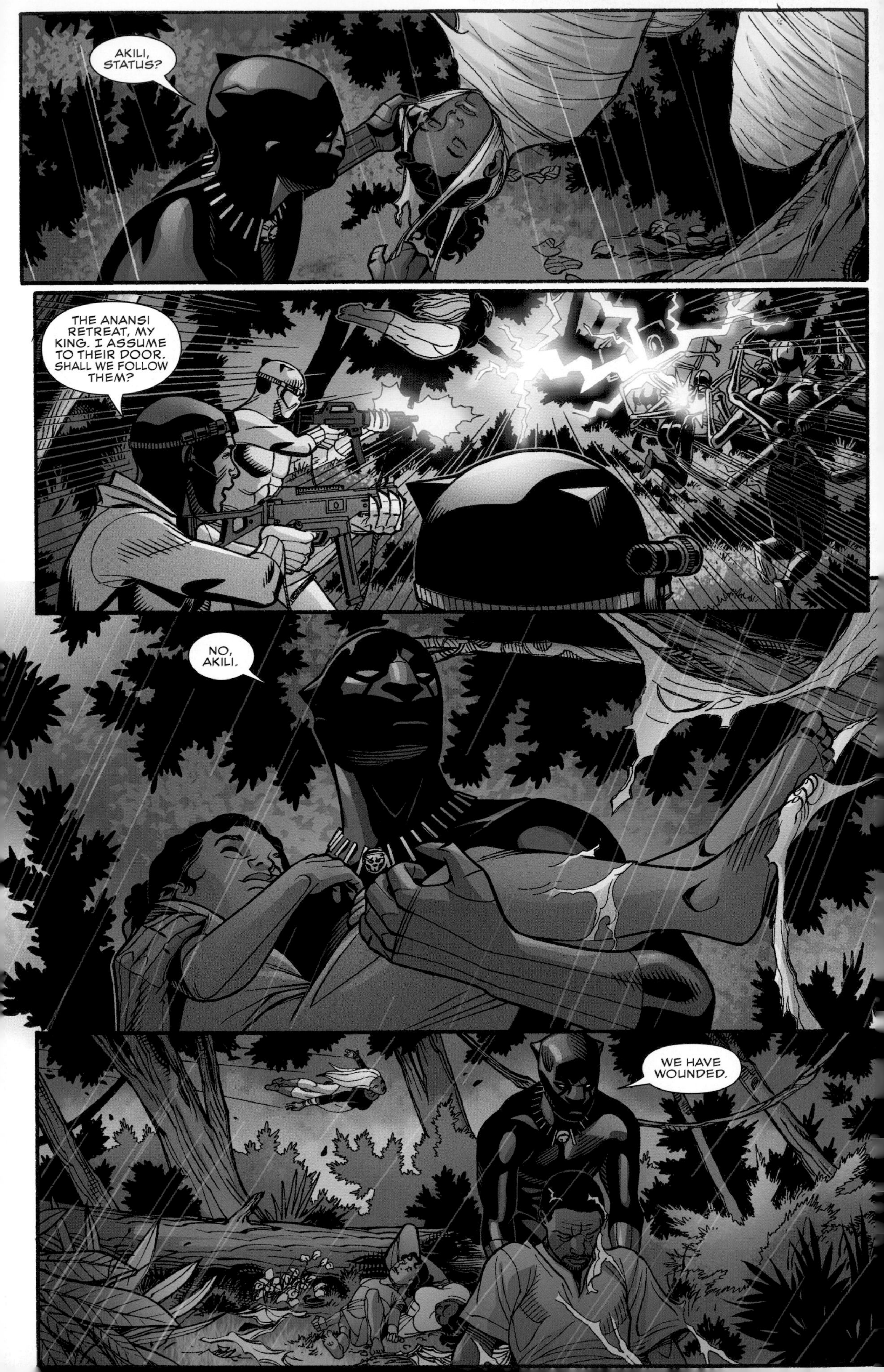
AKILI, STATUS?
THE ANANSI RETREAT, MY KING. I ASSUME TO THEIR DOOR. SHALL WE FOLLOW THEM?
NO, AKILI.
WE HAVE WOUNDED.

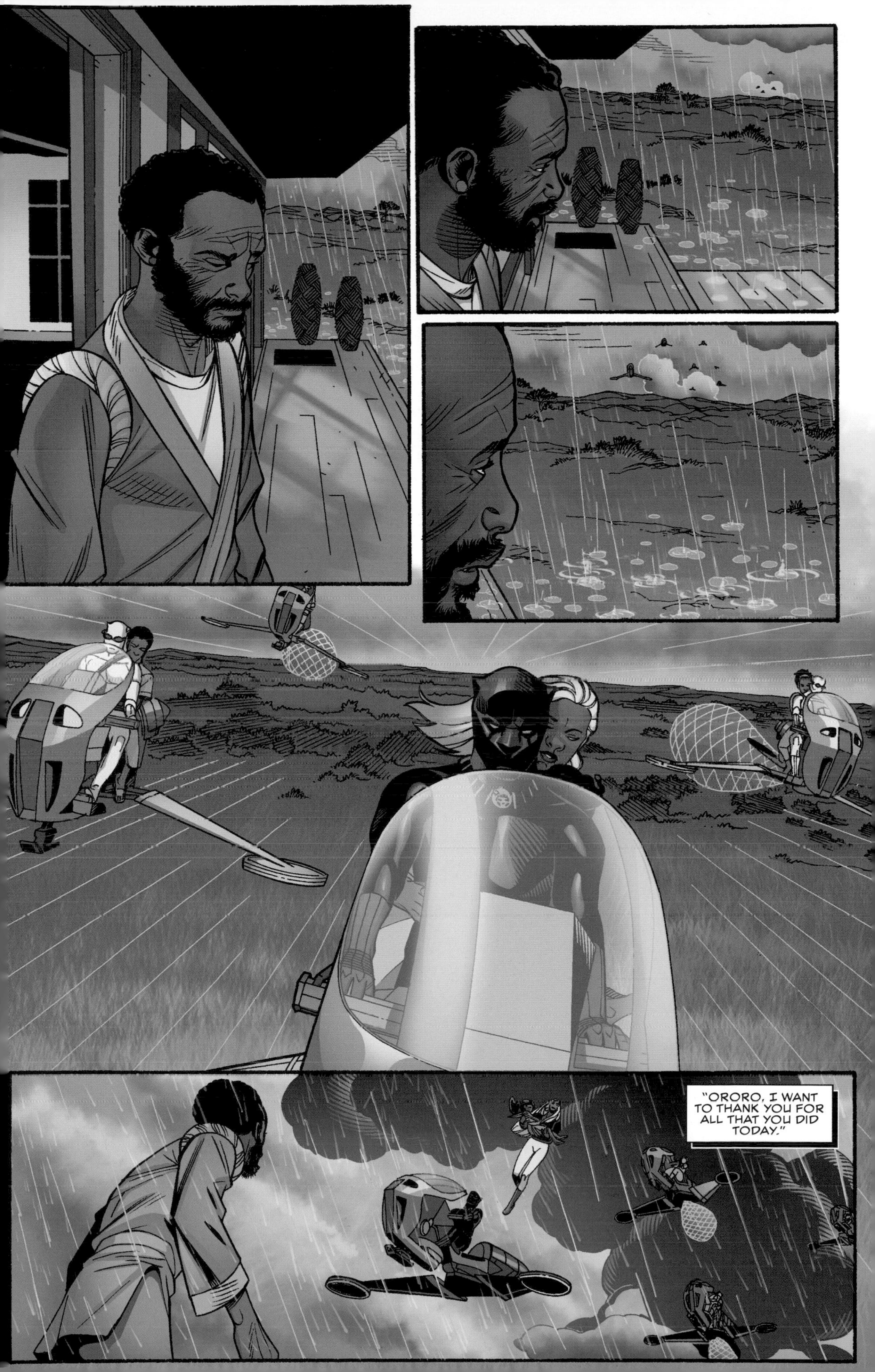
"ORORO, I WANT TO THANK YOU FOR ALL THAT YOU DID TODAY."

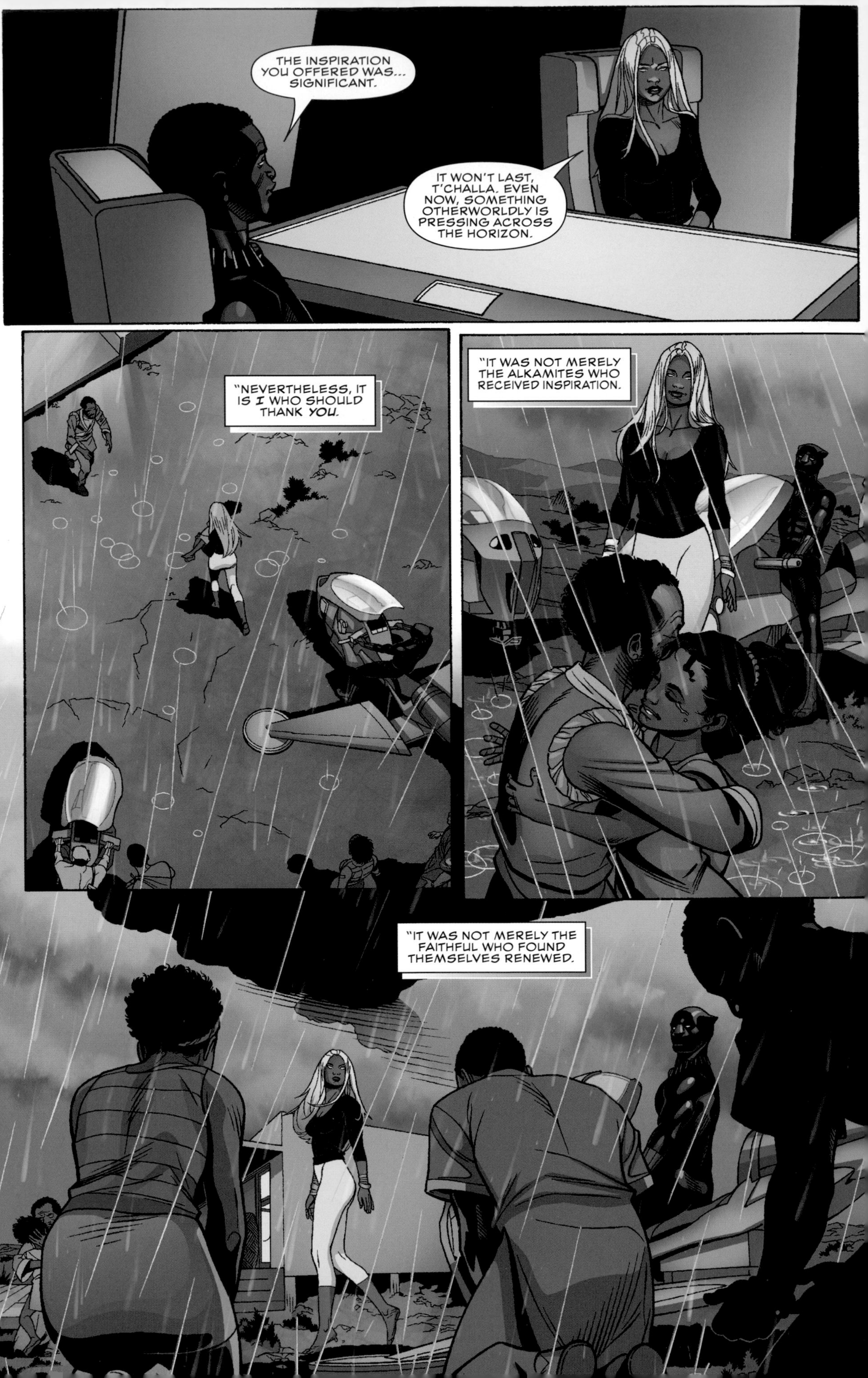
THE INSPIRATION YOU OFFERED WAS... SIGNIFICANT.
IT WON'T LAST, T'CHALLA. EVEN NOW, SOMETHING OTHERWORLDLY IS PRESSING ACROSS THE HORIZON.
"NEVERTHELESS, IT IS I WHO SHOULD THANK YOU.
"IT WAS NOT MERELY THE ALKAMITES WHO RECEIVED INSPIRATION.
"IT WAS NOT MERELY THE FAITHFUL WHO FOUND THEMSELVES RENEWED.

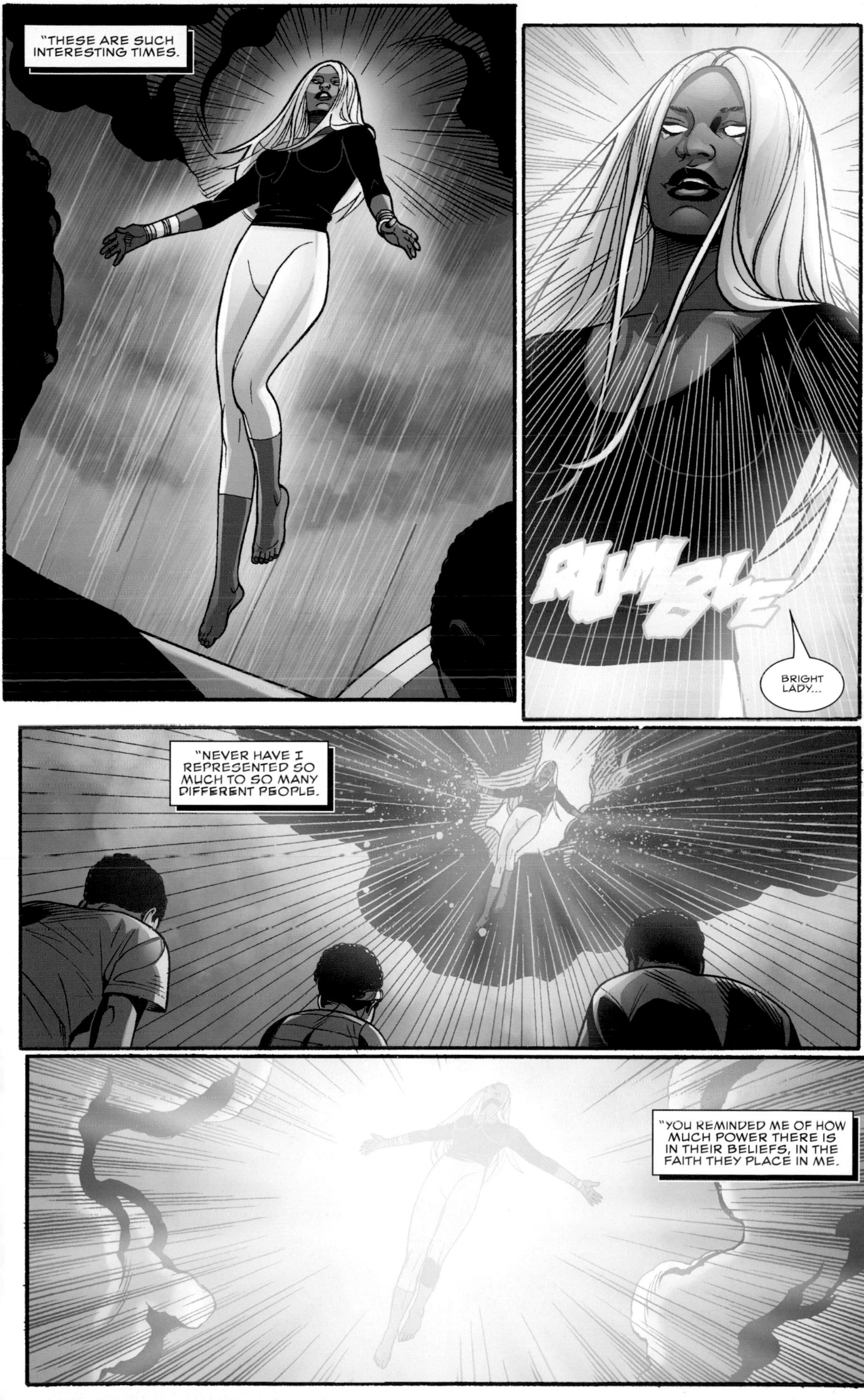
"THESE ARE SUCH INTERESTING TIMES.
RUMBLE
BRIGHT LADY...
"NEVER HAVE I REPRESENTED SO MUCH TO SO MANY DIFFERENT PEOPLE.
"YOU REMINDED ME OF HOW MUCH POWER THERE IS IN THEIR BELIEFS, IN THE FAITH THEY PLACE IN ME.

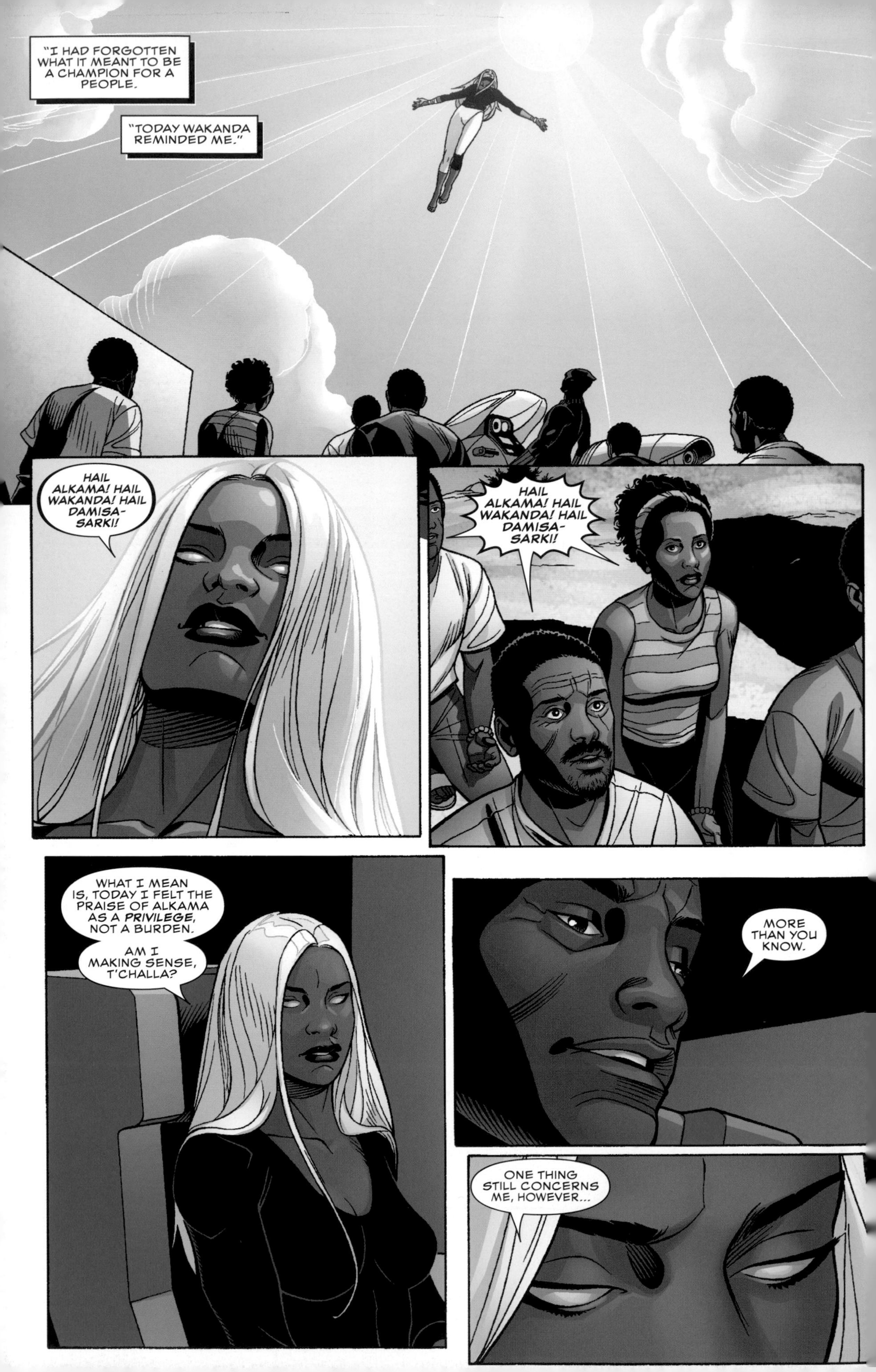
"I HAD FORGOTTEN WHAT IT MEANT TO BE A CHAMPION FOR A PEOPLE.
"TODAY WAKANDA REMINDED ME."
HAIL ALKAMA! HAIL WAKANDA! HAIL DAMISA-SARKI!
HAIL ALKAMA! HAIL WAKANDA! HAIL DAMISA-SARKI!
WHAT I MEAN IS, TODAY I FELT THE PRAISE OF ALKAMA AS A *PRIVILEGE*, NOT A BURDEN.
AM I MAKING SENSE, T'CHALLA?
MORE THAN YOU KNOW.
ONE THING STILL CONCERNS ME, HOWEVER...

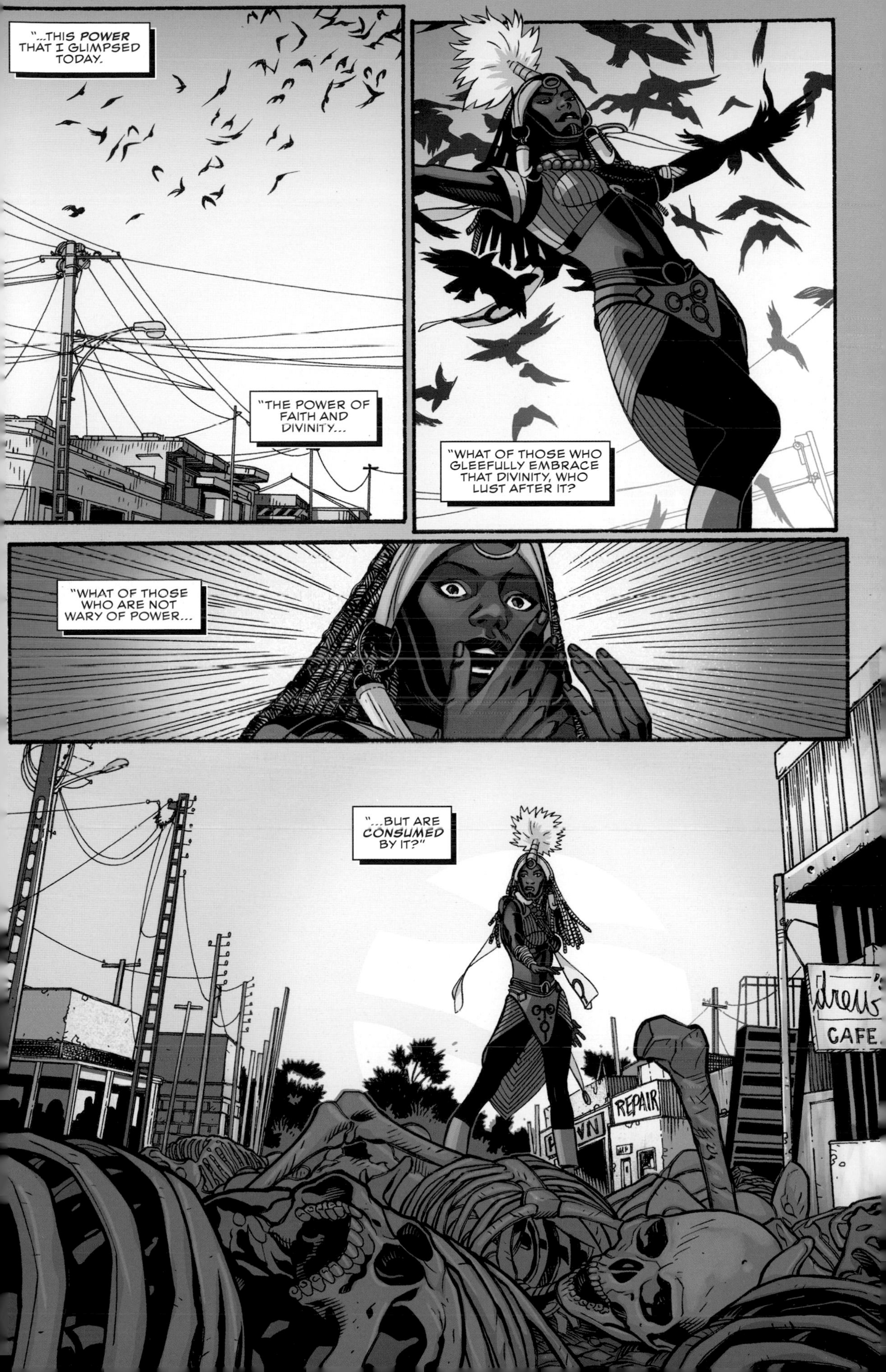
"...THIS POWER THAT I GLIMPSED TODAY.
"THE POWER OF FAITH AND DIVINITY...
"WHAT OF THOSE WHO GLEEFULLY EMBRACE THAT DIVINITY, WHO LUST AFTER IT?
"WHAT OF THOSE WHO ARE NOT WARY OF POWER...
"...BUT ARE CONSUMED BY IT?"
CAFE
REPAIR

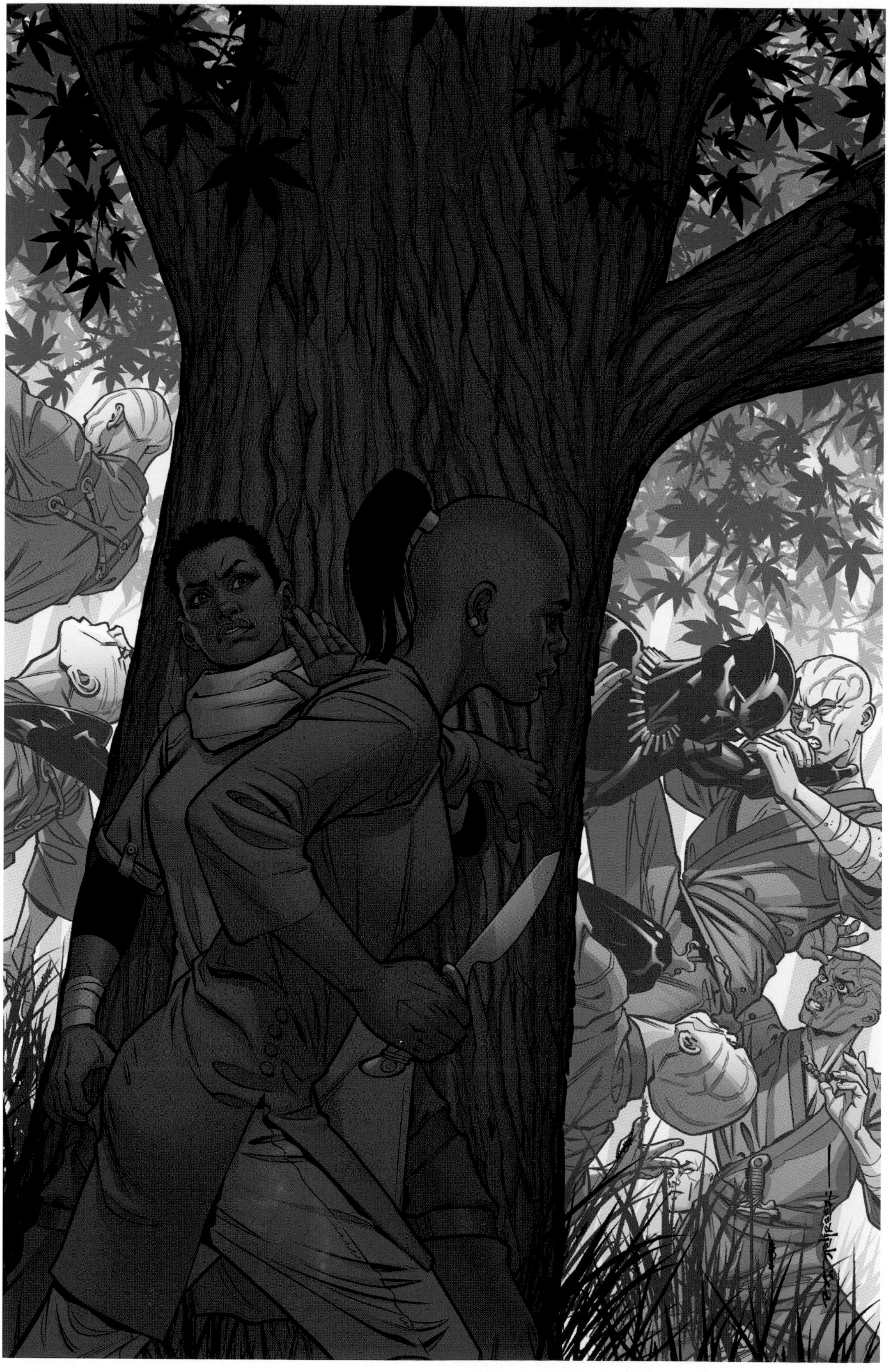

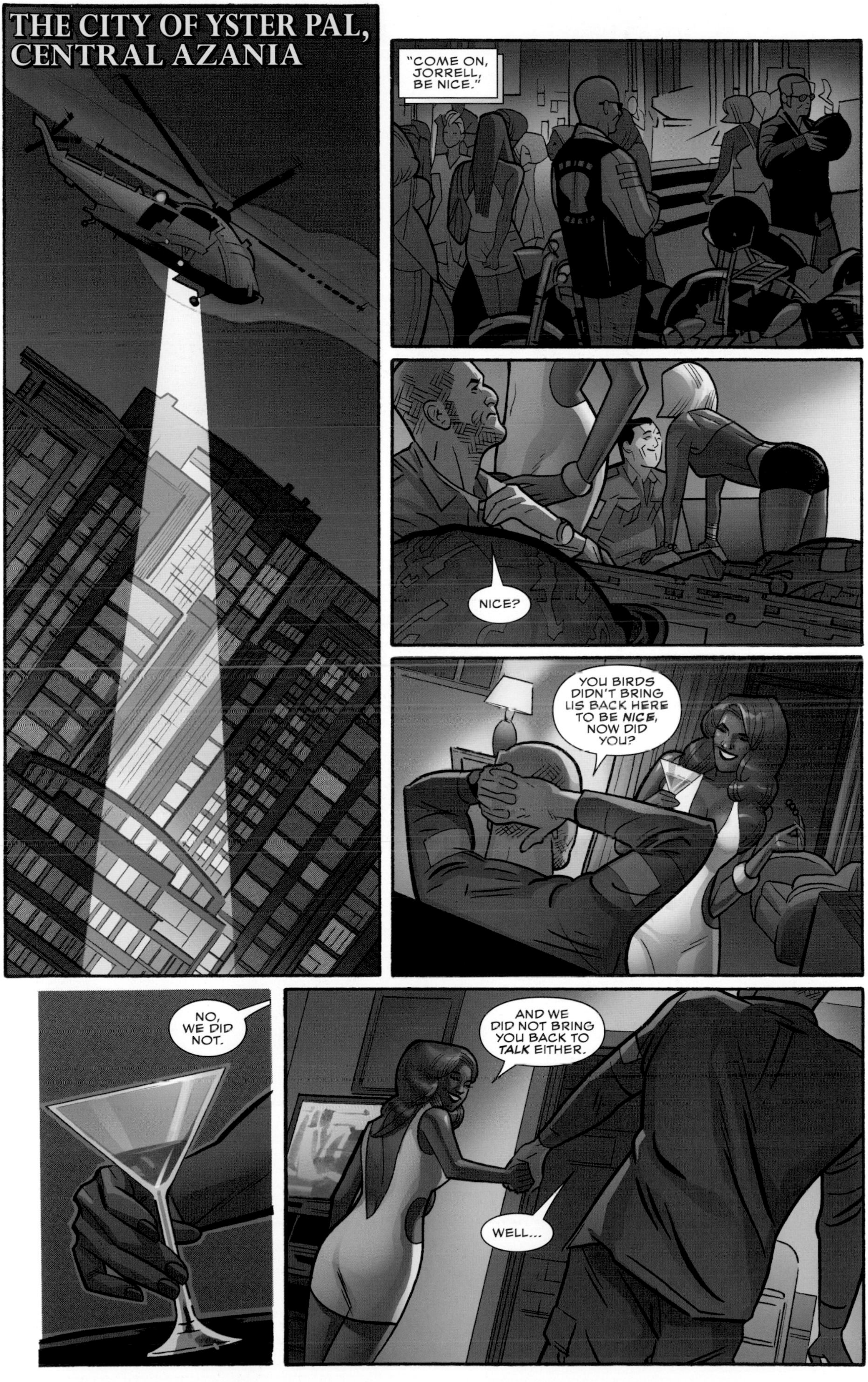
THE CITY OF YSTER PAL, CENTRAL AZANIA
"COME ON, JORRELL, BE NICE."
NICE?
YOU BIRDS DIDN'T BRING US BACK HERE TO BE NICE, NOW DID YOU?
NO, WE DID NOT.
AND WE DID NOT BRING YOU BACK TO TALK EITHER.
WELL...

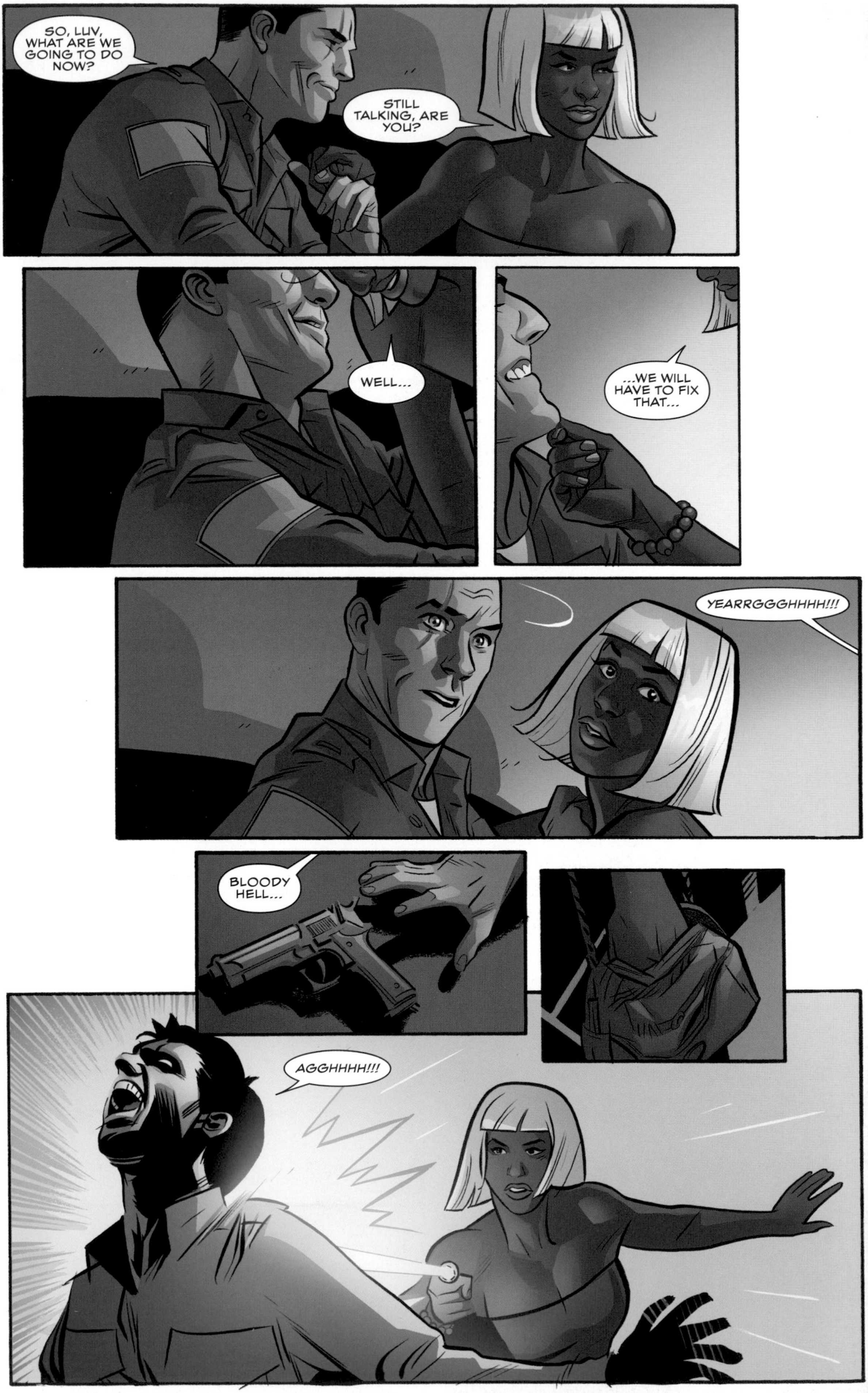
SO, LUV, WHAT ARE WE GOING TO DO NOW?
STILL TALKING, ARE YOU?
WELL...
...WE WILL HAVE TO FIX THAT...
YEARRGGGHHHH!!!
BLOODY HELL...
AGGHHHH!!!

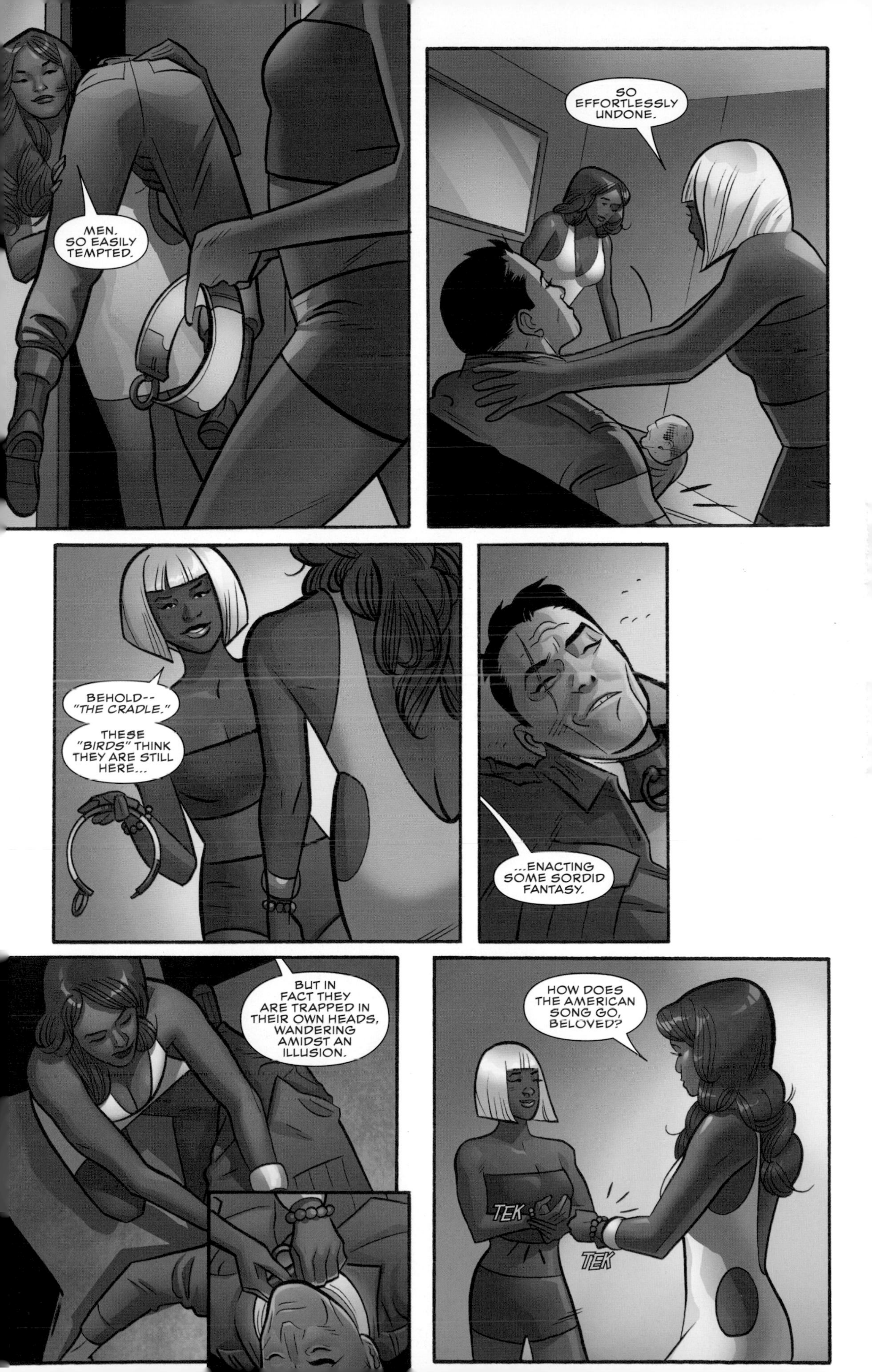
MEN. SO EASILY TEMPTED.
SO EFFORTLESSLY UNDONE.
BEHOLD-- "THE CRADLE."
THESE "BIRDS" THINK THEY ARE STILL HERE...
...ENACTING SOME SORDID FANTASY.
BUT IN FACT THEY ARE TRAPPED IN THEIR OWN HEADS, WANDERING AMIDST AN ILLUSION.
HOW DOES THE AMERICAN SONG GO, BELOVED?
TEK
TEK

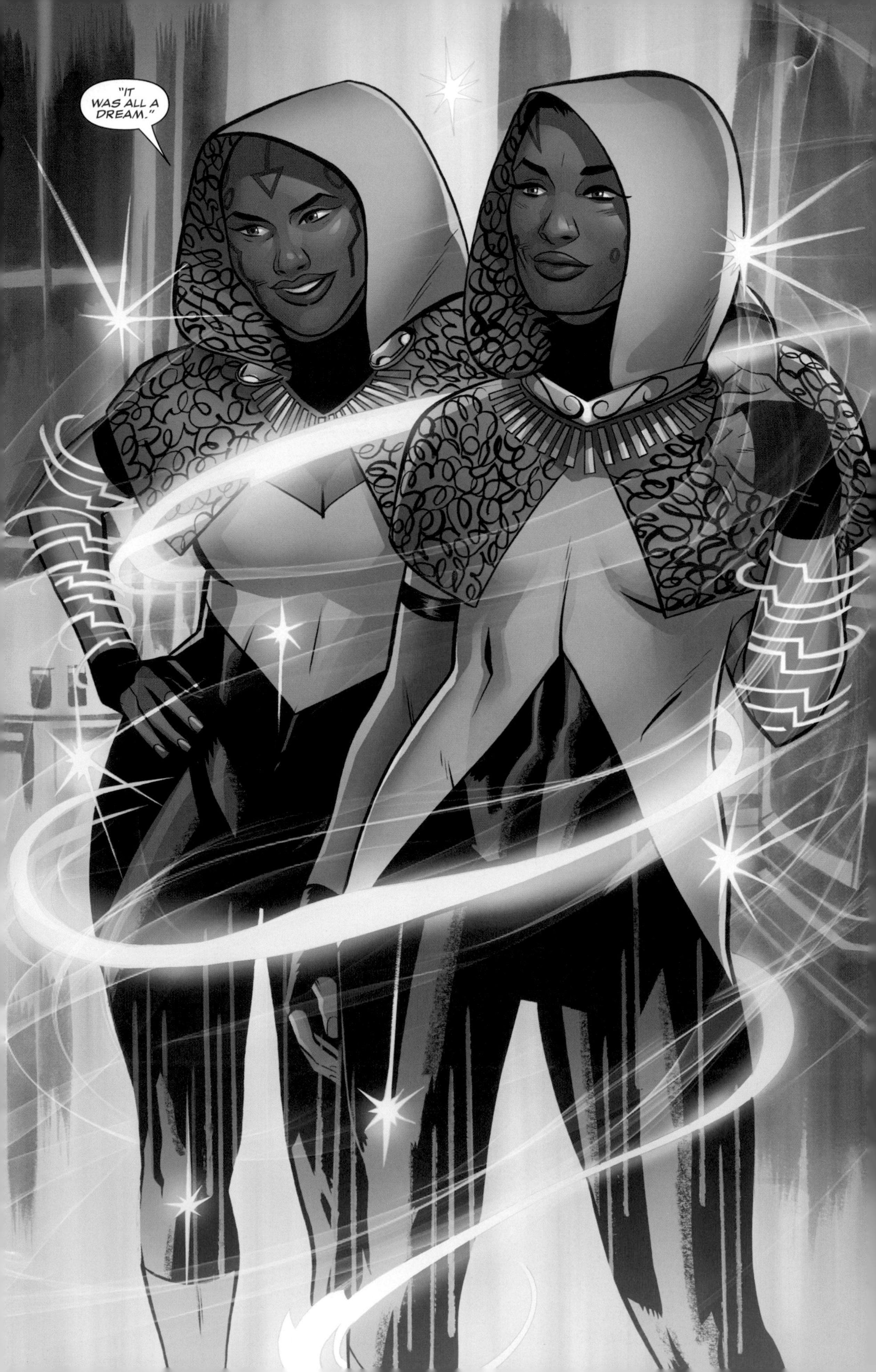
"IT WAS ALL A DREAM."

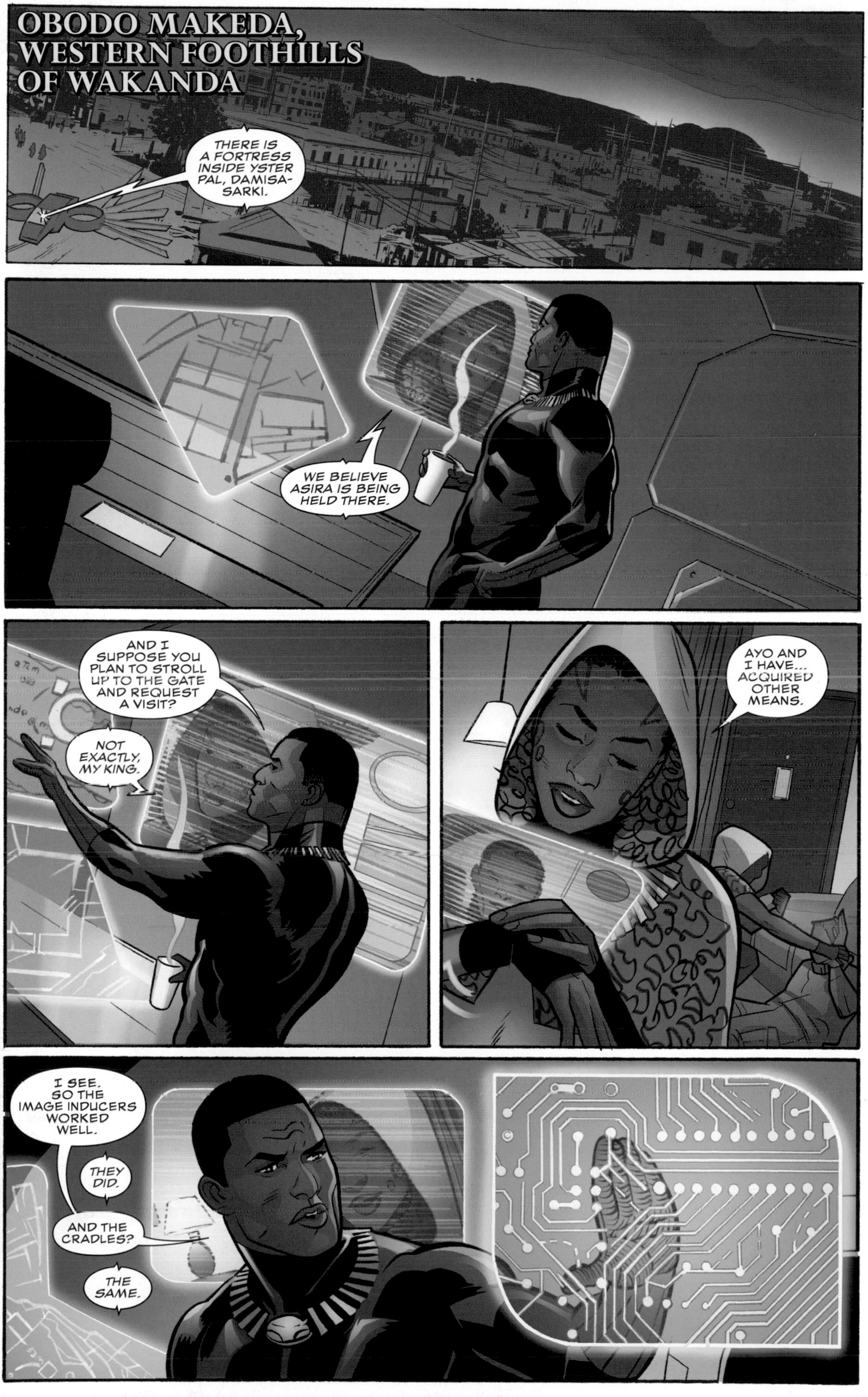
OBODO MAKEDA, WESTERN FOOTHILLS OF WAKANDA
THERE IS A FORTRESS INSIDE YSTER PAL, DAMISA-SARKI.
WE BELIEVE ASIRA IS BEING HELD THERE.
AND I SUPPOSE YOU PLAN TO STROLL UP TO THE GATE AND REQUEST A VISIT?
NOT EXACTLY, MY KING.
AYO AND I HAVE... ACQUIRED OTHER MEANS.
I SEE. SO THE IMAGE INDUCERS WORKED WELL.
THEY DID.
AND THE CRADLES?
THE SAME.

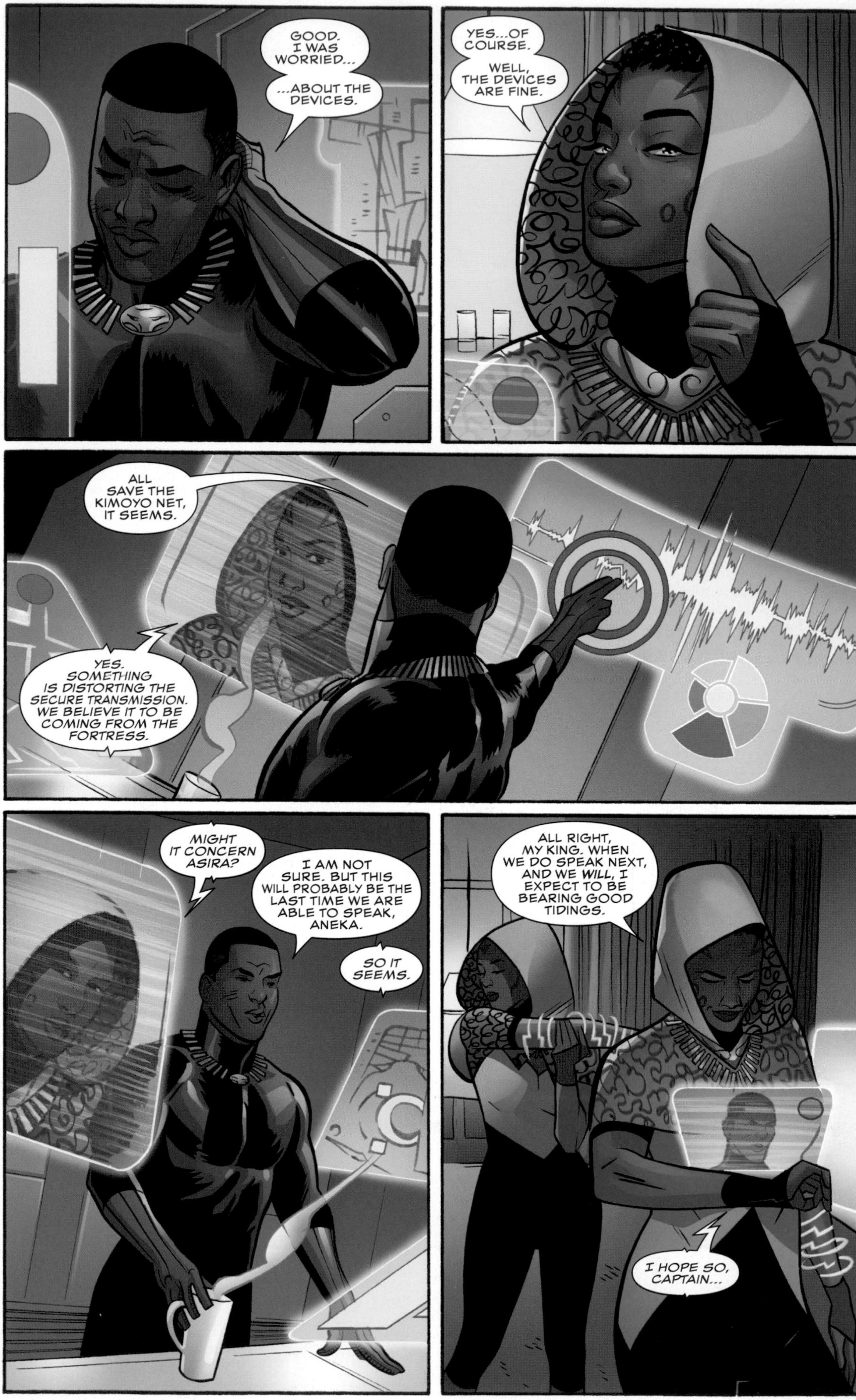
GOOD. I WAS WORRIED...
...ABOUT THE DEVICES.
YES...OF COURSE.
WELL, THE DEVICES ARE FINE.
ALL SAVE THE KIMOYO NET, IT SEEMS.
YES. SOMETHING IS DISTORTING THE SECURE TRANSMISSION. WE BELIEVE IT TO BE COMING FROM THE FORTRESS.
MIGHT IT CONCERN ASIRA?
I AM NOT SURE. BUT THIS WILL PROBABLY BE THE LAST TIME WE ARE ABLE TO SPEAK, ANEKA.
SO IT SEEMS.
ALL RIGHT, MY KING. WHEN WE DO SPEAK NEXT, AND WE WILL, I EXPECT TO BE BEARING GOOD TIDINGS.
I HOPE SO, CAPTAIN...

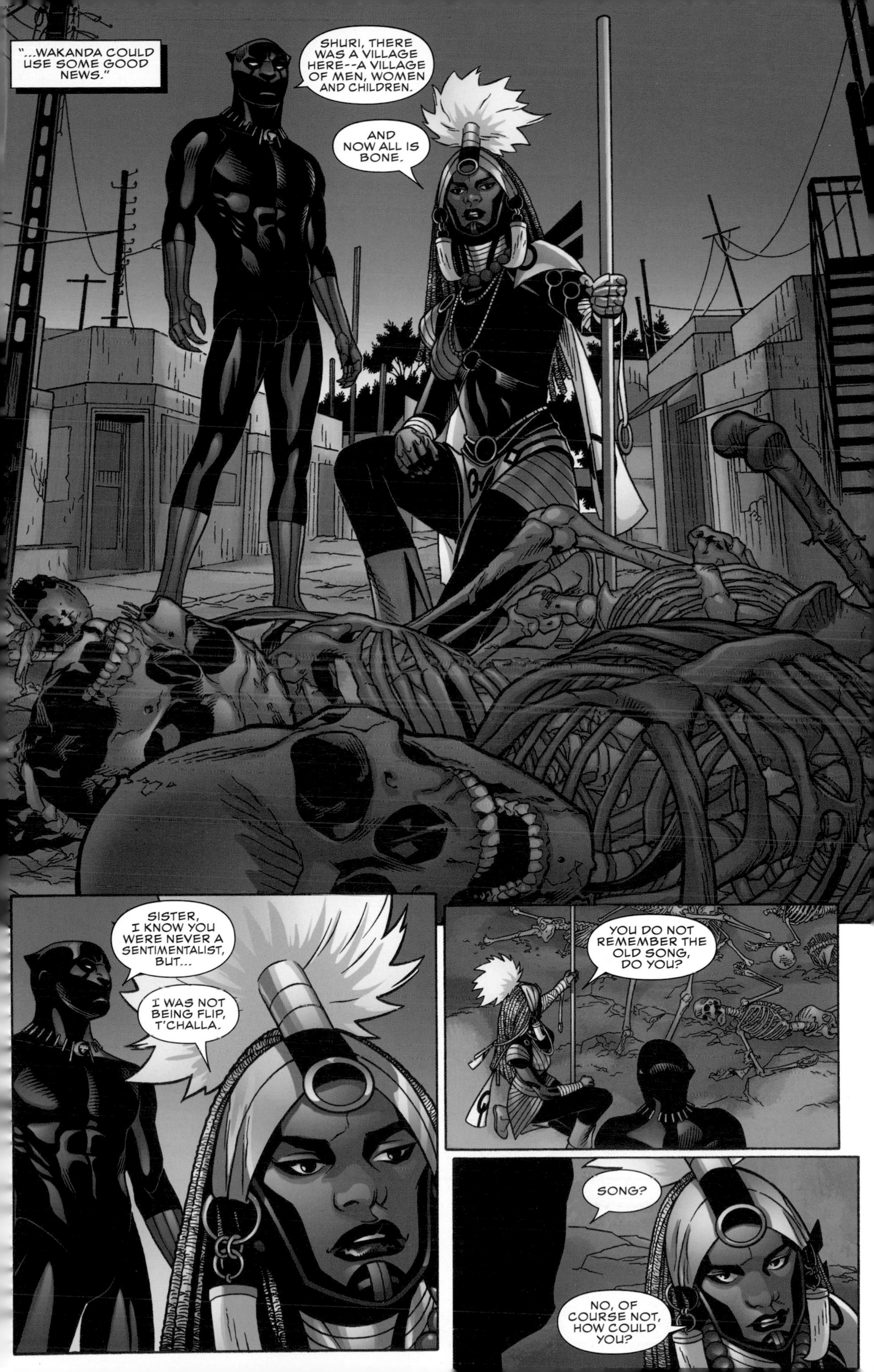
"...WAKANDA COULD USE SOME GOOD NEWS."
SHURI, THERE WAS A VILLAGE HERE--A VILLAGE OF MEN, WOMEN AND CHILDREN.
AND NOW ALL IS BONE.
SISTER, I KNOW YOU WERE NEVER A SENTIMENTALIST, BUT...
I WAS NOT BEING FLIP, T'CHALLA.
YOU DO NOT REMEMBER THE OLD SONG, DO YOU?
SONG?
NO, OF COURSE NOT, HOW COULD YOU?

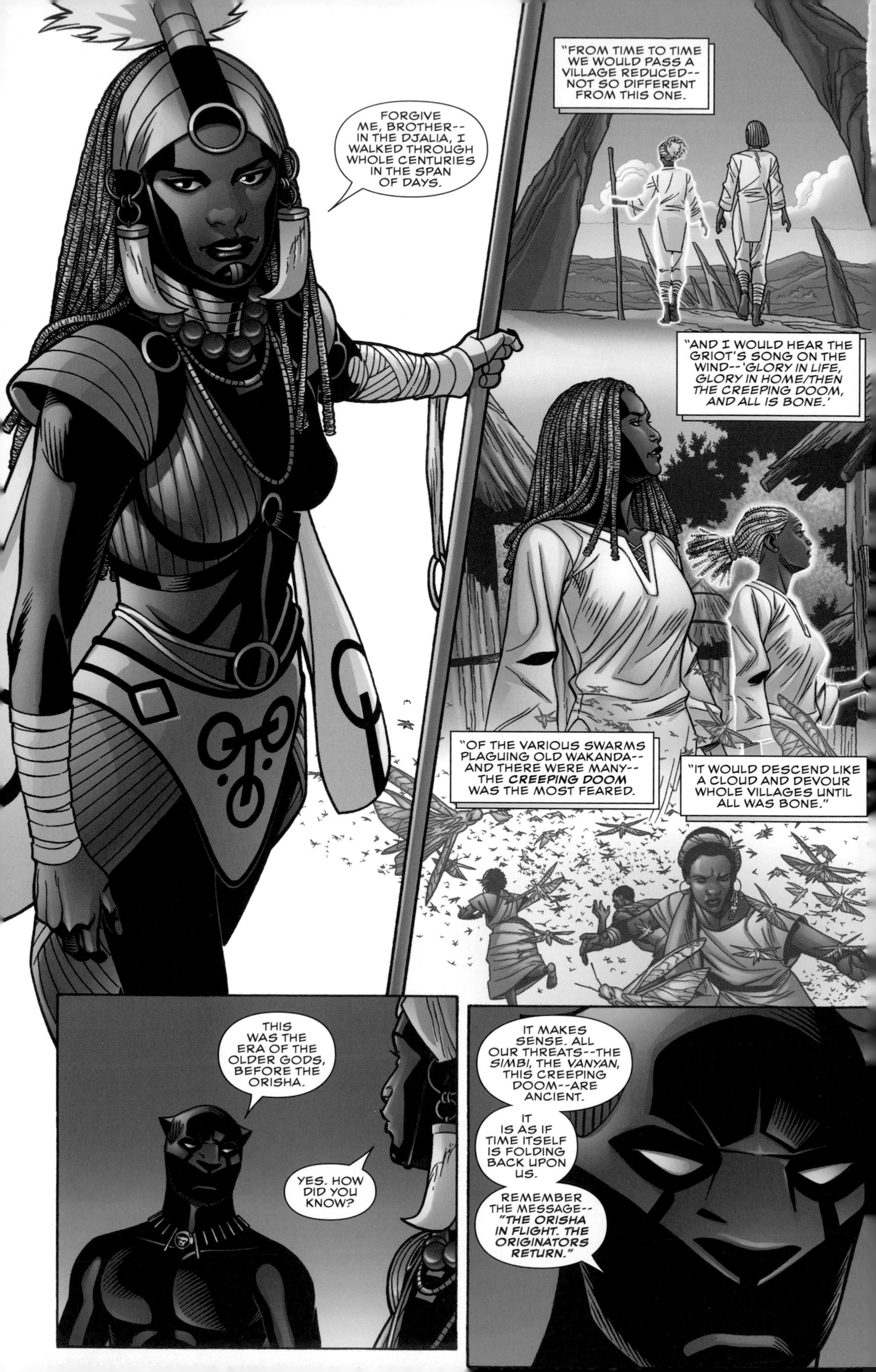
FORGIVE ME, BROTHER-- IN THE DJALIA, I WALKED THROUGH WHOLE CENTURIES IN THE SPAN OF DAYS.
"FROM TIME TO TIME WE WOULD PASS A VILLAGE REDUCED-- NOT SO DIFFERENT FROM THIS ONE.
"AND I WOULD HEAR THE GRIOT'S SONG ON THE WIND--'GLORY IN LIFE, GLORY IN HOME/THEN THE CREEPING DOOM, AND ALL IS BONE.'
"OF THE VARIOUS SWARMS PLAGUING OLD WAKANDA-- AND THERE WERE MANY-- THE CREEPING DOOM WAS THE MOST FEARED.
"IT WOULD DESCEND LIKE A CLOUD AND DEVOUR WHOLE VILLAGES UNTIL ALL WAS BONE."
THIS WAS THE ERA OF THE OLDER GODS, BEFORE THE ORISHA.
YES. HOW DID YOU KNOW?
IT MAKES SENSE. ALL OUR THREATS--THE SIMBI, THE VANYAN, THIS CREEPING DOOM--ARE ANCIENT.
IT IS AS IF TIME ITSELF IS FOLDING BACK UPON US.
REMEMBER THE MESSAGE-- "THE ORISHA IN FLIGHT. THE ORIGINATORS RETURN."

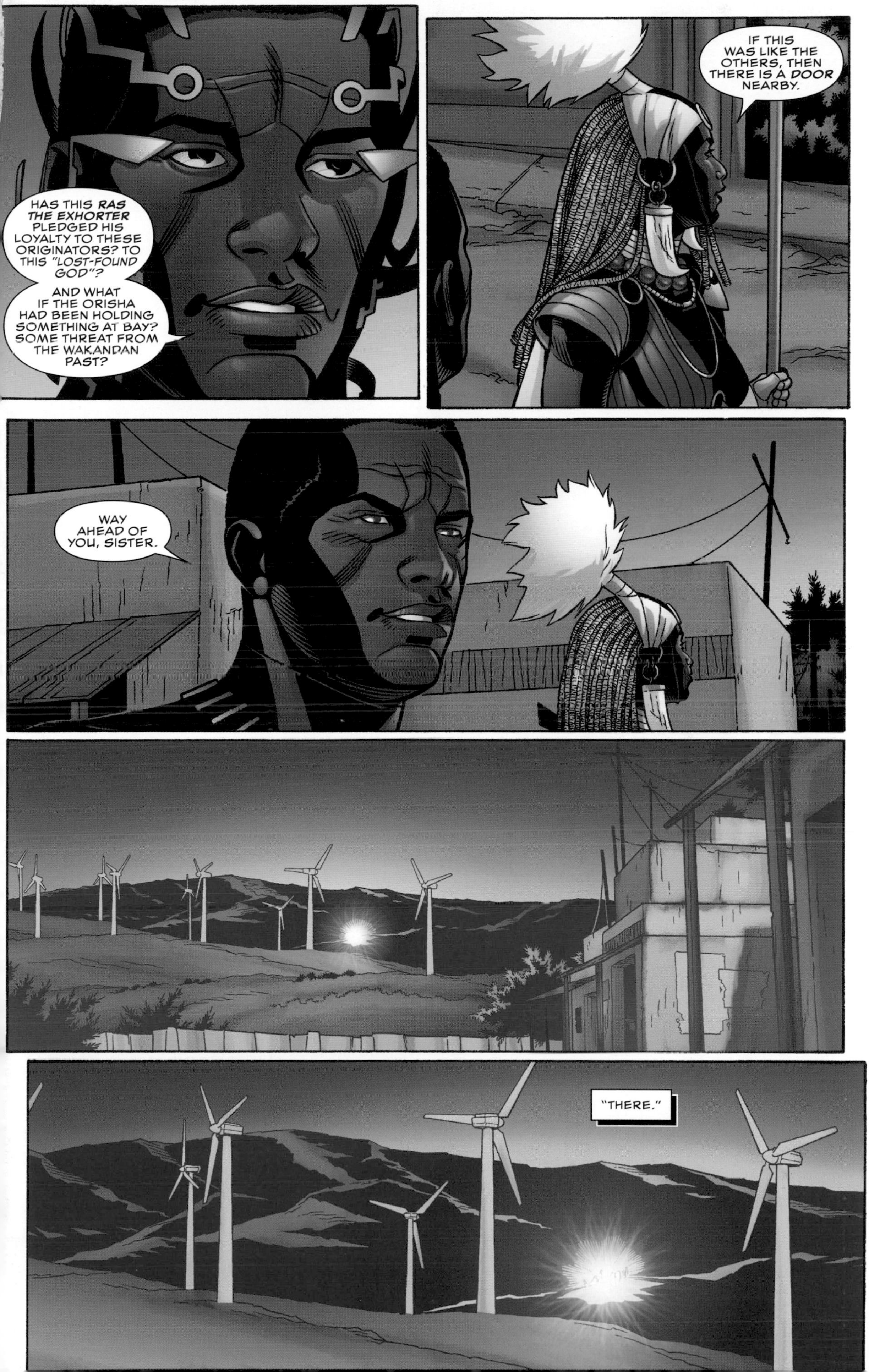
HAS THIS *RAS THE EXHORTER* PLEDGED HIS LOYALTY TO THESE ORIGINATORS? TO THIS "LOST-FOUND GOD"?
AND WHAT IF THE ORISHA HAD BEEN HOLDING SOMETHING AT BAY? SOME THREAT FROM THE WAKANDAN PAST?
IF THIS WAS LIKE THE OTHERS, THEN THERE IS A *DOOR* NEARBY.
WAY AHEAD OF YOU, SISTER.
"THERE."

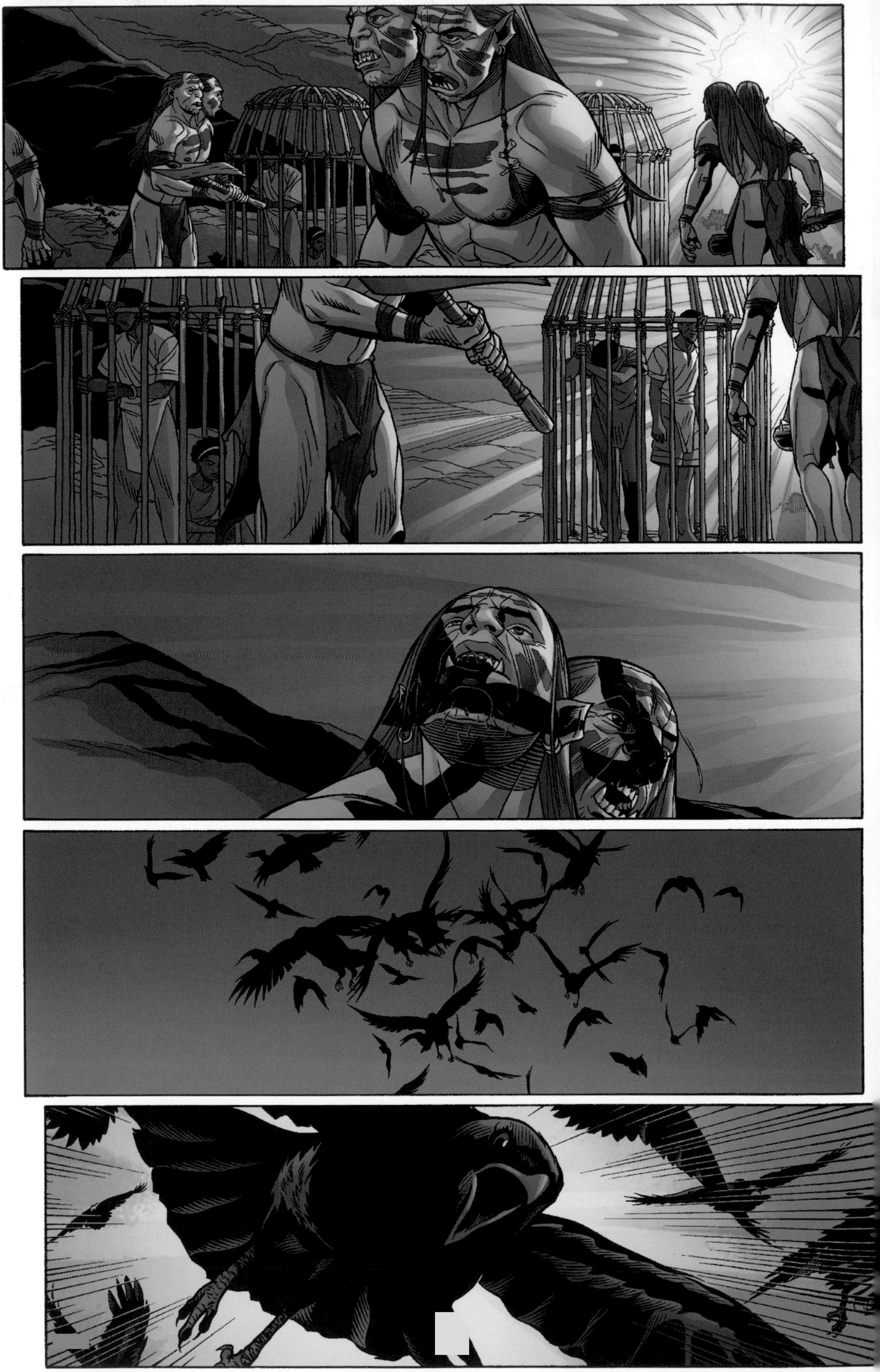

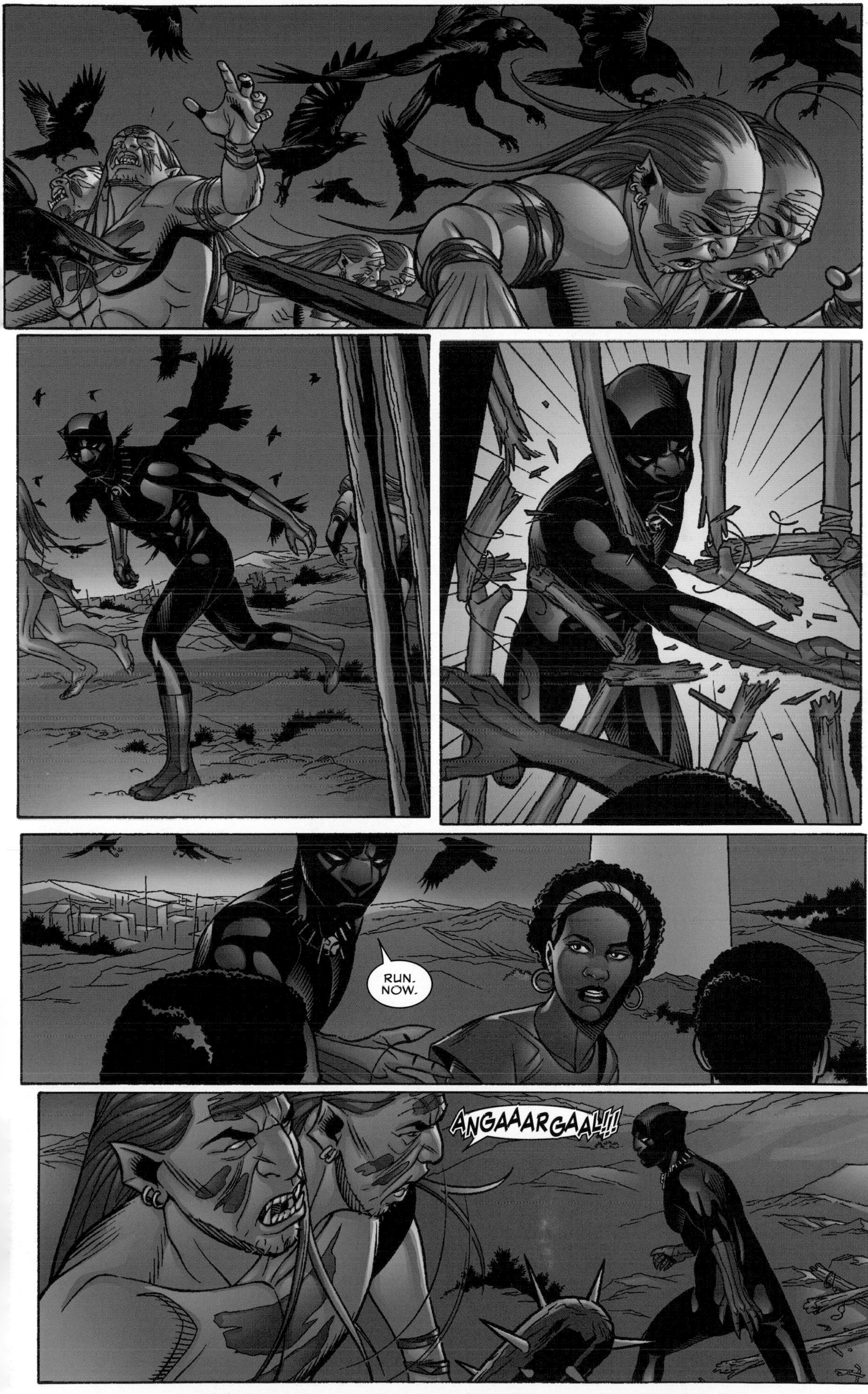
RUN. NOW.
ANGAAARGAAL!!!

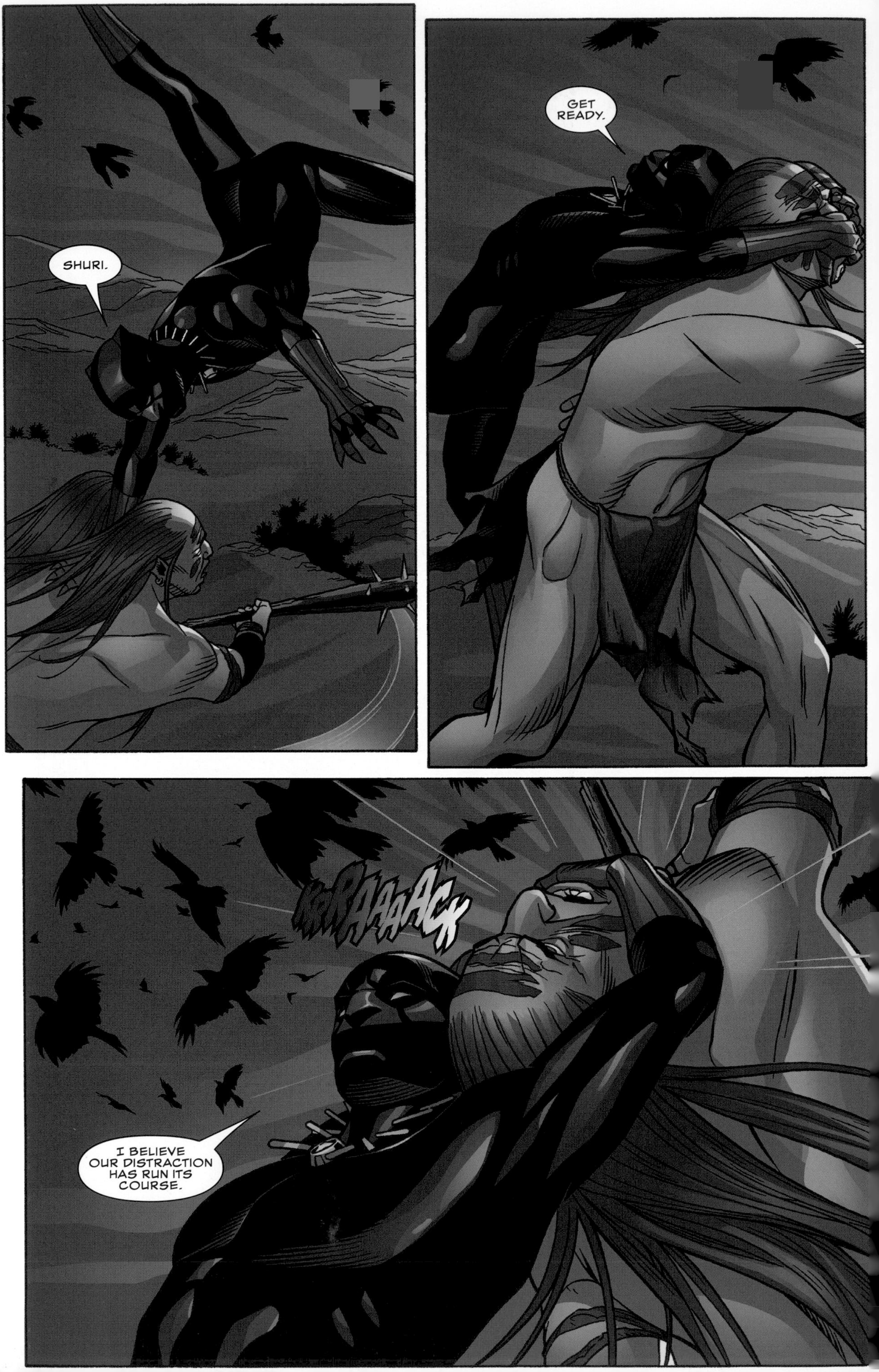
SHURI.
GET READY.
RAAAACK
I BELIEVE OUR DISTRACTION HAS RUN ITS COURSE.

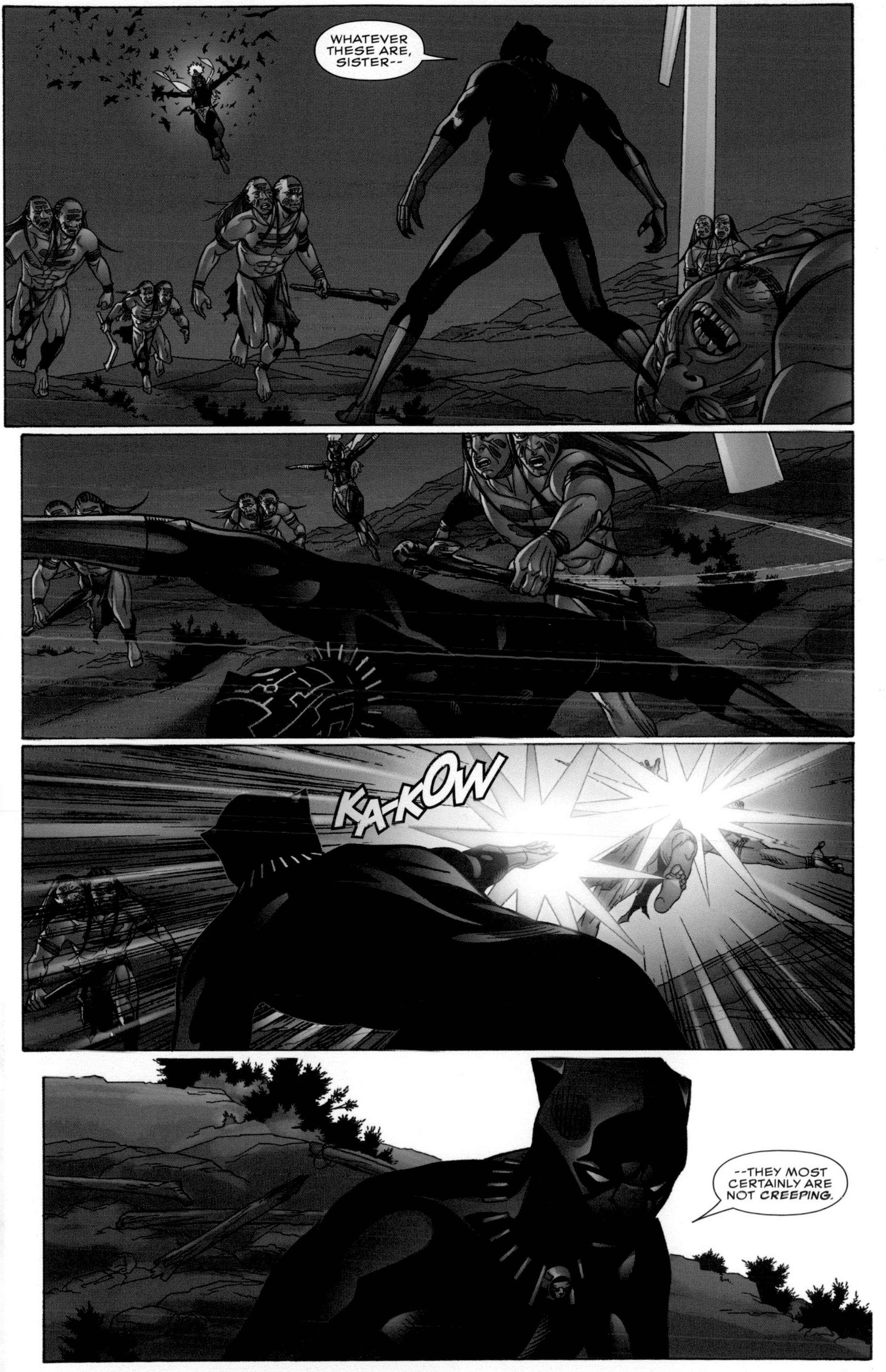
WHATEVER THESE ARE, SISTER--
KA-KOW
--THEY MOST CERTAINLY ARE NOT CREEPING.

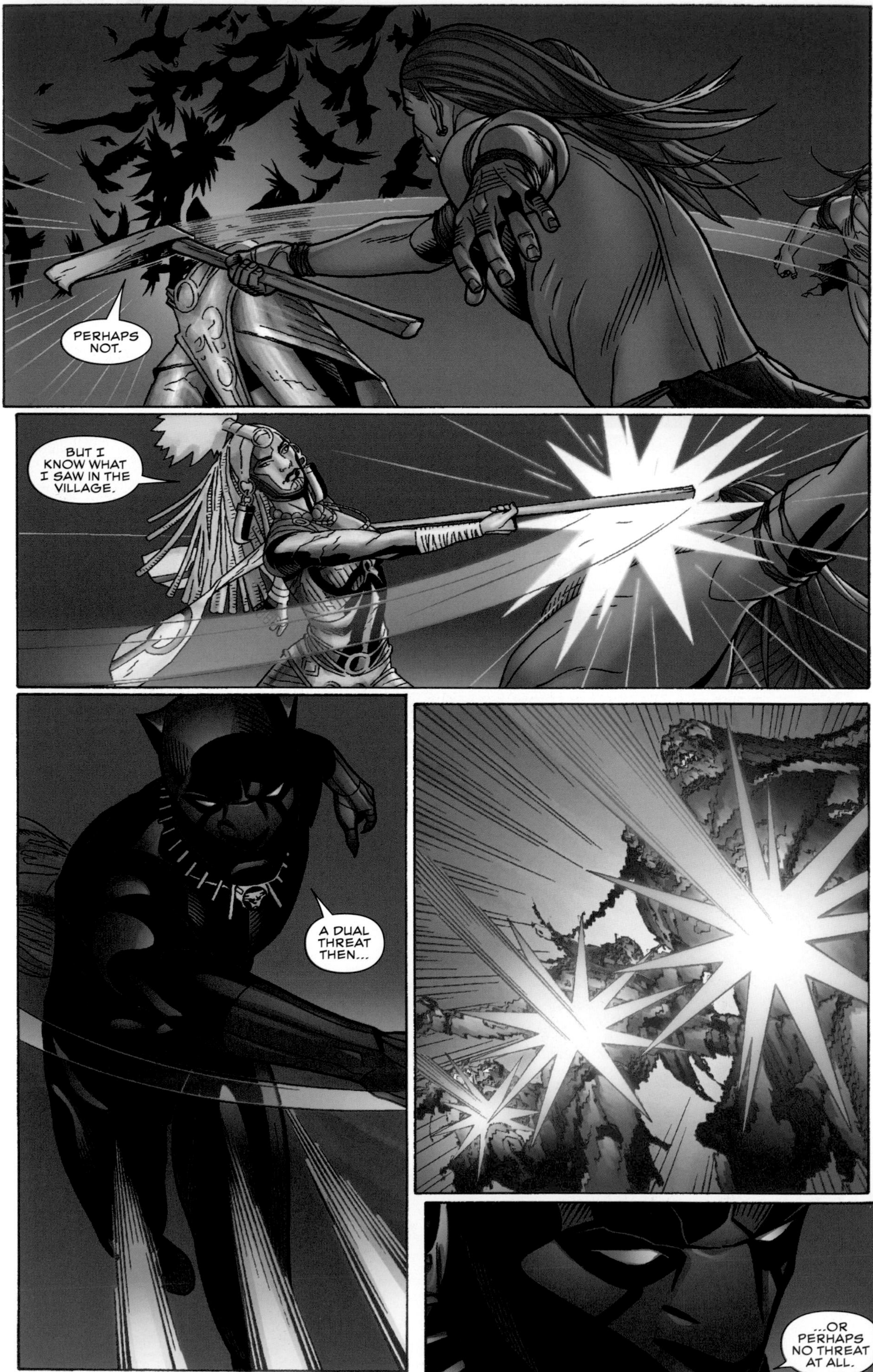
PERHAPS NOT.
BUT I KNOW WHAT I SAW IN THE VILLAGE.
A DUAL THREAT THEN...
...OR PERHAPS NO THREAT AT ALL.

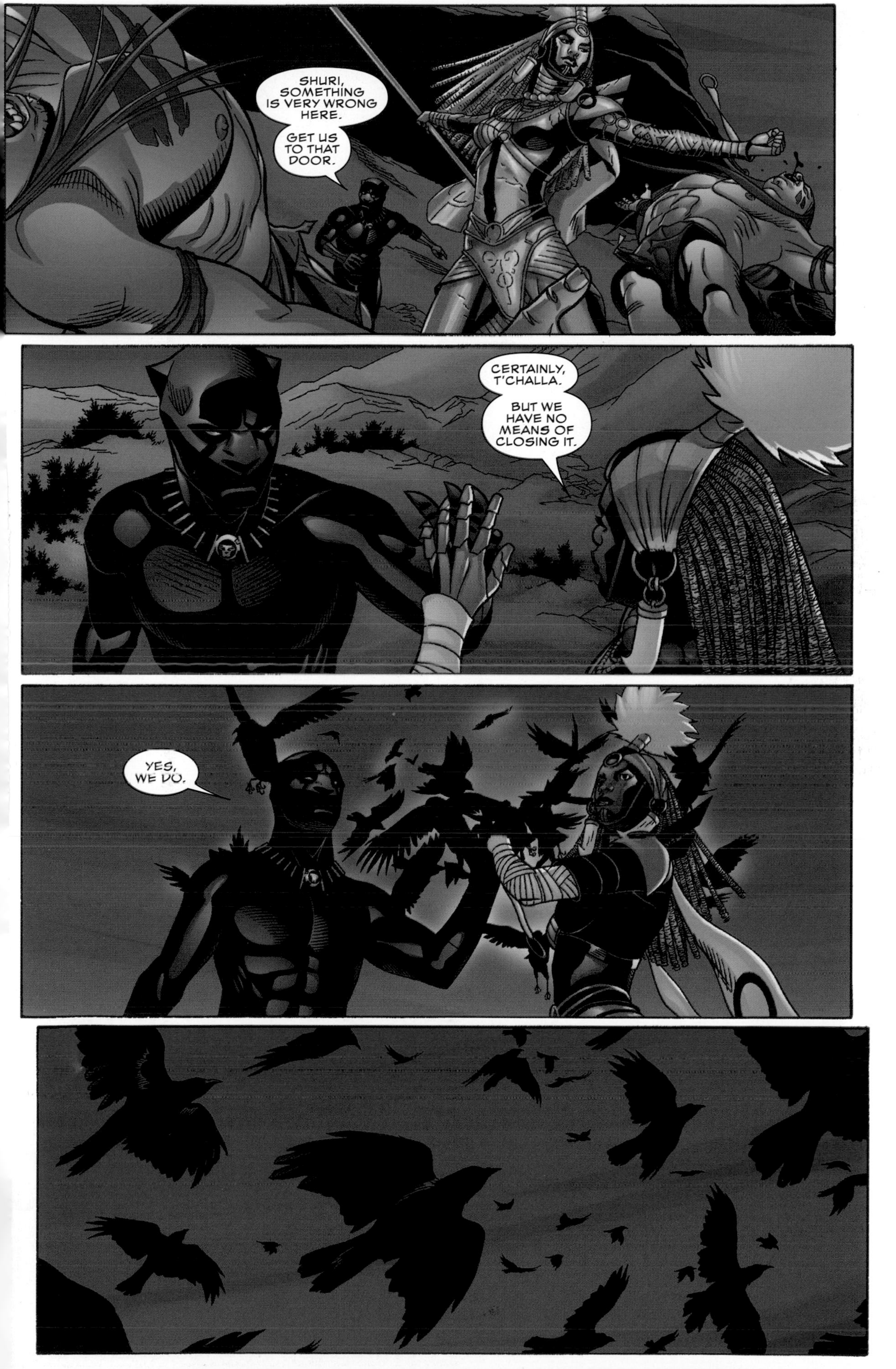
SHURI, SOMETHING IS VERY WRONG HERE.
GET US TO THAT DOOR.
CERTAINLY, T'CHALLA.
BUT WE HAVE NO MEANS OF CLOSING IT.
YES, WE DO.

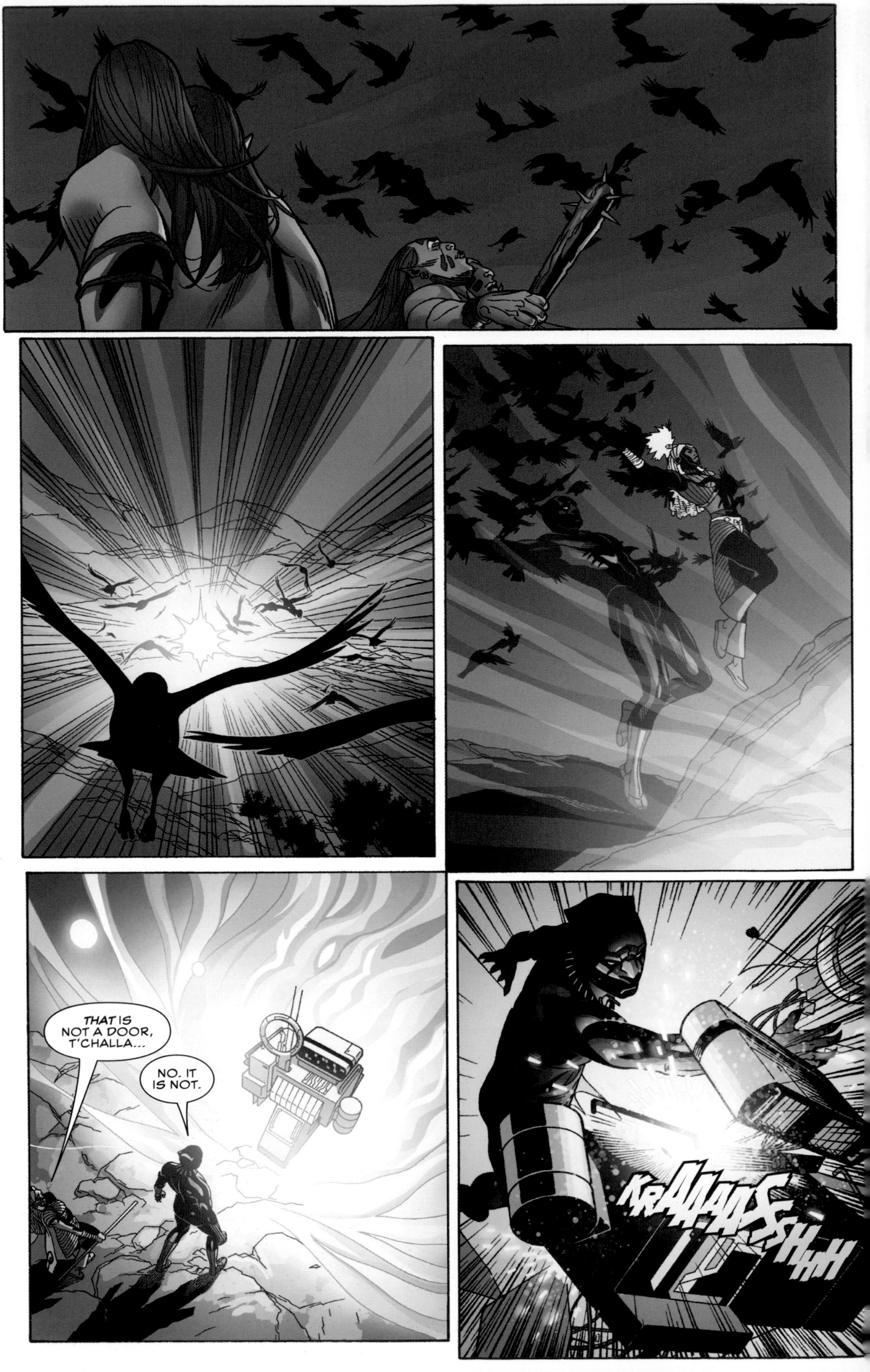

THAT IS NOT A DOOR, T'CHALLA...
NO. IT IS NOT.
KRAAAAASSHHH

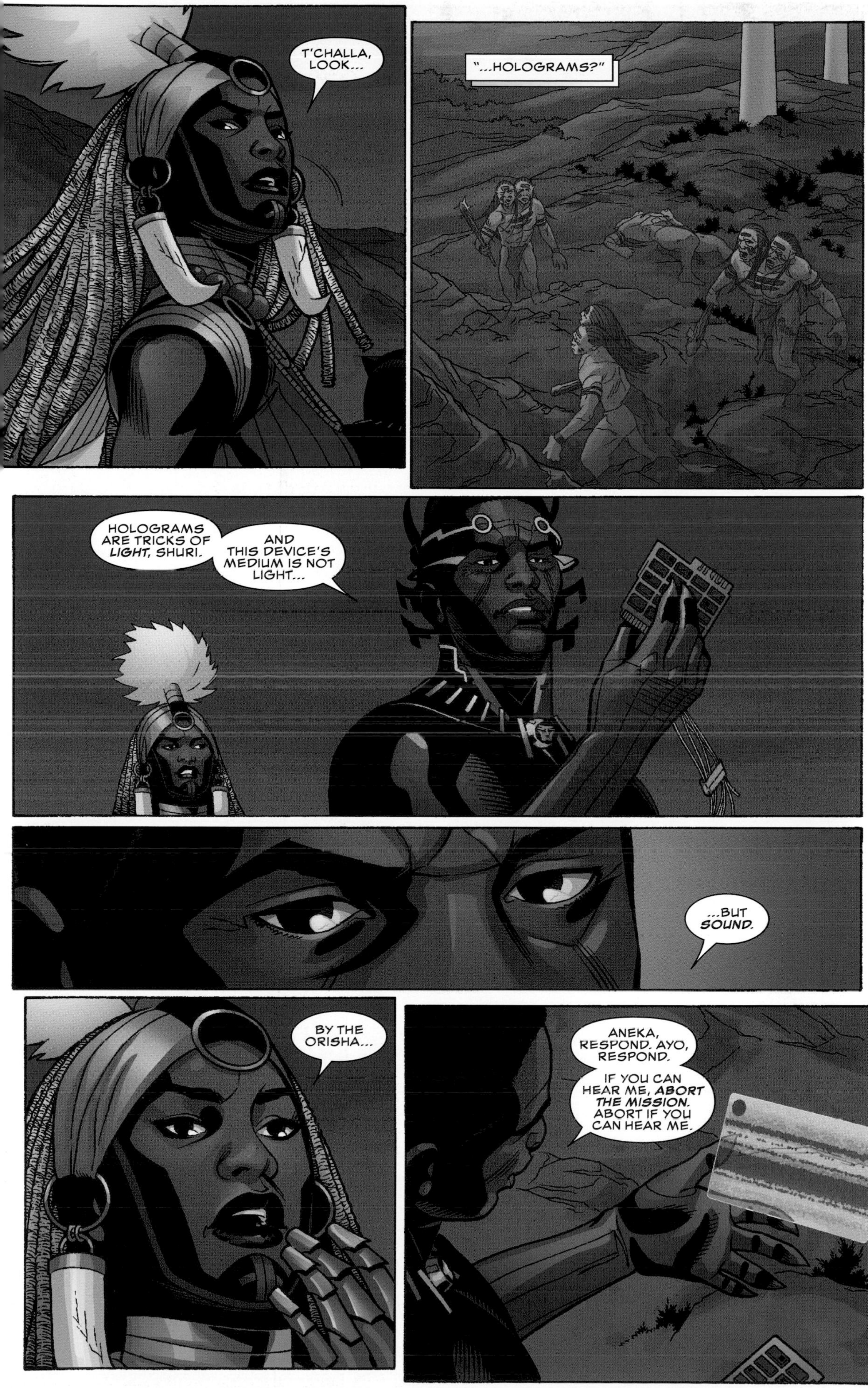
T'CHALLA, LOOK...
"...HOLOGRAMS?"
HOLOGRAMS ARE TRICKS OF *LIGHT*, SHURI.
AND THIS DEVICE'S MEDIUM IS NOT LIGHT...
...BUT *SOUND*.
BY THE ORISHA...
ANEKA, RESPOND. AYO, RESPOND.
IF YOU CAN HEAR ME, *ABORT THE MISSION*. ABORT IF YOU CAN HEAR ME.

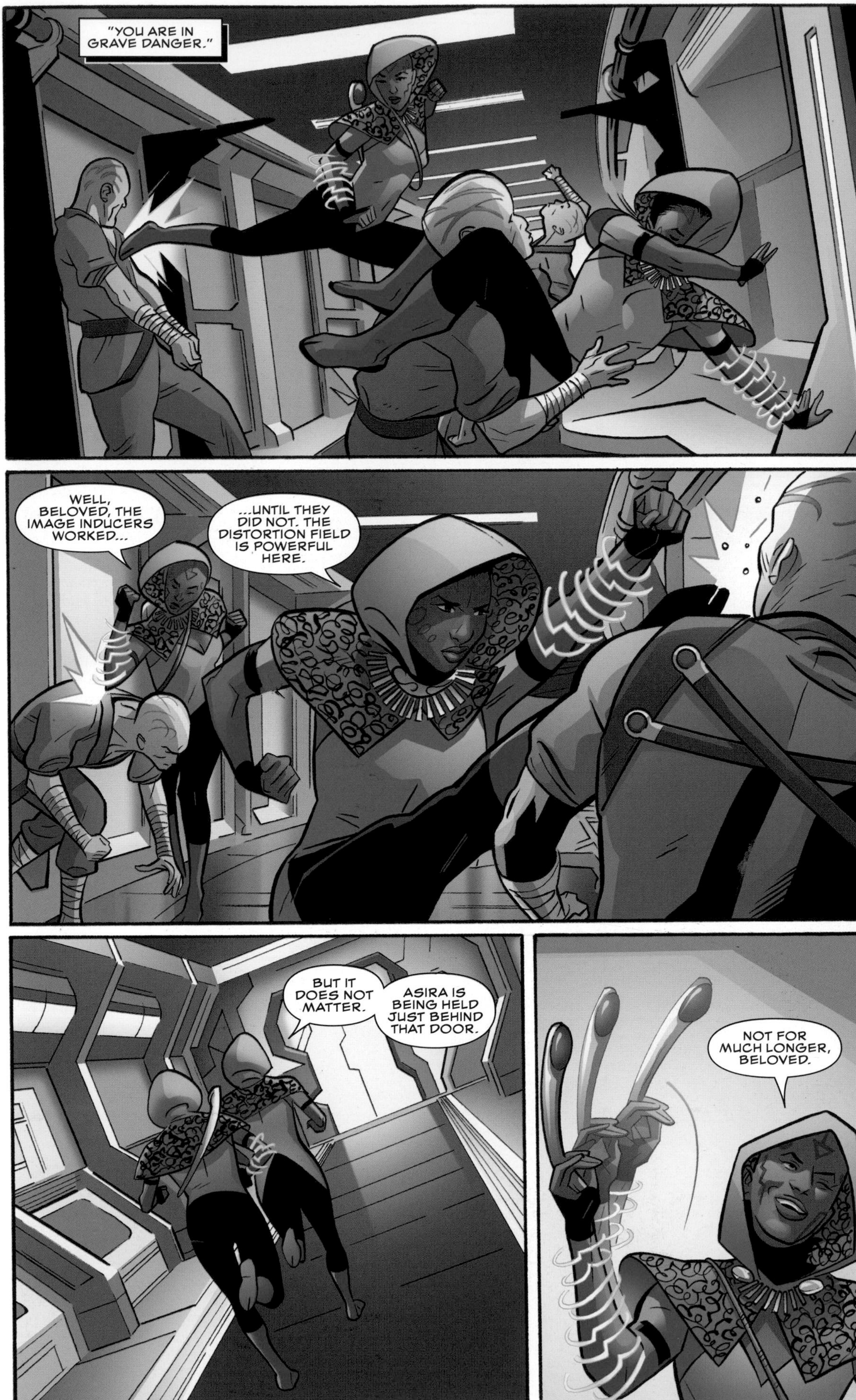
"YOU ARE IN GRAVE DANGER."
WELL, BELOVED, THE IMAGE INDUCERS WORKED...
...UNTIL THEY DID NOT. THE DISTORTION FIELD IS POWERFUL HERE.
BUT IT DOES NOT MATTER.
ASIRA IS BEING HELD JUST BEHIND THAT DOOR.
NOT FOR MUCH LONGER, BELOVED.

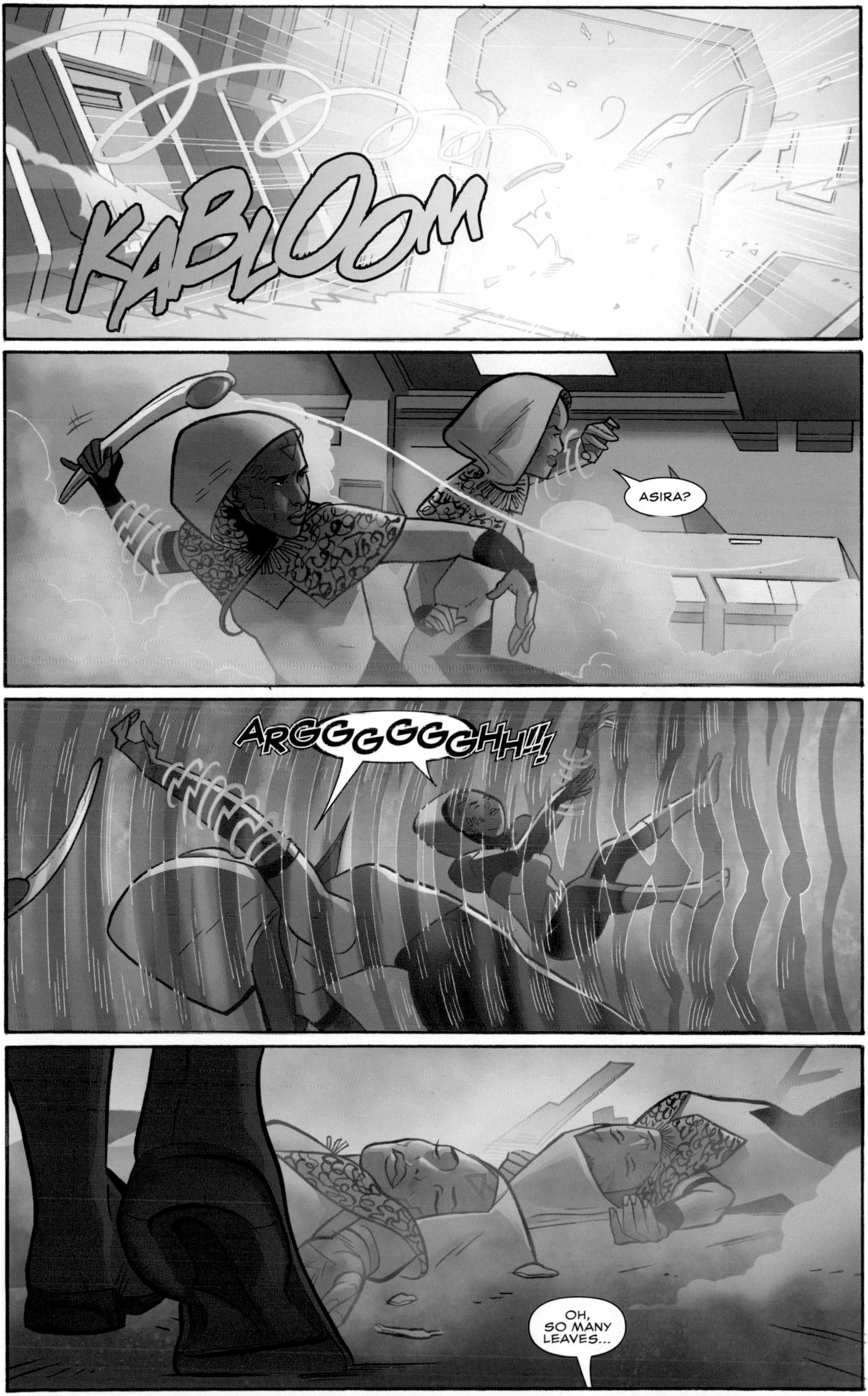
KABLOOM
ASIRA?
ARGGGGGGHH!!!
OH, SO MANY LEAVES...

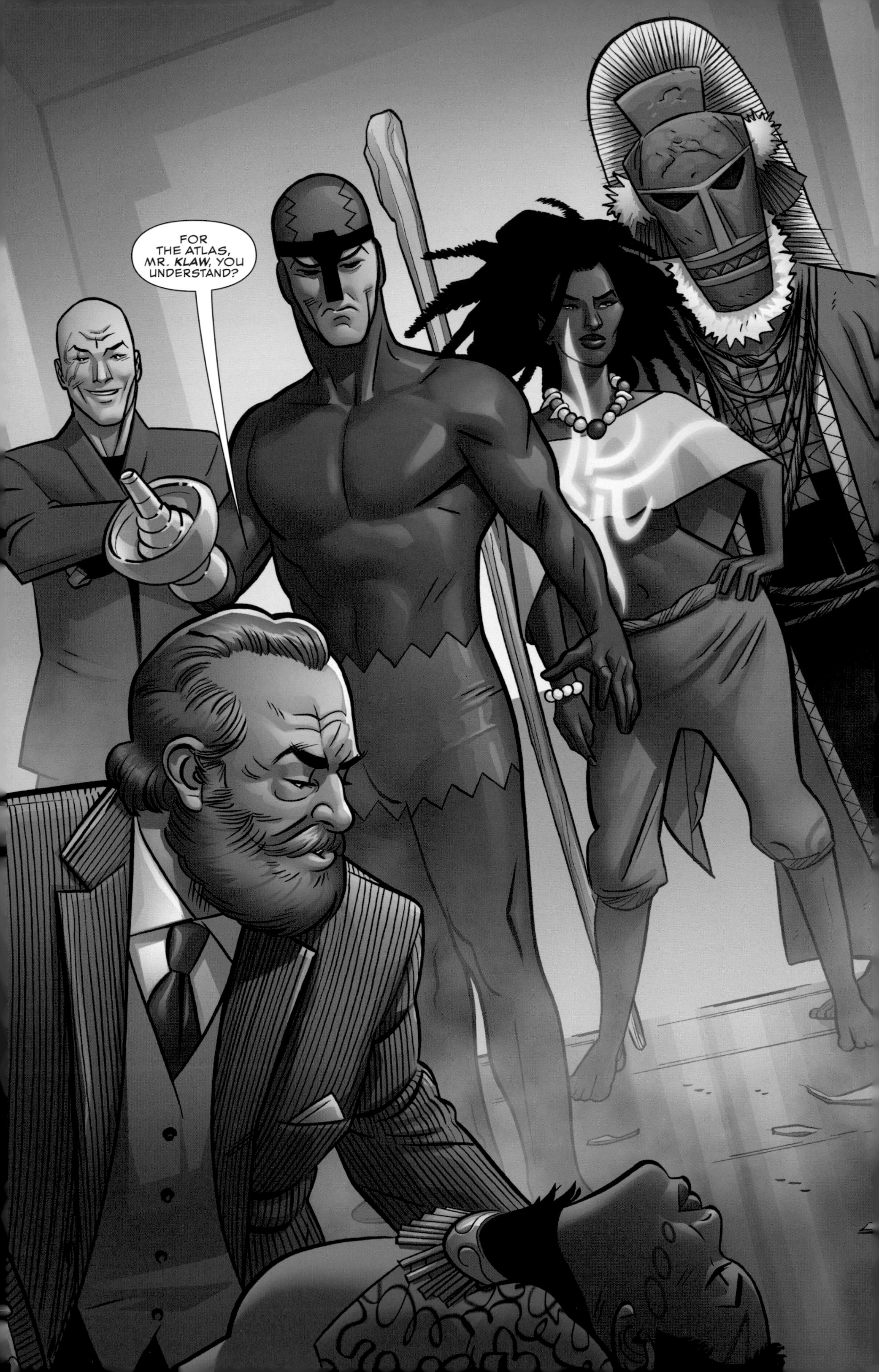
FOR THE ATLAS, MR. KLAW, YOU UNDERSTAND?

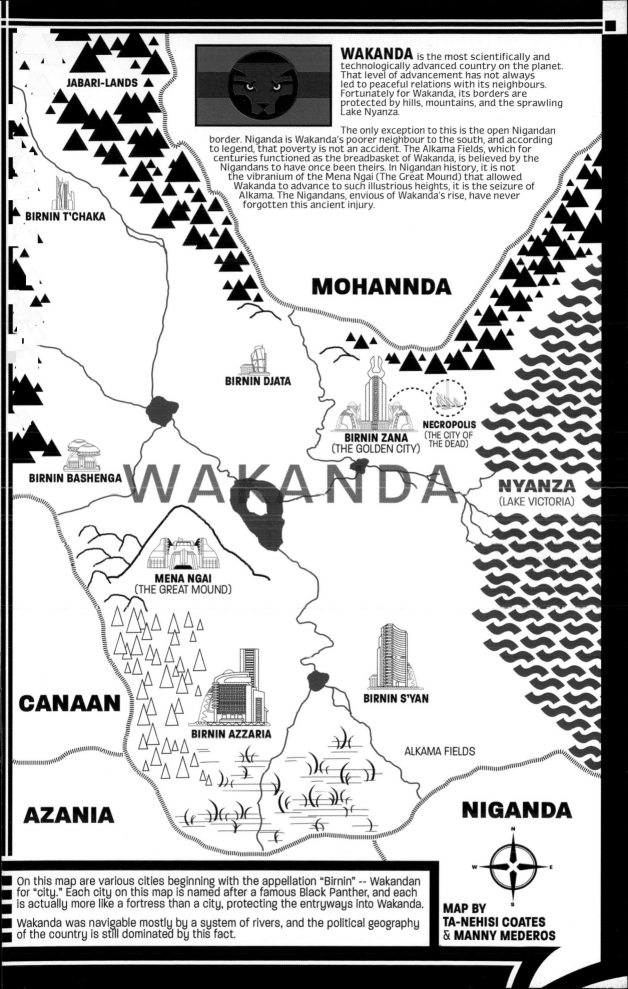

JABARI-LANDS

WAKANDA is the most scientifically and technologically advanced country on the planet. That level of advancement has not always led to peaceful relations with its neighbours. Fortunately for Wakanda, its borders are protected by hills, mountains, and the sprawling Lake Nyanza.

The only exception to this is the open Nigandan border. Niganda is Wakanda's poorer neighbour to the south, and according to legend, that poverty is not an accident. The Alkama Fields, which for centuries functioned as the breadbasket of Wakanda, is believed by the Nigandans to have once been theirs. In Nigandan history, it is not the vibranium of the Mena Ngai (The Great Mound) that allowed Wakanda to advance to such illustrious heights, it is the seizure of Alkama. The Nigandans, envious of Wakanda's rise, have never forgotten this ancient injury.

BIRNIN T'CHAKA

MOHANNDA

BIRNIN DJATA

BIRNIN BASHENGA

NECROPOLIS
(THE CITY OF
THE DEAD)

BIRNIN ZANA
(THE GOLDEN CITY)

W A K A N D A

NYANZA
(LAKE VICTORIA)

MENA NGAI
(THE GREAT MOUND)

CANAAN

BIRNIN S'YAN

BIRNIN AZZARIA

ALKAMA FIELDS

AZANIA

NIGANDA

On this map are various cities beginning with the appellation "Birnin" -- Wakandan for "city." Each city on this map is named after a famous Black Panther, and each is actually more like a fortress than a city, protecting the entryways into Wakanda.

Wakanda was navigable mostly by a system of rivers, and the political geography of the country is still dominated by this fact.

MAP BY
TA-NEHISI COATES
& MANNY MEDEROS

BLACK PANTHER VARIANT COVER GALLERY

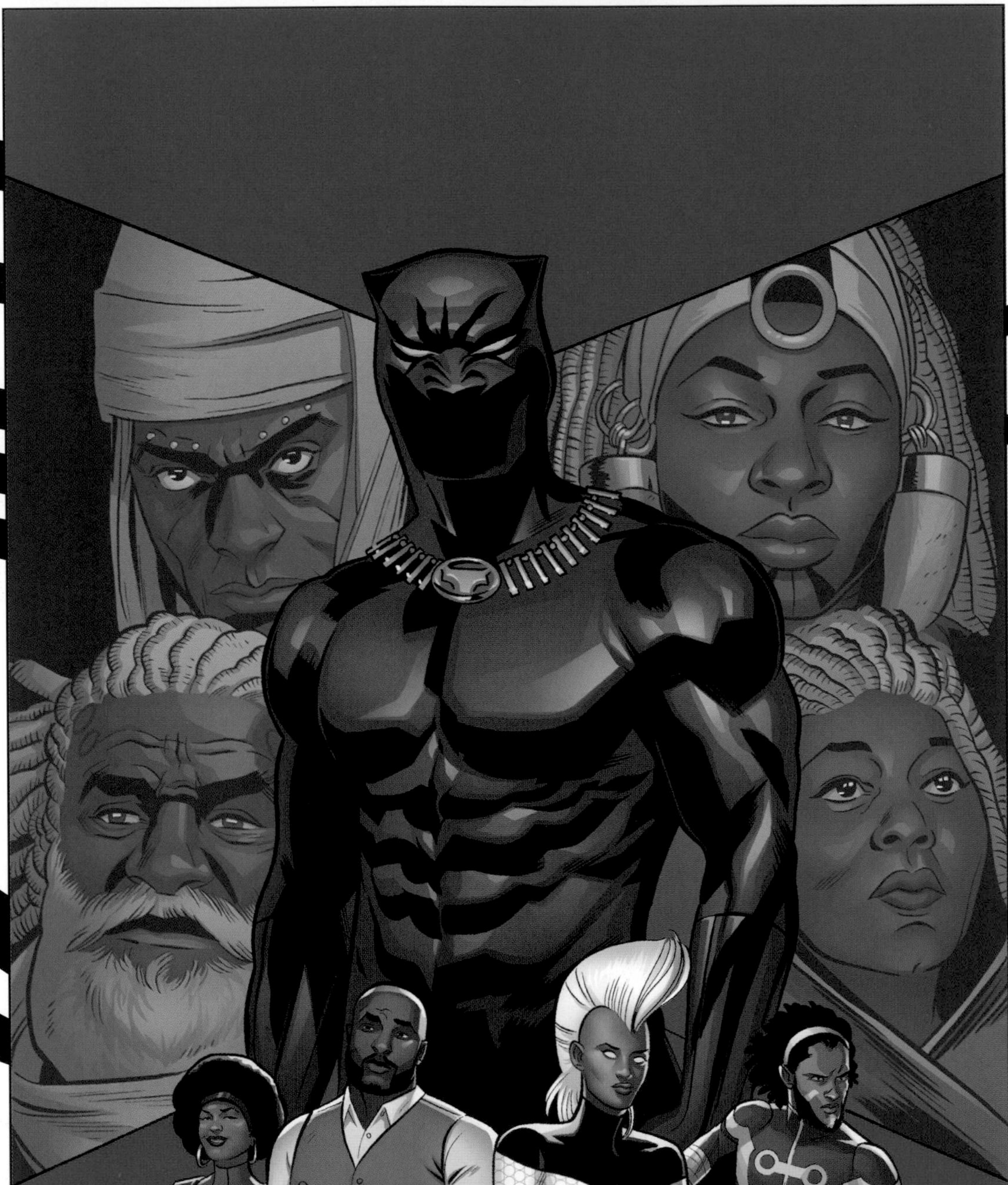

Black Panther #13
by Wilfredo Torres

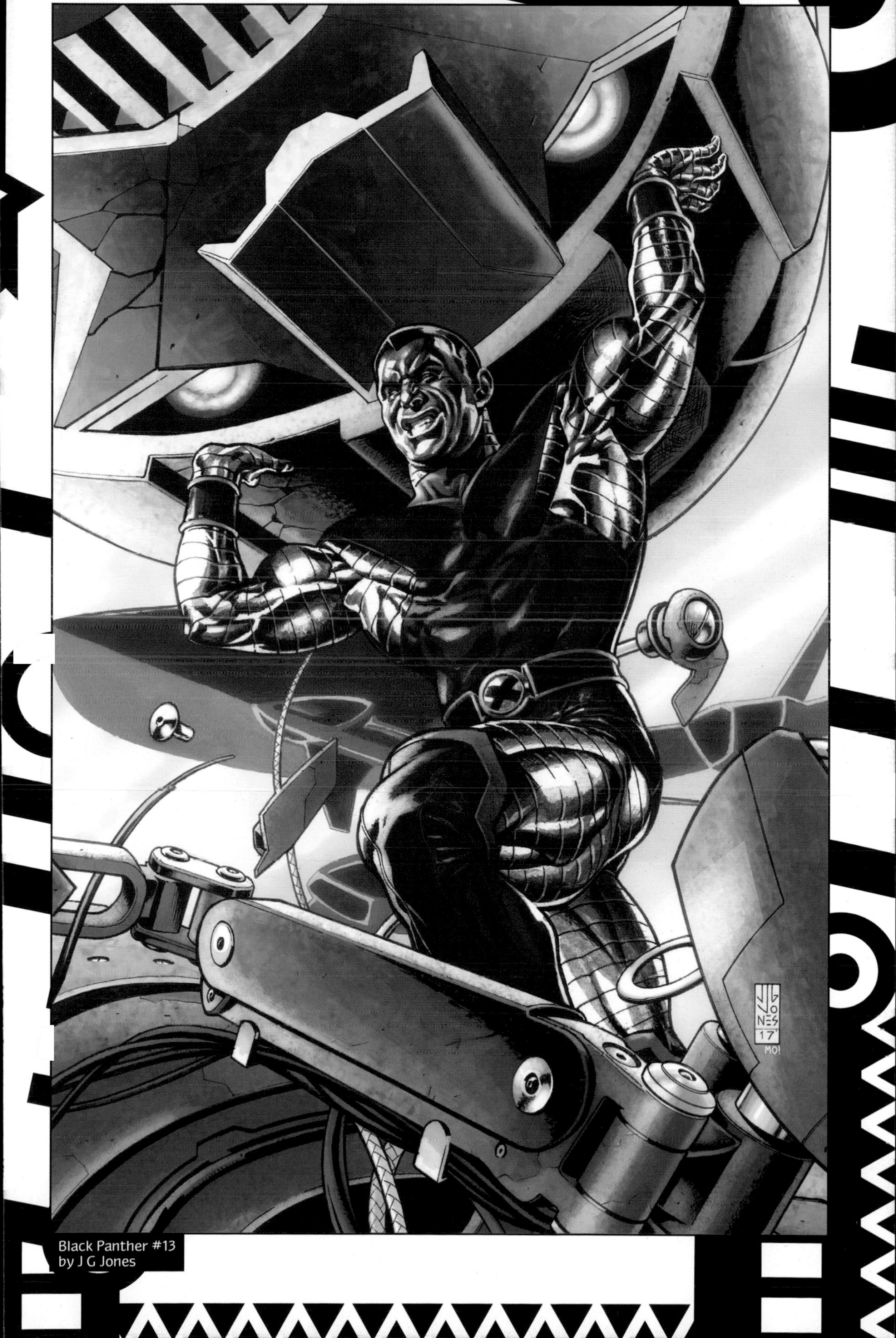
JG JONES 17' MO!

Black Panther #13
by J G Jones

Black Panther #13
by Kris Anka

Black Panther #14
by Andrew Robinson

Black Panther #13
by Jamie McKelvie

Black Panther #14
by Jamie McKelvie

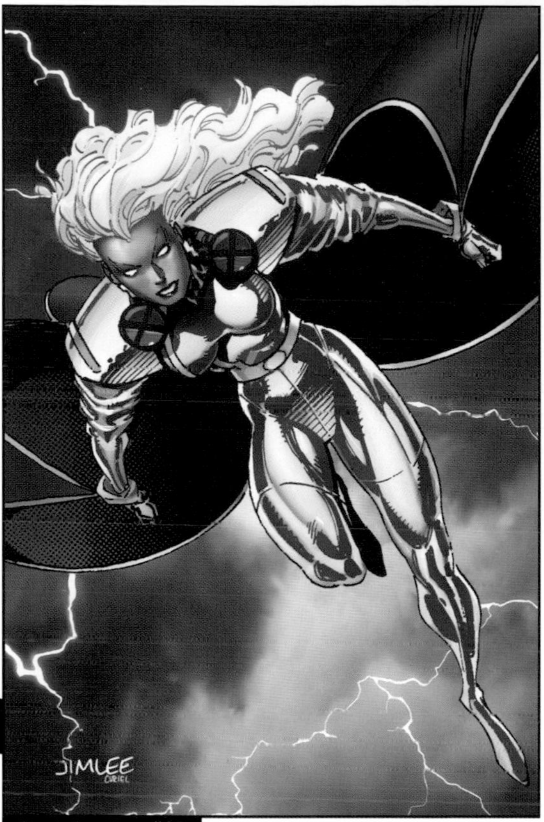
JIMLEE

Black Panther #16
by Jim Lee

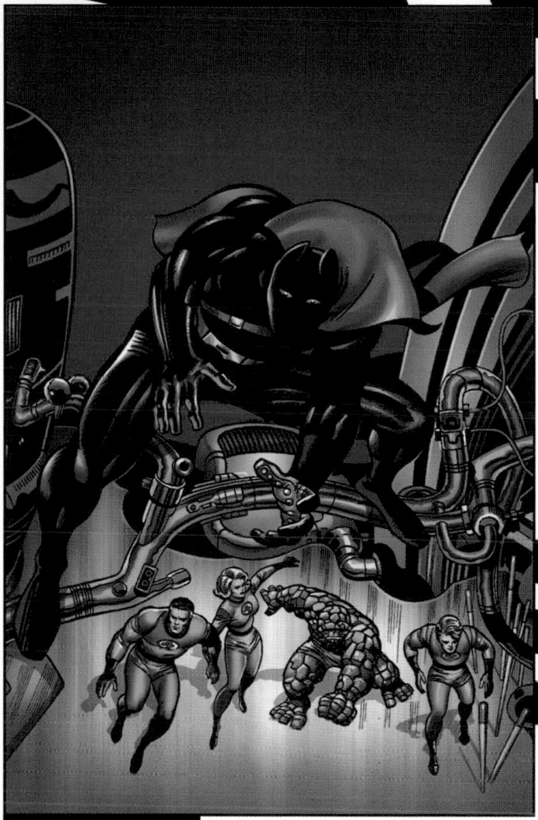

Black Panther #16
by Jack Kirby

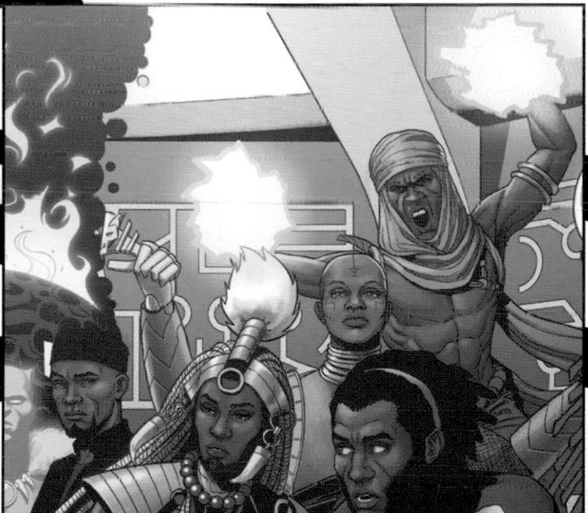

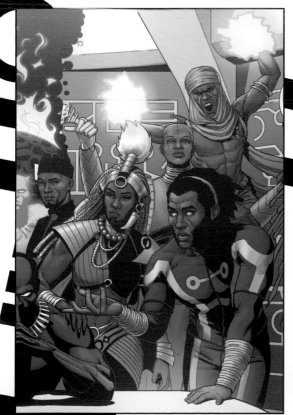

Black Panther #15
by Jamie McKelvie

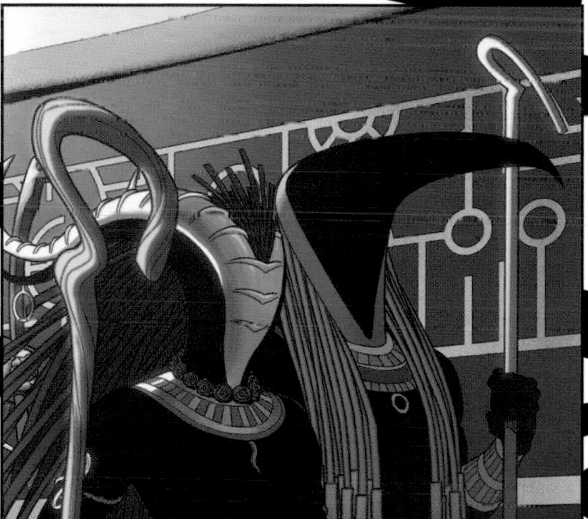

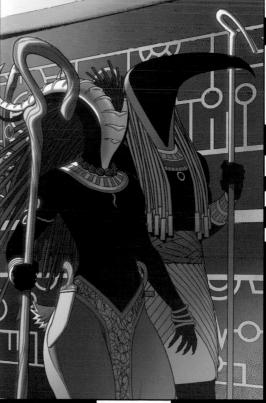

Black Panther #16
by Jamie McKelvie

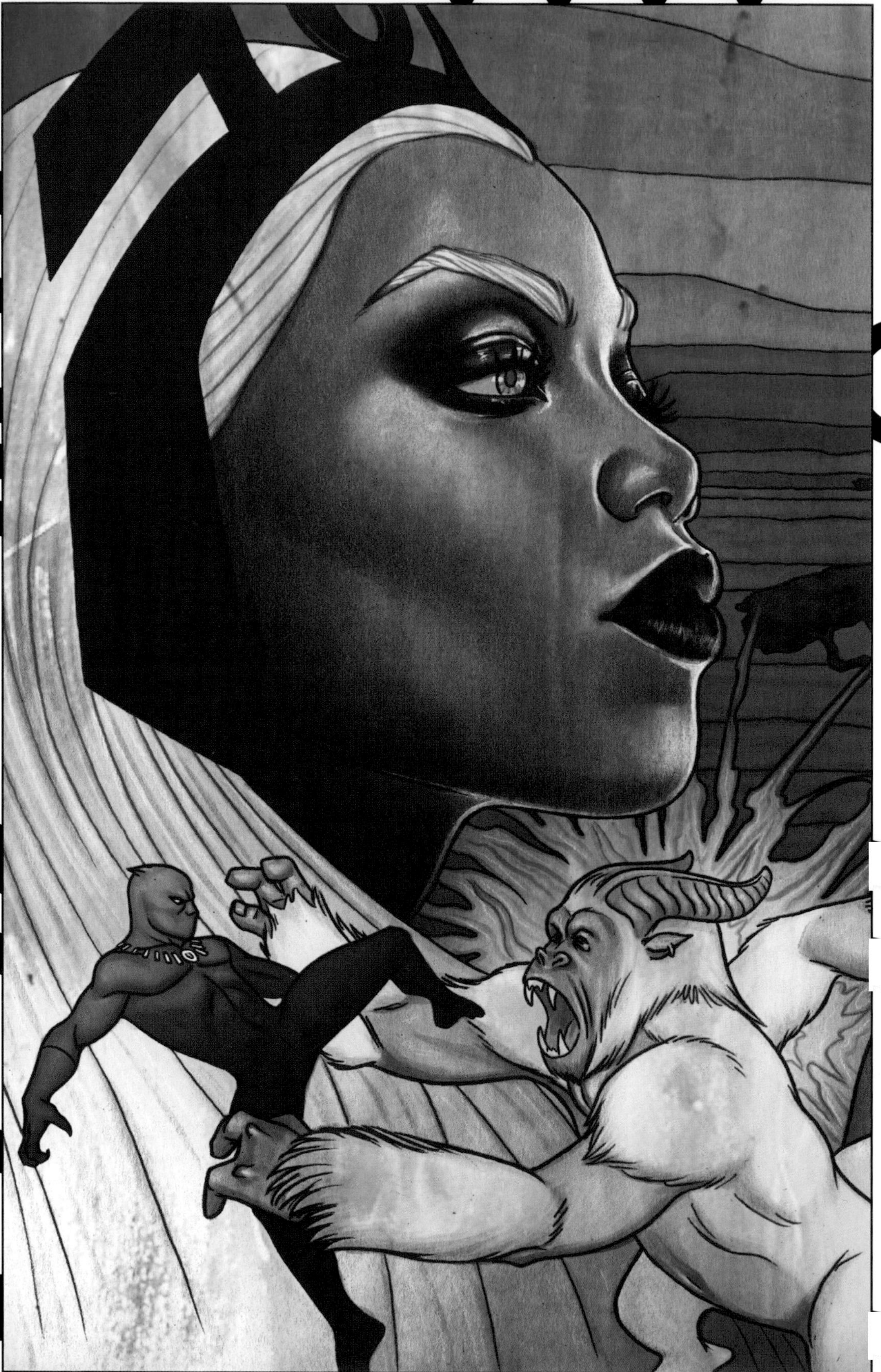

Black Panther #17
by Jenny Frison

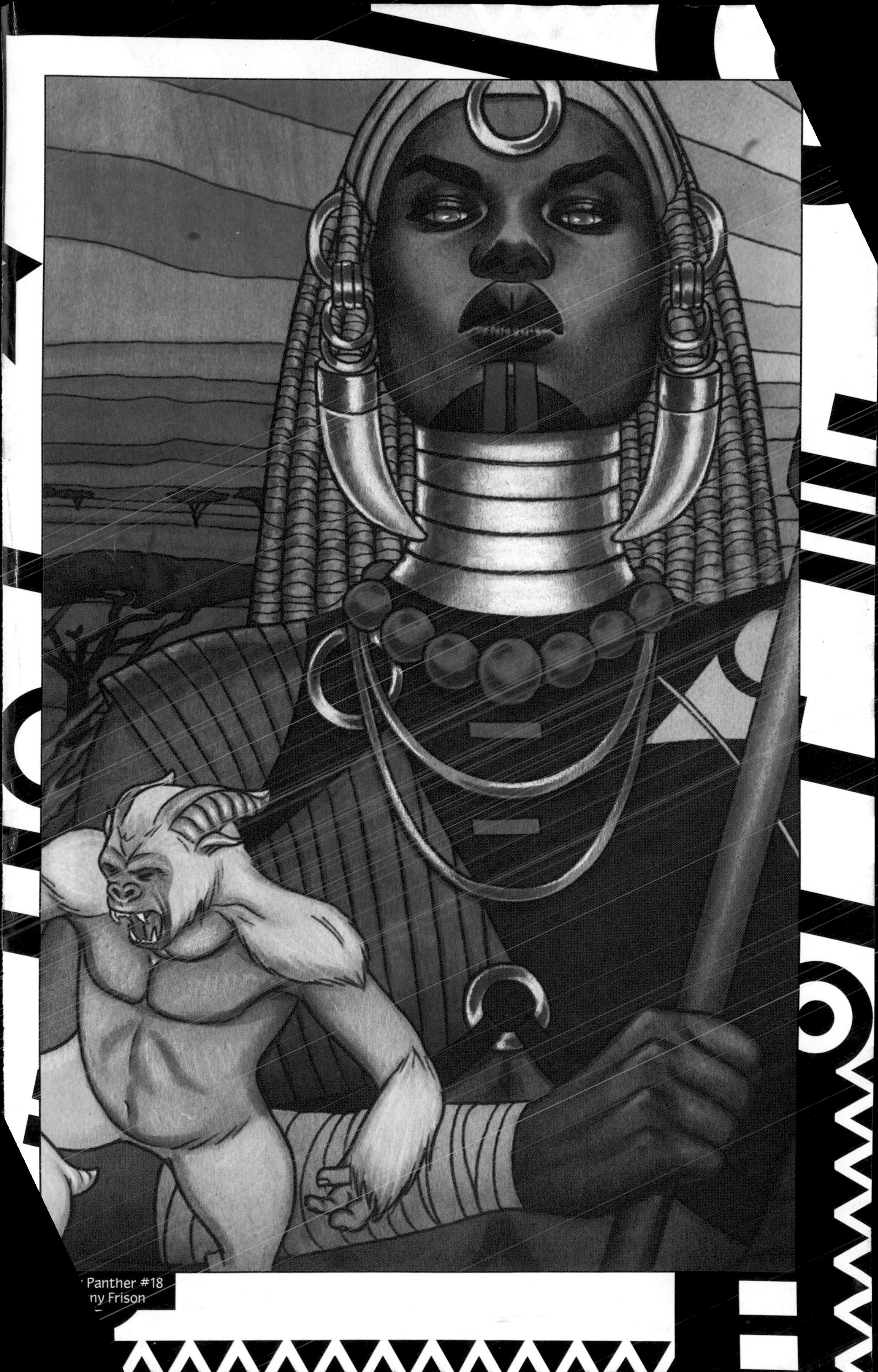

Panther #18
ny Frison

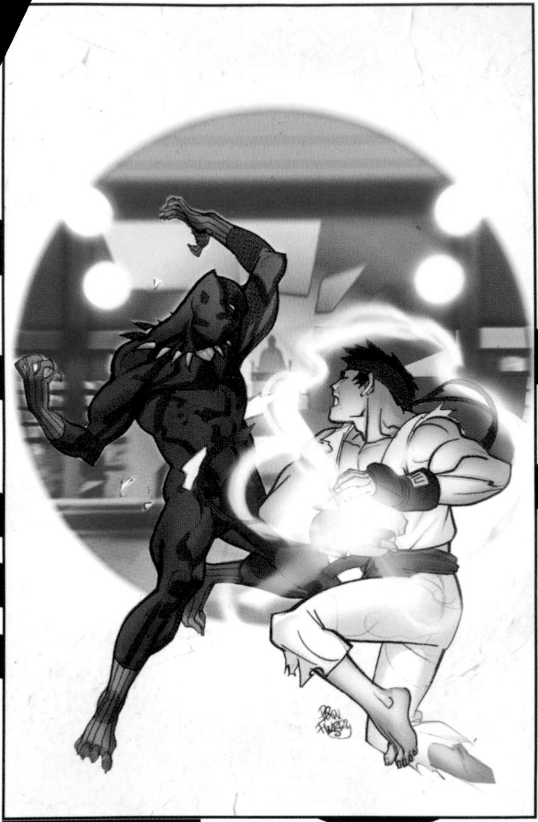

Black Panther #17
by Pasqual Ferry

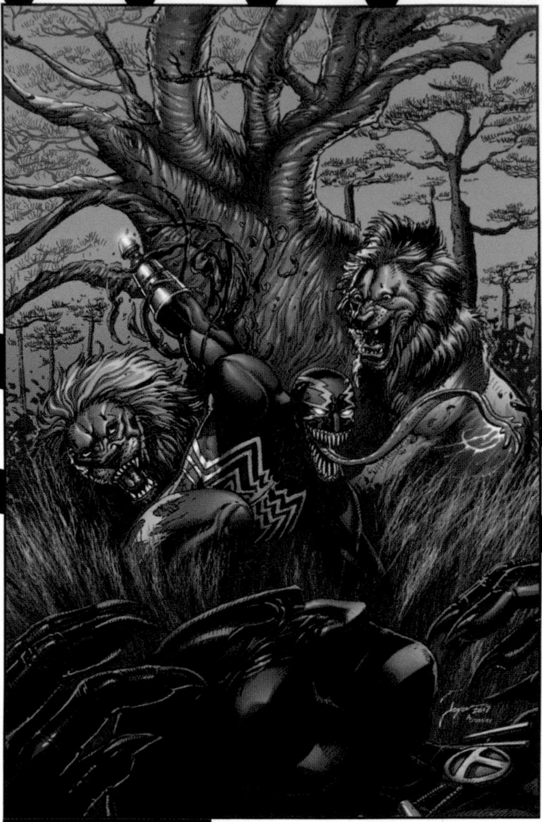

Black Panther #18
by Joyce Chin

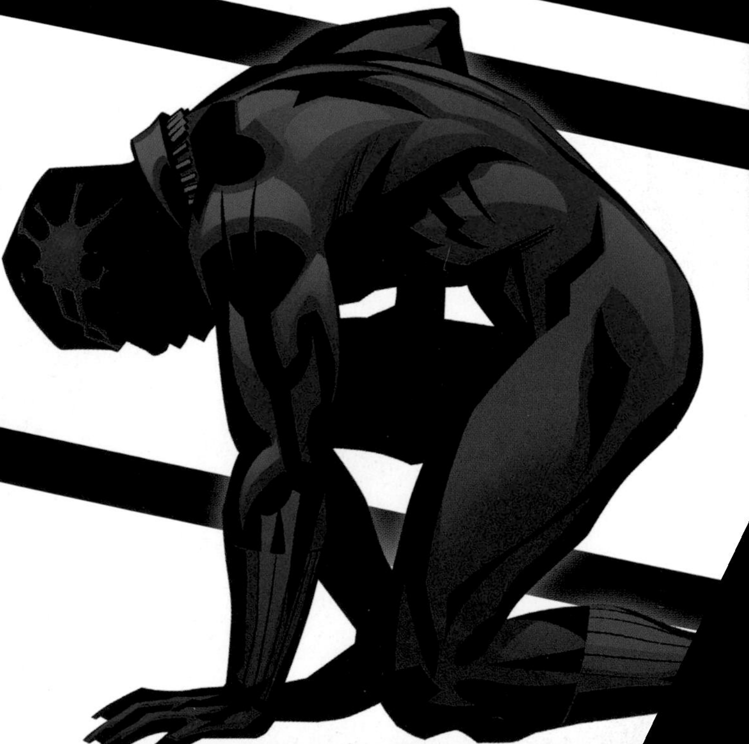

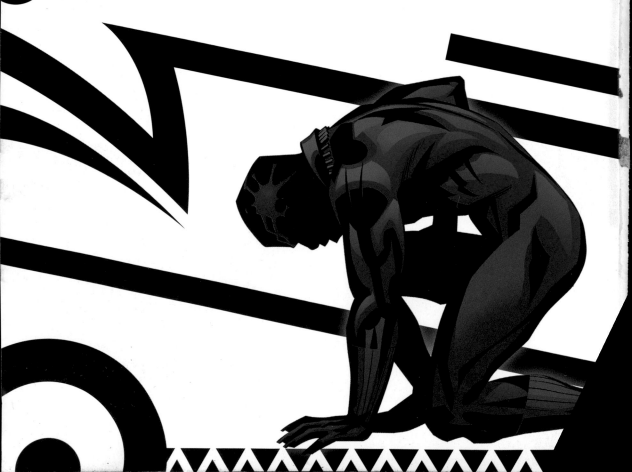